Albert Orville Wright

An Exposition of the Constitution of the United States

Albert Orville Wright

An Exposition of the Constitution of the United States

ISBN/EAN: 9783337119614

Printed in Europe, USA, Canada, Australia, Japan

Cover: Foto ©ninafisch / pixelio.de

More available books at **www.hansebooks.com**

AN EXPOSITION

OF THE

CONSTITUTION OF THE UNITED STATES,

DESIGNED

FOR THE USE OF TEACHERS, AND ADVANCED CLASSES IN
SCHOOLS, AND CITIZENS GENERALLY.

BY

A . O . WRIGHT,

AUTHOR OF AN ANALYSIS AND EXPOSITION OF THE CONSTITUTION OF
THE STATE OF WISCONSIN.

"That which contributes most to preserve the State is to educate children with
reference to the State; for the most useful laws, and most approved by every
statesman, will be of no service if the citizens are not accustomed to and brought
up in the principles of the Constitution."—*Aristotle's Politics*, Book V., ch. 9.

FIFTH EDITION,

MADISON, WIS.
MIDLAND PUBLISHING COMPANY.
1883.

PREFACE.

It is a hopeful sign for the future of our country, that the Constitution of the United States is studied so largely in our schools. In a popular government, the people ought to understand the principles on which the government is based, and the machinery of government by which these principles are to be carried out; that is, they ought to understand the Constitution of their nation. Some confused and imperfect knowledge of this will naturally be picked up by most citizens; and a few lawyers and others will gain a comprehensive knowledge of the Constitution. But a clear and accurate knowledge cannot be generally diffused, except by regular instruction in the public schools. It is therefore a hopeful sign that this instruction is now given in a large number of our schools.

This book is the result of several years' experience in the classroom and in teachers' institutes. That experience has led to certain methods of presenting the subject matter in the text book.

The order of the Constitution is followed. The Constitution of the United States has an order of its own, and a good one, and it is an aid to the memory of the student to observe that order.

Some topics are found scattered in different places, like the topic of impeachment. No arrangement of the Constitution can avoid this difficulty. Topics cross one another, and an arrangement which would bring some topics together would scatter others. The best plan for studying is to follow the order of the Constitution. But an opportunity for considering together all the parts of any topic is given by the analysis at the head of each section.

It is recommended that the text of the Constitution be memorized, or at least all the more important portions of it. As an aid to topical recitation the heading of each paragraph is printed in small capitals. The matter printed in smaller type may be omitted if there is lack of time, or with younger classes.

The author's aim has been to use plain language, and direct and simple forms of statement.

The question of whether we are a Nation or a Confederacy, was settled by the framers of this Constitution. But it has also been setted by our civil war in a more effectual way than by any words written on paper. Any writer on the Constitution who dodges this most important issue is false to his country as well as to truth. On this and other questions about which there is a difference of opinion, the truth ought to be spoken without hesitation or equivocation. This the author has meant to do.

This work has been thoroughly revised in MSS. by the law firm of Lewis, Lewis & Hale, of Madison, the senior member of which is United States District Attorney. Portions of it have also been submitted to officers who have to deal with the subjects treated of in those portions. The author's acknowledgments are also due to many teachers and superintendents of schools for suggestions which have helped to improve this work. Should, however, any errors still be found in it, the author will be thankful for due notice of the same.

Madison, Wis., *August 23, 1880.*

Note.— There is an apparent, but not a real, discrepancy between the property valuations given on pages 34 and 292. The former is the true valuation, the latter the assessed valuation. In estimating the average wealth of our citizens, the true valuation is given. In estimating the effect of a property qualification for the suffrage, the assessed valuation is used, which is the one on which the qualification to vote would be based.

TABLE OF CONTENTS.

"*Thou too — sail on, O, Ship of State!*
Sail on, O Union, strong and great!
Humanity, with all its fears,
With all its hopes of future years,
Is hanging breathless on thy fate!
We know what Master laid thy keel,
What Workman wrought thy ribs of steel,
Who made each mast, and sail, and rope,
What anvils rang, what hammers beat,
In what a forge and what a heat
Were shaped the anchors of thy hope!

"*Fear not each sudden sound and shock,*
'Tis of the wave and not the rock;
'Tis but the flapping of the sail,
And not a rent made by the gale!
In spite of rock and tempest's roar,
In spite of false lights on the shore,
Sail on, nor fear to breast the sea!
Our hearts, our hopes, are all with thee,
Our hearts, our hopes, our prayers, our tears,
Our faith triumphant o'er our fears,
Are all with thee, — are all with thee!"

— LONGFELLOW.

GENERAL PLAN OF THE CONSTITUTION.

THE ENACTING CLAUSE.

ART. I. THE LEGISLATIVE DEPARTMENT.

ART. II. THE EXECUTIVE DEPARTMENT.

ART. III. THE JUDICIARY DEPARTMENT.

ART. IV. RELATIONS OF THE STATES.

ART. V. THE METHOD OF AMENDMENT.

ART. VI. THE SUPREMACY OF THIS CONSTITUTION.

ART. VII. THE RATIFICATION OF THIS CONSTITUTION.

AMENDMENTS I-X. BILL OF RIGHTS.

AMENDMENTS XI-XII. MISCELLANEOUS.

AMENDMENTS XIII-XV. RESULTS OF THE CIVIL WAR.

THE CONSTITUTION OF THE UNITED STATES.

The Original Constitution.

Amendments since added.

THE CONSTITUTION OF THE UNITED STATES.

THE ENACTING CLAUSE.

"A government of the people, by the people, and for the people."
— ABRAHAM LINCOLN.

We, the people of the United States, in order to form a more perfect union, establish justice, insure domestic tranquility, provide for the common defense, promote the general welfare, and secure the blessings of liberty to ourselves and our posterity, do ordain and establish this Constitution for the United States of America.

I. THE UNITED STATES A REPUBLIC. — Governments are classified according to their form as Monarchies, Aristocracies and Democracies.

1. A *Monarchy* is a government by one person. A monarchy may be either absolute or limited. In an absolute monarchy the sovereign is not restricted in his powers by any constitution; in a limited monarchy he is restricted in his power by some kind of constitution, written or unwritten.

2. An *Aristocracy* is a government by a small part of the people, who form a privileged class. An aristocracy may be one of birth, or of wealth, or of both combined.

3. A *Democracy* is a government by the people. A democracy may be either pure or representative. A pure democracy is one in which the voters themselves meet and make laws. In a representative democracy the voters elect representatives to make the laws. A representative democracy is usually called a republic.

It is plain that in so large a country as ours the voters
cannot assemble to make laws, but that they must do
that work by representatives. So that in a large country a pure democracy is impossible. If the government
is democratic it must be a representative democracy.

The United States then is a republic. It is not the
government of One or of the Few, but of the Many.
And as it is representative in form, it is a Republic.

A republican form of government is guaranteed to
every State in the Union, by this Constitution (Art.
IV, Sec. 4). Whatever else this means, it means at
least that no State shall ever become a monarchy or an
aristocracy.

II. THE PEOPLE THE SOURCE OF POWER. — A republic is a government by the people through representatives. The representatives govern, but they do not
govern by any inherent right, but only *as* representatives. The people are the source of power. In the
words of President Lincoln, this is "a government *of*
the people, *by* the people, and *for* the people."

The members of the House of Representatives are
the most direct representatives of the people, as their
name indicates. But every officer of the United States
or of any State, is directly or indirectly chosen by the
people, and is responsible to the people for the faithful
performance of his duties.

The Enacting Clause recognizes this fact, that the
people are the source of power, and says expressly "We,
the people of the United States, do ordain and establish
this Constitution."

III. A POPULAR GOVERNMENT BEST. — A democratic government is best, in any country in which the
people are fitted for it. Rude and barbarous nations,
or nations intelligent, but debased morally, are not

fitted to govern themselves. Hence monarchies or aristocracies are best for such nations. But where the people generally have a fair degree of intelligence and of moral character, a republican government is best.

The people will doubtless make mistakes and do wrongs, but so will any government, and the mistakes and errors of a republic are certainly no worse than those of a monarchy or an aristocracy. No one claims that republics will be perfect. Nothing human is perfect.

But we can reasonably claim that those oppressions and corruptions which are easy to begin and to keep up under other forms of government, are almost impossible under a republic. In an absolute monarchy the interests of the king and his favorites are attended to, without much regard to the interests of the rest of the people. In an aristocracy the interests of the ruling class are the only interests thought of. But in a republic, the interests of one class are balanced by the interests of the other classes. All are represented; and the interests of all are secured as well as is possible in human affairs. The public discussions, which are necessary in a popular government, prevent secret forms of corruption, and help to secure justice and purity of administration.

In short, when the people of any country are fit to take care of themselves, they can do it better than any king or nobles can do it for them.

IV. OBJECTS OF THIS CONSTITUTION. — The objects of this constitution, as here stated, are six:

1. To form a more perfect union.
2. To establish justice.
3. To secure domestic tranquility.
4. To provide for the common defense.
5. To promote the general welfare.
6. To secure the blessings of liberty to the people of the United States and their posterity.

These all refer to the defects in the government of
the United States at that time, under the Articles of
Confederation.

That union was (1.) a very imperfect one; (2.) it did
not establish justice; (3.) it did not ensure domestic tranquility; (4.) it did not provide efficiently for the common defense; (5.) it could do but little to promote the
general welfare; (6.) and therefore it was not strong
enough to secure the blessings of liberty to this country
for any great length of time.

The defects of the Confederation were many; but they
may all be summed up in one phrase: The real power
was vested in the several states, and Congress had no
power to enforce its laws. Congress could *resolve*, but
it could not *execute;* it could *ask* the states to pay taxes,
to furnish troops, to conform to treaties, to do justice
to each other's citizens, but it could not *command* them.

V. THE CONSTITUTION COMPARED WITH THE ARTI-CLES OF CONFEDERATION.

1. This Constitution forms a more perfect union than that under
the Articles of Confederation. It is still not a perfect union; for it
was not wished to destroy the States and make one centralized government, nor would that have been wise. But the loose and ineffi-
cient Confederation was exchanged for a Federation in which a
strong national government was set up over States still retaining
much power.

2. Justice is established by means of a national Judiciary, which
protects foreigners and the citizens of other states against unjust
decisions of any State courts. [See Article III.]

3. Domestic tranquility is ensured by the provision that the
United States shall protect each State against domestic violence.
[Article IV, Sec. 4.] Shays's rebellion in Massachusetts in 1786,
had called general attention to the need of a strong central government to assist the states against such insurrections.[1]

---

[1] Washington wrote at that time to a member of Congress: "You talk,
my good sir, of employing influences to appease the present troubles in Massachusetts. *Influence* is not *government*. Let us have a government by
which our lives, liberties and properties will be secured, or let us know the
worst at once."

4. The common defense could only be provided for by a government capable of raising and supporting armies and navies. Even in the enthusiasm of the Revolutionary War, the central government showed how weak it was, to raise armies or collect taxes, and thinking men saw that in another war it might be still worse.

5. To promote the general welfare is an elastic expression, capable of being lengthened or shortened according to our own ideas of what is for the general welfare. This clause has covered things as different as the purchase of Louisiana, an expedition to the North Pole, a system of weather reports, and the establishment of the Smithsonian Institution. Under this clause the powers of the general government may yet be greatly extended.

6. To secure the blessings of liberty, law is needed as well as liberty. Liberty alone soon degenerates into license, and that into anarchy, which is worse than despotism.

The American idea of liberty is of liberty protected by law. This principle is carried out in our own national government. The power of the general government is given to it in order to secure the blessings of liberty to the people; not to destroy that liberty, but to protect it. Under this government we have flourished during this first century as few nations of the world have ever done. We have also survived the shock of a great Civil War, which settled the question whether this Constitution should be accepted for all it means. We may therefore reasonably hope that our liberty, protected by the strength of our national government, will be handed down to a remote posterity.

VI. THE UNITED STATES A NATION, NOT A CONFEDERACY.

The enacting clause reads, " We, the *people* of the United States, do ordain and establish this *Constitution*." It does not read, " We the *States* do contract and enter into a *treaty* with each other." The United States is therefore *one nation*, and not a confederacy of independent allied states. The source of power is not in the several states, but in the people of the United States. This Enacting Clause was not worded as it is, hastily or inconsiderately. There was a great difference of opinion in the United States, both before and after this Constitution was adopted, upon this very point. The Thirteen Colonies, though all alike dependent upon England, were independent of one another. They had formed several alliances among themselves for defense, and when the struggle with the mother country began they were drawn together by the necessities of the war. Many thoughtful men advocated a much closer union even in 1775; but the Articles of Confederation adopted in 1781, were as much as the states were then willing to concede. And it was not until experience had shown the great evils which come from the jealousies and rivalries of independent states, held together only by a weak confederate government, that the people became willing to establish a real national government. And even then there was a large minority opposed to the Constitution, *because* it took away the independence of the states.

After the Constitution was adopted the contest was carried on by the two parties which were immediately organized, the Federalist and the Anti-Federalist. As the Constitution by its practical workings showed its value, it came to be accepted generally by the people as the bond of our Union. The Supreme Court has decided that these words, " We, the *people* of the United States," etc., declare us to be one nation. And at last our great Civil War has settled the question practically. The seceding States claimed not only the right of revolution, which every oppressed people has, but the right of secession, claiming that we were not one nation but a confederacy of independent allied States, and that any State had a right to dissolve the alliance at pleasure. The result of the war decided that the American people are *one nation*, and mean to remain so.

VII. LOCAL SELF-GOVERNMENT AND NATIONAL UNITY.
    The United States differs from many republics in being composed of several States. It is a Federal Republic in which some powers are given to the state governments and some to the United States government. Just where to draw the line between these two sets of governmental functions, is a difficult question both in theory and in practice. Ever since the Constitution was adopted, there have always been two political parties, the one inclined to limit the powers of the United States government and increase the powers of the states, and the other party inclined to increase the powers of the United States government and limit those of the states. But, on the whole, the general government has been slowly gaining power at the expense of the state governments. This growth in power, however, has not been so great as to change the essential relations of the two sets of governments. These principles may be stated thus:

1. The United States government has all the power needed for national independence.

2. The state governments have all the power needed for local self-government.

Every person in the United States (except in the District of Columbia and unorganized territories, in forts, arsenals, and dockyards, or on the high seas) is thus subject to two jurisdictions. He is subject to two sets of laws, which are made and administered by two different sets of officers, and he pays taxes and owes allegiance to both governments, that of the state or territory in which he is, and that of the United States. For nearly all the ordinary relations of business and society, he looks to his state law and state government. He marries and is divorced, educates his children, transmits his property, buys and sells, and is protected from thieves and murderers, under the laws of the state or territory where he is at the time But he is protected from foreign foes by United States troops and ships; he uses United States money; sends and receives letters through the United States postoffices; and, if he is a foreigner, he can only be naturalized according to United States law. It is plain that in ordinary business and society the state government touches the citizen at far more points than the general government does.

But the principle of local self-government is carried out still further. The states leave the affairs of each township, village, city or county to be regulated by the people thereof, under the general provisions of state laws which limit and define the powers of these subdivisions of a state. There is nothing in the United States Constitution which requires this, and not very much in the constitutions of the several states. But it is a part of the unwritten constitution,— the political habits of the American people. Thus the federal character of our republic harmonizes with the American habit of local self-government, and is thus sustained by a power far more effectual than any written constitution.

ARTICLE I.

THE LEGISLATIVE DEPARTMENT.

"There the common sense of most shall hold a fretful realm in awe.
And the kindly earth shall slumber, lapt in universal law."
— TENNYSON.

I. GENERAL PLAN OF THIS ARTICLE.— This Article is put first, because it is the most important and the longest Article in the Constitution. A republican government is a government of *laws*, not a government of *men*. And therefore in such a government the most important part is to make the laws, which is the duty of the Legislative Department of the government. Laws must be made by the Legislative Department before they can be executed by the Executive Department, or before cases can arise under them to be brought before the Judicial Department.

This Article is divided into ten sections as follows:

Sec. 1, states in whom the Legislative power is vested.
Sec. 2, treats of the House of Representatives.
Sec. 3, treats of the Senate.
Sec. 4, treats of the elections and sessions of Congress.
Sec. 5, treats of the powers of each House separately.
Sec. 6, treats of the privileges of members.
Sec. 7, treats of the process of making laws.
Sec. 8, treats of the powers of Congress.
Sec. 9, treats of the prohibitions on Congress.
Sec. 10, treats of the prohibitions on the States.

SECTION 1.

IN WHOM THE LEGISLATIVE POWER IS VESTED.

All legislative powers herein granted shall be vested in a Congress of the United States, which shall consist of a Senate and House of Representatives.

I. DEPARTMENTS OF GOVERNMENT.—The government of the United States is divided into three departments, Legislative, Executive and Judicial. The legislative department is that part of the government which *makes* the laws; the executive is that part which *carries out* and *enforces* the laws; and the judicial is that part which *applies* and *interprets* ·the laws. These departments are not kept quite distinct, but, as we shall see, the legislative department exercises some judicial functions, and the executive exercises some legislative functions. But these are exceptions to the general rule. Of these three departments the legislative is the most important and has the most power. It therefore needs to be guarded with the greatest care, to prevent its usurping power. For this reason it is divided into two Houses, that each may be a check upon the other; for this reason, the President has a veto; and for this reason, the members of the lower house are reëlected frequently, to make them feel their responsibility to the people. By these expedients, the legislative department is restrained from usurping power that does not belong to it.

II. WHY THERE ARE THREE DEPARTMENTS.

In this division of the powers and duties of government, the framers of our Constitution followed the form to which the people of the United States had always been accustomed. The government of England was divided into these three departments. The legislative power was vested in the Parliament, consisting of a

B

House of Lo ds and a House of Commons; the executive power was vested in the King and his Cabinet ministers; and the judicial power was vested in the judges. This division of powers was not exact and logical, but each branch of government exercised some powers that logically would belong to the others, because it had been found in practice that it worked well so. The King had a legislative power in the veto, as the President also has; the House of Commons had a ju licial pow r in presenting impeachments, and the House of Lords in trying them, just as the House of Representatives and Senate now have.

The colonies had naturally adopted forms of government not differing much from that of England, and had found them to work w d. And when a national government for the United States was formed, the same division of powers was adop ed without any serious question, because the people were accustomed to it, and because experience had shown it to be the best way to divide the powers of a government.

As long as the United States was only a confederation of independent states, a congress of delegates was enough without an executive or a judiciary. But as soon as the United States was made a nation, the three departments of government were made nece sary.

III. THE COLONIAL GOVERNMENTS. — The colonies of Great Britain, which afterwards became the United States of America, had three different forms of government.

1. *The Royal Provinces.* — In these the governor and judges were appointed by the King. The upper house of the legislature was generally appointed by the governor, and only the lower house of the legislature was elected by the people. Both the governor and the king had a veto upon the laws. So that if the representatives of the people passed a law obnoxious to the royal party, it could be negatived by the upper house or vetoed by the governor or annulled at any time by the king. But no tax could be levied without the consent of the legislature. Virginia (after 1624) is the best example of a royal province.

2. *The Proprietary Colonies.* — In these the supreme power was vested in the proprietor, who was either a man or a company. The proprietor, if living in the colony, virtually ruled as king, or if in England, appointed a governor and other officers. In the case of

New York (under both Dutch and English till 1683), the people
had no voice in the government or in taxation.   But in the case of
Pennsylvania, the people elected both houses of the legislature, and
the proprietors appointed the governor.

3. *The Chartered Colonies.* — In these the people elected their
own governor and other officers as well as the legislature.   Connecticut is the best example of a chartered colony.

In general terms with some exceptions we may say, that the New
England colonies were chartered, the Middle colonies proprietary,
and the Southern colonies were royal provinces.

All these governments contained the germs of popular liberty,
excepting only the early proprietary government of New York.   In
all the colonies the people wished to govern themselves, and only
submitted to the arbitrary restriction of the king, and of some of
the proprietors, because they were compelled to.   As soon as they
rebelled against the English government in 1775, they at once expelled their royal or proprietary governors and elected governors of
their own.   They preferred the type of government of the chartered
colonies, and adopted it as soon as they could.   The State governments are now substantially of the form of government in the
chartered colonies.

And when the people came to set up a true national government
for the United States, they adopted the same general form.   The
changes that have been made since the adoption of this Constitution in the forms of the State and National governments, have been
in the direction of popular representation and personal liberty.

IV.   CONGRESS. — The name Congress, was the name
given to the delegates from the colonies under the Articles of Confederation.   This name was retained for the
legislative body of the United States under the Constitution.   Under the Confederation, Congress consisted
of but one House.   But by the Constitution, Congress
was made to consist of two Houses, for several reasons,
[1.] to hinder foolish or unscrupulous legislation, [2.] to
represent the States in one House and the people in the
other, [3.] and because the English Parliament and the
colonial legislatures had two Houses, so that it was one
of the political ideas of the people of the United States
that a legislature should have two Houses.

Each Congress exists two years, beginning on the Fourth of March at noon, every odd numbered year. At that time the term of all the Representatives and of one-third of the Senators expires. And at that time every other odd year, the term of the President also expires. It is usual to refer to the successive Congresses by their number. Thus the Congress which existed from 1789 to 1791, is called the First Congress, and the Congress which existed from 1877 to 1879, is called the Forty-fifth Congress.

SECTION 2.

THE HOUSE OF REPRESENTATIVES.

THE HOUSE OF REPRESENTATIVES.

ORGANIZATION.

1. *Representatives* — Chosen by the people .... **I, 2, 1**

2. *Qualifications of Voters* ....
   - (a.) The same as for voters for State legislature. **I, 2, 1**
   - (b.) But are expected to include all adult male citizens (except felons and traitors) .... **Am. XIV**
   - (c.) And cannot exclude negroes, as such.... **Am. XV**

3. *Term of office* — two years .... **I, 2, 1**

4. *Qualification of Representatives* ..
   - (a.) Age — 25 years .... **I, 2, 2**
   - (b.) U. S. citizenship — 7 years. .... **I, 2, 2**
   - (c.) Residence — in State from which chosen.. **I, 2, 2**
   - (d.) Must not hold U. S. offices .... **I, 6, 2**
   - (e.) Must not be unrepentant rebels.......... **Am. XIV**
   - (f.) Must take oath of office **VI, 3**

5. *Apportionment of Representatives* ..
   - (a.) Basis of apportionment — the population — except wild Indians .... **Am. XIV**
   - (b.) Census — every ten years .... **I, 2, 3**
   - (c.) Limitations on numbers
     - (a.) 1. Not more than one for every 30,000. **I, 2, 3**
     - (b.) 2. One to each State..... **I, 2, 3**

6. *Elections* — *time* — *place and manner* ....
   - (a.) Fixed by State legislatures .... **I, 4, 1**
   - (b.) Or by Congress....... **1, 4, 1**

7. *Vacancies* — filled by special elections............ **I, 2, 4**

8. *Privileges of Members.* (See Section 6.)

POWERS.

9. *Sole Powers* ....
   - 1. To choose officers....... **I, 2, 5**
   - 2. To impeach .... **I, 2, 5**
   - 3. To originate bills for raising revenues .... **I, 7, 1**
   - 4. To elect a President — when the electors fail to elect one .... **Am. XII**

10. *Separate Powers.* (See Section 5.)

11. *Legislative Powers.* (See Sections 7, 8 and 9, also Amendments I to X and XIII to XV.)

CLAUSE 1.

ORGANIZATION.

The House of Representatives shall be composed of members chosen every second year by the people of the several States, and the electors in each State shall have the qualifications requisite for electors of the most numerous branch of the State legislature.

I. REPRESENTATIVES ARE CHOSEN BY THE PEOPLE. — In a free country the people govern. Even in a limited monarchy the representatives of the people have some voice in the government. In a republic all officers, in one sense, are representatives of the people, for they are chosen directly or indirectly by the people, and they are responsible to the people.

But in a special sense the members of the lower house of Congress are called Representatives, because they specially represent the people. Each Representative is chosen to represent the people of his State or district. As the people cannot all go to the Capitol and help to make laws, certain persons are chosen to do the work of legislation for them. It is supposed that each Representative will vote and help to make laws as the people of his State or district wish him to do, and that if questions come up on which he has received no instruction, he will act according to his best judgment for the interests of those who chose him as their Representative.

If each Representative thus represents his State or district, then all together will represent the people of the United States. If the people of a district are divided on certain questions, then their Representative will usually represent the majority of the people of his district. Indeed, he will be chosen over his competitors for the very reason that he does represent the majority

of his district on the leading questions of the day.   And
a majority of the House of Representatives will thus be
almost certain to represent a majority of the nation on
all the leading questions of the day.

II.   THEY ARE CHOSEN FOR A SHORT TERM OF
OFFICE. — Representatives are chosen for two years, so
that they may be responsible to the people.   If a Representative does not truly represent in Congress the people of his district, they need not have him as their Rep-
resentive longer than two years.   Every two years the
people have an opportunity of choosing Representatives
anew.   If a Representative does truly represent his district, he will probably be re-elected.   It is not meant
that a new person should be chosen every two years;
but only that the people should have an opportunity of
endorsing or of rejecting their Representative every
two years.

III.   CONGRESSIONAL DISTRICTS. — The Constitution
says that Representatives shall be chosen by the people
of the several States.   And it also states how they shall
be apportioned among the several States.   [Clause 3.]
But the Constitution leaves to each State to decide how
its Representatives are to be divided among its people.
The Constitution treats each State as a political unit.
Each State is to have so many Representatives according
to its population.   But how these Representatives are
to be apportioned within each State, is left to each State
legislature to determine.

As a rule, the state legislatures have divided the States
into as many Congressional districts as each State has
Representatives; and the people of each district have
elected one Representative.

But in some cases, one or more extra Representatives
have been elected ".at large," that is by the people of

the whole State. Thus after a new apportionment, in which the State of Pennsylvania gained four Representatives, the legislature could not agree on the redistricting of the State. The result of it was that the old districts were left as they had been, and the four extra Representatives were elected " at large," or by the people of the whole State.

If a State chose, it could elect all its Representatives on one ticket, and have no districts. But that is so contrary to the political habits of our people that it is not likely to be done.

IV. QUALIFICATIONS OF VOTERS LEFT TO THE STATES. — When the Constitution says that Representatives shall be chosen by the *people* of the several States, it means by the *voters*, as representing the people. As a fact, not more than one-fourth of the people are actual voters. Women and children are not voters in any State, and some men in all the States are disqualified for various reasons. The voters are supposed to represent the people.

When the Constitution was adopted, the States required different qualifications of voters, as they still do. The United States establishes no uniform qualification for voters, but leaves that matter to the several States. Each State, then, in fixing the qualifications required of those who vote for the lower house of its legislature, also gives the same persons the right to vote for members of the lower house of Congress.

V. TWO RESTRICTIONS ON STATE POWER IN DETERMINING WHO SHALL VOTE. — Two restrictions have since been added. By the Fifteenth Amendment negroes cannot be forbidden to vote because they are negroes. Any reason which would disqualify a white man will also disqualify a negro, but no other reason will. This pro-

vision affects elections for Representatives, as it does all
other elections, State and National.

And by the Fourteenth Amendment it is provided,
that where a State excludes any considerable part of its
inhabitants who are male citizens of the United States,
over twenty-one years old, for any cause except crime
or rebellion, that the number of Representatives to
which that State is entitled shall be proportionately
diminished. This was intended to prevent States from
disfranchising negroes; but it would also work against
a property or educational qualification. It virtually
establishes manhood suffrage throughout the United
States. No case has ever arisen under this amendment
by which the representation of a State has been diminished.

VI. Disputed questions.

1. *Ought a Representative to Vote as the Majority of his Constituents Wish?* There are three questions involved, (*a*) the legal
power, (*b*) the inducements to the Representative, (*c*) the moral
right.

(*a*) The legal power is plain. Once elected and sworn in, no legal
power can coerce a Representative to vote, except as he himself
chooses. He is absolute master of his vote.

(*b*) But powerful inducements are put before him to determine
his vote. There is first his past record, with which he wishes to be
consistent if possible; and his pledges to his constituents expressed
or implied in his acceptance of a nomination by a certain party.
There is, second, his present relations to personal and political
friends at home, and in Congress, whose friendship he wishes to
retain, and whose help he expects to ask for in projects of his own.
This is made very powerful by the institution of the *caucus*. And
last, but not least, are his hopes for his political future, which will
depend largely upon his votes in Congress. These inducements
generally cause Representatives to follow either their party leaders
or the expressed wish of their constituents.

(*c*) But the moral question is a harder one to answer. Usually it
is the obvious duty of a Representative to vote as the majority in

his district wish him to vote. But there may come occasions when he ought to go contrary to his constituents. He ought not to vote for injustice or dishonesty because his constituents demand it. Nor ought he to vote for anything contrary to the real interests of the nation out of a narrow and selfish sectional policy. He is legislating not merely for his district, but also for the nation, and above all for truth and justice.

2. *Should Representatives be changed Frequently?* It is very poor policy for the people of any district to change their Representatives often or for frivolous reasons. The longer a Representative is in Congress, the more influence he gains there. It is almost impossible for a Representative in the first term of his office to do more than vote. The real work of Congress is done in the committees, and members win their places on important committees by long service more than by ability. The longer a district sends a man of ability and integrity to Congress, the more influence he, and therefore his district, will acquire over the business transacted in the House.

It is one of the sophistical maxims of our politics that "rotation in office" is a good thing. It is a good thing for the politicians, because it gives more of them a chance to get positions, but it is not a good thing for the people, who are worse served thereby. Rotation of Representatives is only a good thing where a Representative is corrupt or incompetent, or fails to represent his district on the great questions of the day.

CLAUSE 2.

QUALIFICATIONS OF REPRESENTATIVES.

No person shall be a Representative who shall not have attained the age of twenty-five years, and been seven years a citizen of the United States, and who shall not, when elected, be an inhabitant of that State in which he shall be chosen.

I. AGE OF A REPRESENTATIVE. — A Representative in Congress must be at least twenty-five years old. The object of requiring this is to secure a little more maturity of character and experience of political life than is required of a voter. Most of our Representatives are much older than twenty-five. In the British Parliament a member of either house must be twenty-one years old. The same age is required in most of the State legislatures.

II. CITIZENSHIP OF A REPRESENTATIVE.— A Representative in Congress must have been at least seven years a citizen of the United States. A natural born citizen will of course have been twenty-five years a citizen, when he reaches the age of twenty-five. But a naturalized citizen must have been naturalized at least seven years, whatever his age, before he can be a Representative in Congress.

As the least time under our naturalization laws in which a foreigner can become a citizen is five years, it follows that the least time in which a foreigner, after reaching this country, can become a Representative, is five plus seven, or twelve years. The reason for requiring so long a citizenship is in order that the naturalized citizen may become familiar with our institutions, and outgrow at least in part the political ideas he may have brought from another land.

III. RESIDENCE OF REPRESENTATIVES. — A Representative must be, when he is elected, a resident of the State from which he is chosen. Living in a place constitutes residence in it. In cases of doubtful residence, a person's true residence must be decided by his intention as shown by his words and actions. A person may have several places in which he lives; but only one of them can be his legal residence, for purposes of taxation, voting and holding office.

It is not necessary that a Representative should have resided any time in the State from which he is elected. But he must be a resident of that State when elected.

But it is not required that a Representative shall be a resident of the *district* from which he is elected. Although the usual practice is to elect from each district a resident of that district, there have been several cases of Representatives being elected who were not residents of their districts.

The reason for requiring residence in the State, is that the Representative may be familiar with the local interests and needs of his State. The reason for not restricting the residence to the district is because the Constitution leaves the whole question of the distribution of Representatives inside a State, to the State itself. In Great Britain no qualification is required in regard to residence, and every House of Commons contains many members who do not reside in the county or borough for which they are elected. The same is the case in France.

IV. DISQUALIFICATIONS.— The Constitution also prescribes the following disqualifications:

1. No person holding any office under the United States can be a Member of Congress during his continuance in office. [I. 6, 2.]

2. No person who violates an oath to support the Constitution by engaging in rebellion against the United States, can be a Member of Congress, unless this disability is removed. [Amendment XIV, 3.]

V. SOME DISPUTED QUESTIONS. — The following questions have been raised at various times:

1. *Can a State provide Additional qualifications for its Representatives?* No; for that would be giving a single State the right to amend the United States Constitution. A State can no more add other qualifications t an it can require less. This has been decided by the House of Representatives, under the powers given it

by Section 5. Similar cases have been decided the same way by the Senate.[1]

2. *Can a person be elected who is not twenty-five years of age?* Yes; if he becomes twenty five years of age before he takes his seat. And the House even went so far in one case as to admit a member who was not twenty-five when the first session of the House began. He had to wait a few weeks until he was of the required age, and then he took his seat.

3. *Can a person be elected a Representative who has not been a citizen seven years?* Yes; if he shall have been seven years a citizen before taking his seat.

This is on the same principle as the last case.

4. *Can a person be elected a Representative who is not a voter?* The letter of the Constitution does not prescribe any such qualification.

No such case has yet arisen. But should a woman ever be elected to Congress, or a person who had not a sufficient amount of property in a State where a property qualification is required of voters, we may suppose that the House would decide that he or she was not qualified. But it is not probable that any person not a voter, will ever be chosen a Representative.

5. *If a Representative should remove from his State after being elected would he lose his seat?* No; for the Constitution only specifies that he shall be a resident of the State, when elected.

6. *Can an Ambassador be chosen to Congress, while absent from the United States?* Yes; for he has not lost his residence in the State from which he was appointed.[2]

7. *If an ineligible person receives a majority of votes, does his competitor take his place?* No; in that case no one is elected. There is a vacancy to be filled by a special election. If A. and B. are candidates and A. receives a majority of the votes, but is not eligible for the office, he cannot take his seat. But B. was not elected, and has no claim upon the place, even if A. is not eligible.

---

[1] Some recent text books on the Constitution say that this question is still in doubt. Congress has repeatedly decided that the Constitution prescribes the only qualifications of members, and that no state has a right to require additional qualifications. And this was endorsed by the Supreme Court. *Bailey's Case* (Cl. and Hall, 411).

[2] A public minister residing at a foreign court does not lose his character as an inhabitant of his State. *Bailey's Case* (Cl. and Hall, 411).

CLAUSE 3.

APPORTIONMENT OF REPRESENTATIVES.

Representatives and direct taxes shall be apportioned among the several States which may be included within this Union, according to their respective numbers, [which shall be determined by adding to the whole number of free persons, including those bound to service for a term of years, and excluding Indians not taxed, [three-fifths of all other persons]. The actual enumeration shall be made within three years after the first meeting of the Congress of the United States, and within every subsequent term of ten years, in such manner as they shall by law direct. The number of Representatives shall not exceed one for every thirty thousand, but each State shall have at least one Representative; [and until such enumeration shall be made, the State of *New Hampshire* shall be entitled to choose three, *Massachusetts* eight, *Rhode Island and Providence Plantations* one, *Connecticut* five, *New York* six, *New Jersey* four, *Pennsylvania* eight, *Delaware* one, *Maryland* six, *Virginia* ten, *North Carolina* five, *South Carolina* five, and *Georgia* three.]¹

I. THE ARTICLE AS AMENDED BY THE THIRTEENTH AND FOURTEENTH AMENDMENTS. — If we should reject all obsolete matter, and should change to correspond with Amendments XIII and XIV, this clause would read as follows:

"Representatives shall be apportioned among the several States according to their respective numbers, counting the whole number of persons in each State, excluding Indians not taxed. But when the right to vote at any election for the choice of Representatives in Congress is denied to any of the male inhabitants of such State being twenty-one years of age, and citizens of the United States, or in any way abridged, except for participation in rebellion or other crimes, the basis of representation shall be reduced in the proportion which the number of such male citizens shall bear to the whole number of male citizens, twenty-one years of age, in such State. The actual enumeration shall be made every ten years, in such manner as Congress shall by law direct. The number of Representatives shall not exceed one for every thirty thousand, but each State shall have at least one Representative."

---
¹ The parts of this Clause in brackets are now obsolete.

II.   STATES REPRESENTED ACCORDING TO POPULA-
TION. — As the Representatives are to represent the
people, it is only fair that the States should have Representatives according to the people who are represented.

The theory of our laws is that every man over twenty-one represents a family, and that the exceptions
where men have no families, or families contain no
men, are not enough to require a change of the rule.
And therefore the theory is that the men over twenty-
one will sufficiently represent the women and children.

III.   UNCIVILIZED INDIANS AND NEGRO SLAVES. —
But when the Constitution was adopted, two classes
were entirely disfranchised, those Indians who had not
become civilized, and negro slaves.   It was agreed
by all that Indians who were civilized should be
counted as a part of the representative population, as
they were taxed and subject to the laws of the land.   It
was also agreed that uncivilized Indians should not be
counted, as they neither were taxed nor obeyed the laws.
But the negro slaves made a more difficult problem.
They were human beings, and yet they were property.
The slave States naturally wished to count their slaves
as a part of their representative population, while the
free States protested against it.   A compromise was
finally made upon the basis of counting only three-
fifths of the slaves in the basis of representation.

It would have been shorter and plainer to have said,
"According to their respective numbers, excluding Indians not taxed, and including only three-fifths of the
slaves."   But the authors of the Constitution were
ashamed to confess the existence of slavery in a free
country, and hoped it would soon die out.   They
therefore avoided the use of the words "slave" or

"slavery" throughout the Constitution, as they made it. But these words are used in the amendments adopted after the Civil War. The words, "Persons bound to service for a term of years," mean apprentices. As they are not slaves, they are to be counted in full.

Since slavery is abolished, this three-fifths rule is obsolete. The slave States have gained quite a number of Representatives in consequence of the abolition of slavery.

In this representative population, the population of the Territories and the District of Columbia is not counted, because they send no Representatives to Congress.

IV. TAXATION ON THE SAME BASIS AS REPRESENTATION. — The Revolutionary war had just been fought on the cry of "No taxation without representation." The authors of this Constitution were therefore led to place taxation on the same basis as representation.

A State could be taxed only because it was represented, and only in such proportion as it was represented.[1]

V. THE CENSUS. — The process of counting the population is called a *census*. The first census was taken in 1790, and one has been taken every ten years since. Besides the actual number of inhabitants, a great amount of other useful information is gathered at each census, and published by the government.

VI. THE NUMBER OF REPRESENTATIVES. — There are two limitations upon the number of Representatives:

1. Each State must have at least one.

2. There shall not be more than one to every thirty thousand of the representative population.

---

[1] See section 8 for a full discussion of the subject of taxation.

Congress has from time to time fixed a ratio of representation, generally as soon as possible after each census.   There are now a much less number of Representatives than one to every thirty thousand, or about one to every one hundred and thirty thousand.

If the ratio of representation were still one for every thirty thousand, we should have a House of Representatives containing over thirteen hundred members, a number too large to transact legislative business.

VII.   TERRITORIAL DELEGATES.— Under the Constitution the House of Representatives is composed of members from the States only.   But each organized territory has been allowed to send a delegate, who has no vote, but who can speak on matters affecting the interests of his territory.

VIII.   THE GROWTH OF THE UNITED STATES. — The growth of the United States in population and wealth has been one of unexampled rapidity, as the following table will show:

Census of.	Population.	Ratio of representation.	No. of representatives.
1790............	3,929,214	33,000	105
1800......	5,308,483	33,000	141
1810............	7,239,881	35,000	181
1820............	9,633,882	40,000	212
1830......	12,866,020	47,700	240
1840............	17,069,453	70,680	223
1850............	23,191,876	93,423	237
1860............	31,443,321	127,941	243
1870............	38,558,371	131,425	293
1880............	50,155,783	....	325

The population given is that of the whole United States, not the representative population merely.

The ratio of representation and the number of Representatives is that based on the census named.   But the House elected under any ratio of representation does not begin until three years after the census is taken.

Wealth. — In 1870, the census valuation of all the private property of the United States was a little over thirty thousand million dollars, or on an average of about four thousand dollars to each family. As there are few great fortunes in the United States, this shows a high average of wealth and comfort among the people.

CLAUSE 4.

VACANCIES.

When vacancies happen in the representation from any State, the executive authority thereof shall issue writs of election to fill such vacancies.

I. How MADE. — A vacancy may be created (1) by death, (2) by resignation, (3) by expulsion, (4) by accepting an office under the United States, (5) if an ineligible person is elected.

II. How FILLED. — When a vacancy occurs, the governor of the State from which the vacancy occurs calls a special election. To "issue writs of election," does not mean that the governor appoints some one to fill the vacancy, but only that he calls a special election, when the people elect some one to fill the place. The power which can originally elect can also fill a vacancy. The person then elected does not serve full two years, but only the unexpired part of the term.

CLAUSE 5.

SOLE POWERS OF THE HOUSE.

The House of Representatives shall choose their Speaker and other officers, and shall have the sole power of impeachment.

I. ELECTION OF SPEAKER. — The presiding officer of the House of Representatives is called the Speaker, in imitation of the title of the Speaker of the House of Commons.[1]

---

[1] The Speaker of the House of Commons was called thus originally, because he was their spokesman in communicating their wishes to the king.

The Speaker of the House is one of the members of the House, and as such he can vote and speak on all questions. But when he takes part in the debates, he must call some other person to the chair. He appoints all committees, and as legislation is mostly decided in the committee work, he has thus a great influence upon legislation. The real power of the Speaker is thus only second to that of the President. He holds his office at the pleasure of the House, but no instance has occurred of a Speaker being removed. Each new House elects its own Speaker. A Speaker is frequently reëlected.

II. OTHER OFFICERS. — The other officers of the House are not members of the House, and are appointed and removed at the will of the House. They are a Clerk, Sergeant-at-arms, Door-keeper, Postmaster and Chaplain. Besides these there are many persons employed in various positions about the House. These employees are appointed by the Speaker, Clerk, Sergeant-at-arms, Door-keeper or Postmaster, according to the nature of their duties.

III. POWER OF IMPEACHMENT. — The House of Representatives has also the power of impeachment, and the Senate of trying all impeachments. An impeachment trial is a political trial of some officer for a political offense, for the sake of removing him from office. An impeachment by the House only brings the case before the Senate. A committee of the House are appointed to conduct the prosecution. The whole subject of impeachment will be treated in another place.

IV. ANOTHER SOLE POWER. — The House of Representatives also has the sole power of originating bills for raising revenue. (See section 7.)

SECTION 3.

THE SENATE.

THE SENATE.

ORGANIZATION.

Senators
- How chosen — by State Legislatures ... I, 3, 1
- Numbers — two from each State ... I, 3, 1
- Term of office — six years. I, 3, 1
- Voting power — one vote each ... I, 3, 1
- Classification — into three classes; one class to go out every other year. ... I, 3, 2

Qualifications of Senators
- (a.) Age — thirty years .... I, 3, 3
- (b.) U. S. Citizenship — nine years ... I, 3, 3
- (c.) Residence — in State from which chosen .. I, 3, 3
- (d.) Must not hold a U. S. office ... I, 6, 2
- (e.) Must not be an unrepentant rebel ... Am. XIV
- (f.) Must take oath of office VI, 3

Officers
- (a.) President — Vice President of the U. S..... I, 3, 4
- (b.) President *pro tempore* and other officers chosen by the Senate I, 3, 5

Vacancies
- (a.) Filled temporarily, in recess of legislature, by governor ... I, 3, 2
- (b.) Filled in other cases by legislature ... I, 3, 3

Elections
- (a.) Time and manner — fixed by State legislature ... I, 4, 1
- (b.) Or by Congress ... I, 4, 1

Privileges of Senators. See Section 6.

POWERS.

Sole powers
1. To choose officers, except President ... I, 3, 5
2. To try all impeachments I, 3, 6
3. But judgment can only extend to removal from office and disqualification for holding office ... I, 3, 7
4. To elect a Vice President when the electors fail to choose one Am. XII
5. To confirm certain officers nominated by the President ... II, 2, 2
6. To confirm treaties proposed by the President ... II, 2, 2

Separate powers. (See Section 5.)
Legislative powers. (See Sections 7, 8, and 9, also Amendments I to X, and XIII to XV.)

CLAUSE 1.

ORGANIZATION.

The Senate of the United States shall be composed of two Senators from each State, chosen by the legislature thereof, for six years; and each Senator shall have one vote.

I. THE SENATE REPRESENTS THE STATES. — As the House of Representativee represents the *people*, so does the Senate represent the *States*. Under the confederation the Delegates to Congress were sent by the States and not by the people. But now that a true national government was being organized, it was claimed with justice that the people should be represented, and not the States. But the smaller States refused to part with the power they had. At last the compromise was made that the House should represent the people and the Senate the States.

II. EQUALITY OF REPRESENTATION. — Under the confederation each State had one vote; and if the delegates from any State were equally divided, the State lost its vote. A large State had no more voice in the affairs of the general government than did a small State. As long as these States were each in theory an independent sovereignty, it was fair enough that each should have one vote; just as a large man or a small man, a rich man or a poor man have each one vote. And under this Constitution, as a result of the compromise which left the Senate to represent the States, each State has an equal voice. But instead of giving each State one vote, with as many delegates as it pleases, the same end is attained in a simpler way by giving each State two Senators, and each Senator one vote. Under the present plan, if the two Senators from any State are opposed upon any question, instead of the State losing its vote, it has one vote on each side of that question.

III. How CHOSEN. — As Senators represent States, they are chosen by the government of the State, that is by the State legislature. (See section 4.)

This manner of choice also makes the office of Senator more dignified than that of Representative, as each Senator represents a whole State, while most Representatives represent a part of a State only.

When a State legislature wishes the Senators and Representatives from that State to vote in any particular way, it always recognizes the difference between Senators and Representatives. The resolution which is passed in such a case is always to *instruct* the Senators and *request* the Representatives.

IV. TERM OF OFFICE. — The term of office of a Senator is six years, three times as long as that of a Representative, and half longer than that of President. The object is to raise Senators above the whims and caprices of their constituents, so that they may consult their solid interests, rather than their immediate wishes.

A Senator can be re-elected. Thomas Benton represented Missouri in the United States Senate for thirty years, which is the longest term ever served by one person in either House of Congress.

CLAUSE 2.

CLASSIFICATION AND VACANCIES.

Immediately after they shall be assembled in consequence of the first election, they shall be divided as equally as may be into three classes. The seats of the Senators of the first class shall be vacated at the expiration of the second year; of the second class, at the expiration of the fourth year, and of the third class, at the expiration of the sixth year, so that one-third may be chosen every second year; and if vacancies happen by resignation or otherwise, during the recess of the legislature of any State, the executive thereof may make temporary appointments until the next meeting of the legislature, which shall then fill such vacancies.

I. CLASSIFICATION OF SENATORS. — Senators are so classified that one-third of them go out every other year. This object is accomplished by the following process:

1. The first Senate which met in 1789, was divided by lot into three classes, as equal as possible, the first class to serve two years (till 1791); the second class to serve four years (till 1793), and the third class to serve six years (till 1795). Care was taken that the two Senators from the same State should not be put in the same class, so that no state should change both its Senators at the same time.

2. After the first classification, each *class* holds for six years, and Senators come in and go out with the class to which they are elected.

3. But whenever a new State is admitted to the Union, the two new Senators are assigned to the next classes in order, so as to keep the classes as nearly equal as possible. But the two Senators determine by lot between themselves which has the longer and which the shorter term, and the length of term of the new Senators will depend on the length of time before the classes go out to which they are assigned.

The Senate is thus a permanent body. There are always two-thirds, or nearly two-thirds, of the Senators in office, while the House every two years is dissolved, and must be reorganized.

II. VACANCIES. — A vacancy in the Senate may occur for the same reasons as a vacancy in the House. A vacancy in the Senate is filled by the State government of the State which the Senator represented,— by the legislature, if in session, or by the governor, if the legislature is not in session. When the governor appoints, the Senator then appointed only holds until the legislature can elect. But when the legislature elects, it is for the unexpired portion of the term.

Thus it often happens that a vacancy occurs in the Senate, which is filled, first by the appointment of the governor for a few months, and then by election by the legislature for the rest of the unexpired term. But if the vacancy occurs when the legislature is in session, the governor cannot appoint a Senator, but the whole matter is in the hands of the legislature.

CLAUSE 3.

QUALIFICATIONS OF SENATOR.

No person shall be a Senator, who shall not have attained to the age of thirty years, and been nine years a citizen of the United States, and who shall not, when elected, be an inhabitant of that State for which he shall be chosen.

THE QUALIFICATIONS FOR SENATORS.—These are placed a little higher than for Representatives. They are:

1. Age — thirty years.
2. Citizenship of the United States — nine years.
3. Residence — of the State from which elected.

Two cases have occurred of ineligibility, Albert Gallatin (born in Switzerland), who was elected from Pennsylvania; and Gen. Shields (born in Ireland), who was elected from Illinois.

Both seats were declared vacant by the Senate. But Gen. Shields was re-elected as soon as he was eligible.

The disputed questions about Representatives apply also to Senators. (See page 28.)

CLAUSE 4.

THE PRESIDENT OF THE SENATE.

The Vice President of the United States shall be President of the Senate, but shall have no vote unless they be equally divided.

THE PRESIDENT OF THE SENATE. — In order to give the Vice President of the United States something to do, he was made President of the Senate. As he is not, a member of that body, he has no vote, and no right to discuss questions. But when the Senate is equally divided, he has a casting vote.

It is often erroneously supposed that the President *pro tem.* of the Senate or the Speaker of the House has a casting vote. This is not true. Each of these presiding officers has one vote as a member of the body over which he presides, but no casting vote. If in such a case the vote is a tie, it is lost, as it requires a majority to carry a vote, and a tie lacks one vote of a majority.

The Vice President can appoint no committees in the Senate, because he is not elected by the Senate, and does not represent them as the Speaker does the House. The Senate elects its own committees.

The Vice President of the United States when acting President of the Senate, is simply a presiding officer. He puts motions, preserves order, and decides questions of order, subject to an appeal to the Senate, but cannot debate or vote (except the casting vote).

CLAUSE 5.

OTHER OFFICERS.

The Senate shall choose their other officers, and also a President *pro tempore* in the absence of the Vice President, or when he shall exercise the office of President of the United States.

OTHER OFFICERS OF THE SENATE. — The other officers of the Senate are the same as in the House, and are appointed and removed by the Senate at pleasure. In the absence of the Vice President, or when he acts as President, the Senate elect one of their own number as President *pro tempore*, that is temporary President. The custom of the Senate is to elect a President *pro tempore* the first day of each session, who presides whenever the Vice President is absent. Whenever the office of Vice President of the United States becomes vacant by death, resignation, removal or promotion to the office of President, the President *pro tempore* becomes President of the Senate, but he is not Vice President of the United States, though often erroneously called so.

The President of the Senate *pro tempore*, when acting in place of the Vice President of the United States as President of the Senate, has the same duties as presiding officer, but he has not the privilege of the casting vote, and has the privilege of his own vote as Senator on all questions. He has also the privilege of speaking on any question, by calling some other Senator to the chair. Except in the appointment of committees, he has the same duties as the Speaker of the House.

CLAUSES 6 AND 7.

IMPEACHMENT.

The Senate shall have the sole power to try all impeachments. When sitting for that purpose, they shall be on oath or affirmation. When the President of the United States is tried, the Chief Justice shall preside; and no person shall be convicted without the concurrence of two-thirds of the members present.

Judgment in cases of impeachment shall not extend further than to removal from office, and disqualification to hold and enjoy any office of honor, trust or profit under the United States; but the party convicted shall nevertheless be liable and subject to indictment, trial, judgment and punishment, according to law.[1]

I. THE HIGH COURT OF IMPEACHMENT. — As the House of Representatives alone impeaches, the Senate alone tries all cases of impeachment. In an impeachment trial the Senate sits as a High Court of Impeachment, and acts in a judicial capacity. Senators are therefore in such a case put upon oath or affirmation to try the case justly. A majority of two-thirds is needed

---

[1] See comments on Article II, section 4 (page 199).

to convict. When the President of the United States is tried, the Vice President or the President *pro tempore* of the Senate might be interested to have him convicted, in order to succeed to the place of President. It is therefore provided that when the President of the United States is tried, the Chief Justice shall preside.

II. JUDGMENT IN CASES OF IMPEACHMENT. — As an impeachment trial is a political, and not a criminal trial, the punishment is a political, not a criminal one. Conviction on impeachment carries with it removal from office; and the officer convicted may also be declared disqualified from ever holding a United States office again.

If the offense is a criminal one as well as a political one, the political trial will not prevent a criminal trial also.

SECTION 4.

ELECTIONS AND SESSIONS.

CLAUSE 1.

ELECTIONS TO CONGRESS.

The times, places, and manner of holding elections for Senators and Representatives shall be prescribed in each State by the legislature thereof; but the Congress may at any time by law make or alter such regulations, except as to the places of choosing Senators.

I. THE CONSTITUTIONAL PROVISIONS. — The Constitution provides in relation to election of Senators and Representatives,

1. That each State may prescribe the time and place and manner of holding elections for Senators and Representatives;

2. But that Congress may assume control over a part or all of the subject, at any time;

3. But Congress is forbidden to prescribe the place of choosing Senators. As these are chosen by the State legislatures, it is wise to forbid Congress to prescribe where the election shall be held. Otherwise, Congress might prescribe that Senators should be chosen at some other place than the State capitol, or even outside of the State altogether.

When Congress has made any regulations relating to time, place and manner of choosing Senators or Representatives, that supersedes any State law. But, so far as Congress has not prescribed any of these things, the State laws govern it.

II. PROVISIONS MADE BY CONGRESS. — For a long time Congress left this whole matter to the several States, and the greatest variety prevailed. A part of the States elected Representatives in the spring, a part in October, and a part in November. A part of the States elected by ballot and a part by *viva voce* vote.

Recently Congress has by law prescribed certain things in relation to the time and manner of these elections, leaving other questions still open. The elections of United States Senators have been fully provided for by act of Congress; the regulations respecting the election of Representatives are not so minute. Both are given below.

III. ELECTION OF SENATORS. — Senators are chosen as follows:

The last session of a legislature before the term of a Senator from that State expires is the time; and the day is the second Tuesday after the legislature has met and organized; the place, of course, is the capitol of the State, except when in time of public danger the legislature is called to meet at some other place. Each house first votes separately by a *viva voce* vote. Next day a joint convention of both houses is held, when the result in each house is read. If the same person has a majority of all the votes in each house, he is declared elected. But if no one has such a majority of each house of the legislature, the members of both houses in joint convention immediately proceed to vote for Senator. They must meet in joint convention and vote at least once each day until a Senator is elected. All votes must be *viva voce*, that is, as the roll is called each member of the legislature must rise in his place and name the person he votes for. A majority of all the votes cast is required to elect.

In case of a vacancy, the legislature proceeds to fill the vacancy in the same way, on the second Tuesday of the session after the vacancy occurs; or if the legislature is in session when the vacancy occurs, on the second Tuesday after it is notified of the vacancy.

IV. ELECTION OF REPRESENTATIVES.

Representatives must be elected from districts of contiguous territory on the Tuesday after the first Monday of November in 1876, and every two years thereafter. Vacancies are filled by a special election called by the Governor. All votes must be by ballot. In a few States which find it difficult to change their State constitution, Congress has suspended the operation of this law, but as soon as possible all the States must arrange to hold their election for Representatives and for Presidential Electors on the Tuesday after the first Monday of November.

CLAUSE 2.

SESSIONS OF CONGRESS.

The Congress shall assemble at least once in every year, and such meeting shall be on the first Monday in December, unless they shall by law appoint a different day.

I. WHEN CONGRESS MEETS. — Congress must meet at least once each year. As a Congress lasts two years, each Congress has at least two sessions, and may have more.

The regular sessions of Congress begin on the first Monday of December each year.[1] The first regular session of Congress lasts until the adjournment some time in the next summer, and is called the *long session*. The second regular session lasts until the fourth of March, at noon, when the terms of office of all the Representatives and of one-third the Senators expire. This is therefore called the *short session*.

A special session may be called by the President for extraordinary reasons. (II, 3.)

A session of Congress may be ended in one of three ways:

---

[1] For a few years Congress had three sessions, the first beginning on the fourth of March, and the other two on the first Monday of December.

1. The two Houses may agree to adjourn.

2. The term for which all the Representatives and one-third of the Senators were elected may expire. This happens every odd year on the fourth of March.

3. In case the two Houses disagree in respect to the time of adjournment, the President can adjourn them. This case has never occurred, but it is provided for in the Constitution. (II, 3.)

II. WHERE CONGRESS MEETS. — The Constitution does not fix the place where Congress shall meet. But the place now provided is the Capitol at Washington. But when, in case of invasion or contagious disease, it would be unsafe for Congress to meet at Washington, the President is authorized by law to convoke Congress at some other place. Or Congress, when in session, has the right to adjourn to meet at some other place, if it so chooses. But since the seat of government was established at Washington, Congress has always met there.[1]

III. THE ORGANIZATION OF CONGRESS.

On the fourth of March, at noon, every odd year, one Congress closes its existence, and a new Congress begins. The entire House of Representatives goes out of office, those members who have been re-elected as well as those who are elected for the first time. One-third of the Senate also goes out of office.

As the Senate is a permanent body, it does not need to reorganize when it meets. The Vice President takes his place as President of the Senate, or, if he is absent, a President *pro tempore* is chosen, the new members are sworn in, and the Senate is ready for business. If there are two claimants for a seat, neither is sworn in till the case is decided by the Senate, when the one whom the Senate decides to have been lawfully elected is sworn in.

---

[1] The Continental Congress met in the following places: Philadelphia, 1774–76; Baltimore, 1776; Philadelphia, 1777; Lancaster and York, 1777; Philadelphia, 1778–83; Princeton, 1783; Annapolis, 1783; Trenton, 1784; New York, 1785–9. The Constitutional Convention was held at Philadelphia in 1787, this Constitution was ratified in 1788, and went into effect in 1789. The seat of government since then has been: New York, 1789–1790; Philadelphia, 1790–1800; Washington, 1800 to the present time.

But when a new House of Representative meets, the scene is different. The Clerk of the last House makes out the roll of the members who hold certificates of election, who are sworn in, and who then proceed to elect a Speaker. Sometimes this is done at once; but sometimes, when parties are closely balanced, it takes weeks, and even months, to elect a Speaker. Until that is done, the House can do no business, and has no legal organization. But as soon as a Speaker and other officers are elected, the House is organized and ready for business.

In case there are two claimants for a seat, the Clerk puts upon the roll the name of the one who has a certificate of election from the proper state authorities, who therefore votes in the election of officers. But it often happens that when the contest for the seat is decided by the House, the sitting member is ousted and his oppo·nent is seated. It is usual to vote a salary and expenses of contest to both claimants. Thus it is sometimes a good thing to be a defeated candidate for Congress.

SECTION 5.

POWERS OF EACH HOUSE SEPARATELY.

CLAUSE 1.   (Part First.)

JUDGE OF ELECTIONS.

Each House shall be the judge of the elections, returns, and qualifications of its own members, and a majority of each shall constitute a quorum to do business; but a smaller number may adjourn from day to day, and may be authorized to compel the attendance of absent members, in such manner and under such penalties, as each House may provide.

I. **Each house the judge of elections, returns and qualifications.**—In Parliament and in

D

the State legislatures when this Constitution was adopted, each House was the judge of the elections, returns and qualifications of its own members. Consequently the same power was given to each House of Congress.

When it is said that each House shall be a judge of the elections and returns of its members, it is meant that each House has the power to decide whether a member was lawfully elected or not, or of two persons both claiming to be elected, to decide which one is justly entitled to the seat.

When it is said that each House shall be a judge of the qualifications of its members, it is meant that each House has the power to decide whether any particular member has the qualifications required under the Constitution. (See sections 2 and 3.)

Taken together, these powers give each House of Congress power to decide who are its members and who are not. The decision of each House is final and cannot be reviewed by the other House or by the courts.

II. THE PROCESS OF DECIDING CONTESTED ELECTIONS.

After each election for Representative, the proper officers in each State canvass the votes actually cast and decide which of the candidates are elected. A certificate of election is then given by the Governor or Secretary of State to the candidate who has the largest number of votes, as decided by the canvassing officers.

Should the defeated candidate claim that he was rightfully elected, and was cheated out of it by some fraud or mistake in the election or in counting the returns of the election, he can appeal to the House of Representatives, who will decide his case upon the merits. But meanwhile the person who has the certificate of election, takes the seat and votes.

The process of contesting an election is now specified by law. Within thirty days after the result of the election has been declared, the defeated candidate must give notice to the successful candidate that he will contest his election and specify the grounds upon which he will contest it. Within thirty days after that the successful candidate must reply, stating the grounds upon which he relies to support his case. The case then goes before some judge, who takes all the testimony brought by both sides and their written statements and forwards them to the clerk of the House of Representatives.

As soon as the House is organized, the Speaker appoints, with other committees, a committee on Elections. All contested cases are referred to this committee, who examine the evidence sent them, and hear the arguments of lawyers on each side, and then report to the House which of the two claimants is entitled to the seat.

The House then votes on the report, and decides which candidate was lawfully elected. In deciding this question, the committee on Elections and the House go back of the returns, and decide on the evidence presented, whether any illegal votes were cast, whether any mistakes were made in making out the returns, and so on, and then aim to decide according to the real wish of the people of the district without regard to legal technicalities.

The process of deciding a contested election in the Senate is simpler. The question goes directly to the committee on Elections, and by them is reported to the Senate, who decide, as in the House of Representatives.

But the power to decide contested election cases has proved a dangerous power in the hands of a partisan majority. Whichever party has the majority, is very apt to decide contested elections in favor of its own side, rather than in favor of justice.

When the question is one of qualification, it goes to the committee on Elections and then to the House. But in such a case there is no contest. For to prove a member elect to be disqualified, does not seat his opponent; but only creates a vacancy to be filled in the regular way.

III. RECOGNITION OF STATES.

Incidental to the question of qualification is the question whether the State from which the Senator or Representative comes accredited is a State in the Union or not.

If either House does not recognize a State as a State in the Union, it of course refuses to receive the members from that State.

When a new State is received into the Union, its formal recognition as a State is made by receiving its Senators and Representatives into the Senate and House. When the conquered rebel States were received back into the Union, it was by receiving their Senators and Representatives into Congress.

It follows from this that a State may be recognized by one House and not by the other.   But the two Houses have always tried to work in harmony on this question.

CLAUSE 1.   (SECOND PART.)

QUORUM.

IV.   WHAT IS A QUORUM? — A quorum is a sufficient number to do business legally.

In a large body like either House of Congress, it is plain that it would not do to require all the members to be present before any business can be done.   It would be very difficult to have all attend any one day.   And yet it would not be fair for a few members to do business in the absence of the rest, whose votes would perhaps have decided the business in a different way.   Some number must be fixed as a quorum.

The Constitution fixes that number at a majority.

But when the House of Representatives is called on to choose a President, a quorum for that purpose consists of a member or members from two-thirds of the States (Am. XII).

V.   POWERS OF A LESS NUMBER. — But it often happens that a majority are not present to do business. And it has sometimes happened that a number of members absent themselves purposely to prevent business being done.

Two powers are therefore given to a less number than a quorum:

1. They may adjourn till the next day, and so on day after day, till a quorum is present.

2. Or they may compel the attendance of absent members, in accordance with the rules already fixed by the House.

Under the rules of the House of Representatives, no

member has a right to stay away from a session of the House, unless he is excused or is sick. Absentees, who are not excused or sick, can be arrested by special messenger and brought into the House. By the rules, fifteen members, including the Speaker, can compel the attendance of absent members.

VI. PAIRS.

If a member is absent on an important vote, his party will lose his vote. In order to obviate this evil, there is an understanding among the members of both parties, that if a member must be absent, he can agree with some member of the other party to *pair* with him. The member who is absent cannot vote, and the member who is paired with him is allowed by the courtesy of the House not to vote. The result is the same, as if both were present and voted on opposite sides.

CLAUSE 2.

DISCIPLINE.

Each House may determine the rules of its proceedings, punish its members for disorderly behavior, and with the concurrence of two-thirds, expel a member.

I. RULES OF EACH HOUSE.— The rules adopted are the general code of Parliamentary practice, with some special changes and additions to suit the circumstances of each House. The rules of Parliamentary practice, as they are called, grew up in the growth of the English Parliament, and have now been adopted with slight changes by all deliberative bodies where the English language is spoken.[1] Under this section, either the Senate or House of Representatives can alter any of these rules or make new ones for itself, whenever it chooses. And the rules of the two Houses need not be the same. Each House makes its own rules. Of course

[1] The usual Parliamentary rules can be found in any good manual like Robert's Rules of Order, Cushing's Manual, or Jefferson's Manual. The rules of the Senate and House of Representatives are published each year in the Manual of Congress.

the rules must be subject to the Constitution. Thus, a rule making a greater or less number than a majority a quorum would be unconstitutional.

II. POWER TO PUNISH ITS OWN MEMBERS.—Rules would be of no use, unless there were some power to enforce them, and to punish for disobedience. Therefore, each House has the right, not only to make the rules for its own proceedings, but to punish those who violate those rules. The offenses which may be punished are not exactly defined, nor are the kind of punishments; but the punishments for members are usually reprimand or fine, and in extreme cases expulsion. For expulsion, a two-thirds vote is needed. A large discretion is thus given to either House, which might be abused, but is not likely to be.

The power over members is not limited to offenses committed by members in their capacity as members, or during the session of Congress. But a member may be punished for any disorderly or unparliamentary action, or for any conduct which renders him unfit to be a member.[1]

As Senators or Representatives cannot be impeached or removed in any other way or by any other power, this power of expulsion is the only safeguard against unworthy members.

III. POWER TO PUNISH PERSONS NOT MEMBERS. — Besides this power over its own members, each House

---

[1] In July, 1797, William Blount was expelled from the Senate for a high misdemeanor entirely inconsistent with his public trust and duty as a Senator. "The offense charged against him was an attempt to seduce an American agent among the Indians from his duty and to alienate the affection and confidence of the Indians from the public authorities of the United States, and a negotiation for services in behalf of the British government among the Indians. It was not a statutory offense, nor was it committed during the session of Congress, nor at the seat of government. Yet by an almost unanimous vote, he was expelled from that body." (Story, 838.) A Representative from South Carolina was expelled for receiving money for appointing a cadet to West Point, and other members have been expelled for various offenses.

has the power to punish other persons for a breach of its privileges, for disorderly conduct, or for contempt. No such power is expressly given by the Constitution. But it is a principle of the common law, that the power to preserve order and to punish for contempt belongs to courts of law and to legislative bodies. The power of either House to punish for contempt or disorderly behavior, is limited to reprimand, fine, or imprisonment, and to the session of Congress at which the offense is committed.[1]

IV. SOME DISPUTED QUESTIONS.

1. *Can a member be punished for an offense committed before he became a member?* Probably not; the decisions have thus far been to that effect. And the House of Representatives has gone so far as to decide that it could not even punish a member for corrupt conduct in a previous term. But these decisions do not legally bind future Houses, and a flagrant case may arise sometime which will lead to an opposite decision.

2. *Can either House imprison a person not a member?* Yes; but only during the session. When the session of Congress closes the prisoner must be released. The imprisonment in such cases is in one of the committee rooms, under guard of the Sergeant-at-Arms or one of his subordinates.

CLAUSE 3.

PUBLICITY.

Each House shall keep a journal of its proceedings, and from time to time publish the same, excepting such parts as may in their judgment require secrecy, and the yeas and nays of the members of either House on any question shall, at the desire of one-fifth of those present, be entered on the journal.

I. THE VALUE OF PUBLICITY. — In a popular government like ours, the people ought to be able to know

---

[1] The Supreme Court has repeatedly decided, that either House may punish persons not members for a breach of the privileges of the House, and that there is no appeal from the decision. Persons have actually been punished for the following offenses: An attempt to corrupt a member; a challenge sent a member to fight a duel; a printed libel on the Senate; an assault upon a member for words spoken in debate; refusal to testify before a committee of investigation.

what their representatives are doing. It is a good to the legislators and it is a good to the people. The members of Congress need publicity, to check them in corrupt or unwise conduct, by the condemnation of the people. They also need it to secure public applause for any ability they may show in advocating or carrying through wise measures. The people need publicity in the proceedings of Congress, so that they may know whether their representatives are worthy of re-election, and they also need to read the discussions and votes in Congress for their own education in political questions.

II. How PUBLICITY IS SECURED. — Publicity of the proceedings in Congress is secured by the Constitution in two ways:

1. By keeping and publishing a journal of their proceedings.

2. By recording the vote of each member, when one-fifth of those present call for it.

Besides these ways, publicity is effectually secured in three other ways:

1. Spectators are admitted to the proceedings. Galleries are built expressly for the public, and certain distinguished persons are admitted to the floor of each House. Among these are the President and Vice President, Cabinet officers, the members of the other House, U. S. Judges, State Governors, the chief officers of the Army and Navy, and foreign ambassadors.

2. The reporters of newspapers are admitted, and are furnished every facility for reporting the proceedings in full. By the aid of the telegraph, the proceedings of each day in Congress are now printed the next morning in all the leading newspapers, which in the course of that day reach almost every village in the land. These reports are often fuller and more correct than the

official report. Hundreds of thousands of voters read them with the closest interest.

3. Members are in the habit of having their speeches printed and sent to everybody who is likely to take an interest in them.

III. PUBLISHING THE JOURNAL. — The journal of the proceedings of each House is kept by Clerks, and is printed and laid on the desk of each officer and member of each House the next morning. It is published in volumes in the Congressional Globe.

Those parts which require secrecy are not published. The House of Representatives usually has no secret sessions, and the Senate only when it does business which it shares with the President, hence called *executive business*. Such sessions are called *executive sessions*.

Executive business is of two kinds: the confirmation or rejection of appointments to office, and the confirmation or rejection of treaties. It is obvious that secrecy is proper in both of these cases. When the Senate goes into executive session, all persons are shut out except the Vice President, the Senators and a few trusty officers, who are sworn to secrecy. Yet the reporters for the press generally manage to find out and publish what was done in executive sessions, in spite of all these precautions.

The case might arise, that would require both Houses to go into secret sessions; but it would be a very extraordinary case indeed, such as the question of a great foreign war, or the insanity of the President.

IV. METHODS OF VOTING IN CONGRESS. — There are three ways of voting in Congress.

1. By acclamation. The presiding officer puts the question, and all who are in favor of it say " aye," then after a pause, all who are opposed say " no." If they

are nearly all one way or the other, it is easy to decide, and time is saved.

2. If the vote by acclamation is nearly balanced, the presiding officer either says he cannot decide, or some one calls for a division of the House, when a rising vote is taken, and the members are counted. If this is not satisfactory, a call may be made for tellers. The presiding officer then appoints two tellers, who take their position in front of the speaker, and the members, first those in the affirmative, then those in the negative, pass between the tellers and are counted by them.

3. But in important questions, where a record of each member's vote is wished, the ayes and noes (or yeas and nays) are called for. The method of calling for them is thus: Some member addresses the chair, and says, "I call for the ayes and noes," the chair then says, " Is the call sustained?" All those rise who are in favor of the call, and if there are one-fifth of all present, the call is sustained; the roll is then called and each member's vote is recorded.

V. THE OBJECT OF CALLING THE YEAS AND NAYS. — The object of calling the yeas and nays is to make an official record of each member's vote, so that his constituents and the country generally may know how he voted. When such record is made, members are apt to be more careful how they vote. At least one-fifth of those present must call for the yeas and nays, because to call the roll of members takes a long time, and if one or two members could compel such a call, business would be constantly delayed. But on the other hand, if it required a majority vote to record the ayes and nays, a corrupt majority could easily refuse to record their votes, and thus rush through bad measures without any check. As it is, one-fifth of the members can always compel a call of the yeas and nays, and thus make each member give his vote in such a way that the responsibility for it can be proved upon him.

As it is, this power of calling for the yeas and nays is often used by the minority to stave off a measure which they cannot prevent by a direct vote. Thus when a bill is before the House whose passage the minority are anxious to hinder as long as they can, they will make what are called "dilatory motions," that is they will move to adjourn, to lay the bill on the table, to refer it to one of the standing committees, to refer it to a special committee, or to amend it in various ways, and on all these motions will call for the yeas and nays, besides having the right to make speeches on most of them. By these expedients the passage of any bill may be delayed for several days.

CLAUSE 4.

ADJOURNMENT.

Neither House, during the session of Congress, shall, without the consent of the other, adjourn for more than three days, nor to any other place than that in which the two Houses shall be sitting.

ADJOURNMENT.—If either House could adjourn to any time or place, without the consent of the other, it might cause a great deal of trouble and inconvenience, which is prevented by this clause.

The two Houses must be in session at the same time and place. Only one exception is allowed.

Either House may adjourn for three days or less without asking the consent of the other. This is to allow for Sundays and holidays, and other special occasions.

In case the two Houses cannot agree upon the time of adjournment, the President has the power to adjourn them to any time he may think proper (II, 3). This power has never been exercised.

SECTION 6.

POWERS OF MEMBERS.

POWERS OF MEMBERS.	I. PRIVILEGES	1. *Salary*...	(a.) Fixed by law	I, 6, 1
			(b.) Paid from the U. S. Treasury	I, 6, 1
		2. *From arrest*...	(a.) During session and going and returning	I, 6, 1
			(b.) Except for treason, felony, and breach of the peace.......	I, 6 1
		3. *Of Speech*	(a.) For speeches in the House	I, 6, 1
			(b.) Can be punished by the House.	I, 6, 1
			(c) But by no other power	I, 6, 1
	II. RESTRICTIONS....	1. Cannot hold U. S. office		I, 6, 2
		2. Cannot be appointed to an office created or made more valuable for his sake..............		I, 6, 2
		3. Cannot be Presidential elector.........		II, 1, 2

CLAUSE 1.

PRIVILEGES OF MEMBERS.

The Senators and Representatives shall receive a compensation for their services, to be ascertained by law, and paid out of the Treasury of the United States. They shall in all cases except treason, felony and breach of the peace, be privileged from arrest during their attendance at the session of their respective Houses, and in going to and returning from the same; and for any speech or debate in either House, they shall not be questioned in any other place.

I. SALARY PAID BY THE UNITED STATES. — In England members of Parliament are not paid. Under the Confederation, the delegates were paid by the States that sent them. Members of Congress are paid for their services, so that poor men can afford to go to Congress; and they are paid by the United States, so that their pay shall be equal, and that they may be independent of dictation by their State legislatures. Besides, they act for the whole United States, and not for their own State only, and therefore it is fair that they be paid by the United States.

The pay of Senators and Representatives was originally six dollars a day for each day's service, and six dollars for every twenty miles of travel to and from the seat of government. It is now fixed at $5,000 a year, and twenty cents a mile for traveling expenses. The Speaker of the House receives $8,000 a year, and the President *pro tempore* of the Senate the same, when he acts as President of the Senate.

Congress fixes the salaries of its own members. Several times a Congress has raised the salaries of its members, not only for the rest of its term, but has made the increase apply back to the beginning of its term.

There is nothing in the Constitution to prevent this, although it is evidently unjust. An amendment was proposed in 1789, which, if it had been adopted, would have prevented these " back salary grabs " (see page 251).

II. PRIVILEGE FROM ARREST. — The privilege of members of Congress from arrest is common to all legislative bodies, here and in Europe, and for the same reason, that their constituents may not be defrauded of their voices and votes for any frivolous reason. This freedom from arrest does not cover:

1. Arrest on the charge of treason.

2. Arrest on the charge of a felony, that is, any crime which is punishable by death or imprisonment in a penitentiary.

3. Arrest for breach of the peace, that is, any act that disturbs public order, such as assault and battery.

But it does cover:

1. Arrest for any misdemeanor, except breach of the peace.

2. Service of any civil process, such as a suit for debt, a subpœna as a witness, or a summons to serve on a jury.

This privilege from arrest covers the time of the session, and the time necessary to go to Washington before the session and to return after it. It is not necessary for a member to be sworn in before enjoying this privilege, otherwise he might be arrested when going to the first session in order to be sworn in, and thus be prevented from taking his seat at the proper time.

III. FREEDOM OF DEBATE. — The privilege of freedom of speech is given to members of Congress.

This freedom differs from the freedom of speech outside of Congress, granted to all citizens by Amendment II, in giving freedom from libel suits, as well as all other freedom of speech.

Members are privileged from arrest for words spoken in debate. For indecent or libelous words spoken in debate they may be punished by their own House, but not by any court of law. As the debates in Congress are always printed, this privilege extends to their official publication. But it does not extend to their publication in any other way. A member is free to speak a libel on the floor of the House to which he belongs, if the House allows it, and is not liable for its official publication. But if he or any one else publishes such a libel in any other form, it is not protected by this privilege.

CLAUSE 2.

RESTRICTIONS ON MEMBERS.

No Senator or Representative shall, during the time for which he was
elected, be appointed to any civil office under the authority of the United
States, which shall have been created, or the emoluments whereof shall
have been increased during such time; and no person holding any office
under the United States, shall be a member of either House during his
continuance in office.

I. WHAT THIS CLAUSE DOES NOT PROHIBIT. — This
clause is remarkable rather for what it does not prohibit than for what it does.

1. It does not prohibit an officer of the United States
from being elected to Congress and holding his office
till he is ready to take his seat in Congress.

2. It does not prohibit a member of Congress from
being appointed to a *military* office, which was created
or the salary of which was increased for his special
benefit.

3. It does not prohibit a member of Congress being
appointed *as soon as his term is out* to an office which
was created, or the salary of which was increased for
his benefit, perhaps only a few days before.

4. It does not prevent a member of Congress securing
the appointment of a relative or intimate friend to an
office, which was created or the salary of which was increased for his benefit.

5. It does not prohibit a member of Congress from
resigning his seat at any time to take an office, which
was not created or whose salary was not increased
during his term of office.

II. WHAT THIS CLAUSE DOES PROHIBIT. — It does
guard against two sources of corruption.

1. It prohibits any member of Congress getting a

civil office created, or the salary of such an office increased, and then being appointed to it himself, before his term of office is out.

2. It prohibits any one being at the same time a member of Congress, and an officer of the United States. A member of Congress is not an officer of the United States, but a representative of a State or of the people.

III.   ADDITIONAL RESTRICTIONS. — Besides these restrictions, the following may be added:

1. No Senator or Representative can be a Presidential Elector.   (II, 2.)

2. In all the States, the State Constitutions prohibit United States Senators and Representatives from holding any State office, or being elected to the State Legislatures.

SECTION 7.

THE PROCESS OF MAKING LAWS.

CLAUSE I.

WHERE BILLS MAY ORIGINATE.

All bills for raising revenue shall originate in the House of Representatives; but the Senate may propose or concur with amendments as on other bills.

I. Bills which the House of Representatives only can originate. — Most bills may originate in either the Senate or the House of Representatives; but revenue bills must originate in the House of Representatives.

This provision is taken from the unwritten Constitution of England. There the House of Commons alone can originate money bills, and the House of Lords can only accept or reject them, but cannot propose amendments to them. Here the House of Representatives only can originate money bills; but the Senate has the right to propose amendments. The reason for requiring bills for raising taxes to originate in the House of Representatives, is because that body represents the people directly, and it is the people who are to pay the taxes.

E

II. Bills which either house may originate.—
The Senate may, however, originate bills which raise
revenue indirectly, so long as their main object is not
to raise revenue. For instance, a law to levy a direct
tax or a law to assess duties on certain imported goods
must originate in the House of Representatives, but a
law the violation of which was to be punished by fines
to be paid into the treasury, or a law to regulate the
sale of public lands, might originate in either House.
Any bill which does not relate to raising revenue may
originate in either House.

CLAUSE 2.

HOW BILLS MAY BECOME LAWS.

Every bill which shall have passed the House of Representatives and the
Senate, shall, before it become a law, be presented to the President of
the United States; if he approve, he shall sign it; but if not, he shall
return it, with his objections, to that House in which it shall have
originated, who shall enter the objections at large on their journal, and
proceed to reconsider it. If, after such reconsideration, two-thirds of
that House shall agree to pass the bill, it shall be sent, together with the
objections, to the other House, by which it shall likewise be reconsid-
ered, and if approved by two-thirds of that House, it shall become a law.
But in all cases the votes of both Houses shall be determined by yeas
and nays, and the names of the persons voting for and against the bill
shall be entered on the journal of each House respectively. If any bill
shall not be returned by the President within ten days (Sundays ex-
cepted) after it shall have been presented to him, the same shall be a
law, in like manner as if he had signed it, unless the Congress, by their
adjournment, prevent its return, in which case it shall not be a law.

I. The different ways in which a bill may
become a law. — There are three ways in which a bill
may become a law:

1. It may pass both Houses and be signed by the
President.

2. It may pass both Houses, be vetoed by the President, and be passed over his veto by a two-thirds majority of each House.

3. It may pass both Houses, and the President may fail to sign it within ten days (when these are not at the close of the session).

A bill becomes a law as soon as any one of these conditions is complied with. And it goes into operation as a law at once, unless it is expressly provided in the law that it shall go into operation at some future time.

There are four ways in which a bill may be lost:

1. It may not pass the Senate.

2. It may not pass the House of Representatives.

3. It may be vetoed by the President, and not passed over his veto by Congress.

4. It may be retained by the President within ten days of the end of the session, without either his signature or his veto.

II. The president's veto. — The power of the President to reject a bill is generally called the *veto* power.

The veto power of the President is derived from the veto power of the English sovereign. A king (or reigning queen) of England has an absolute veto, but the President has a limited veto. The veto of a bill by the king of England is final. The act cannot be reversed by Parliament. But the President has a limited veto. A bill vetoed by him may become a law in spite of his veto, by a two-thirds vote of each House of Congress. But the absolute veto of the English sovereign is rarely used, while the limited veto of the President is frequently used. [1]

----

[1] The last veto by an English sovereign was by Queen Anne in 1707. It is very unlikely that any English sovereign will ever again exercise that power, for reasons which the student of the English constitution will understand.

Most of our Presidents have used the veto power, but always sparingly. President Johnson, in course of the struggle with Congress which culminated in his impeachment, vetoed twenty-one bills, seventeen of which were passed by Congress over his veto. He also retained nineteen bills, which became laws without his signature. No other President vetoed more than five bills, and several did not veto any. The veto power is one to be rarely used, and only to prevent measures which are obviously very bad.

III. Passage of a bill over the president's
veto.— When the President vetoes a bill, he sends it
with his objections to the House in which the bill originated.   These objections are to be entered on the journal of the House, so that there may be a permanent
record of them in connection with the legislative action
upon that bill.   If the bill thus vetoed fails of a two-
thirds majority in the House to which it is first sent,
that is the end of it.   But if it passes that House, then
it is sent to the other House.   If it fails of a two-thirds
majority there, that is the end of it.   But if the bill
receives a two-thirds majority in that House also, it becomes a law in spite of the President's veto.   The vote
in each House on a vetoed bill must be by ayes and
noes, and must be recorded in the journal, to make each
member as responsible for his vote as the President is
for his veto.

IV.   How a bill may become a law without the
president's signature or veto.— The time in which
the President can consider a bill is limited to ten days,
not counting Sundays.   Otherwise, the President might
embarrass legislation by holding bills indefinitely without signing or vetoing them.   If the President fails to
sign a bill within ten days (not counting Sundays), the
bill becomes a law without his signature.

V.   Pocketing a bill.— The President has a veto
power, which is practically that of an absolute veto,
over those bills which are passed in the last ten days of
the session.   He can refuse either to sign or veto those
bills, which kills them.   This is called " pocketing " a
bill.

When the President " pockets " a bill, Congress can
do nothing about it, because it is not in session.   But
the same bill may be introduced as a new bill at the

next session. The larger part of all bills which pass Congress are passed in the closing days of a session; and therefore this power of the President is more important than it may seem at first.

CLAUSE 3.

JOINT RESOLUTIONS.

Every order, resolution, or vote to which the concurrence of the Senate and House of Representatives may be necessary (except on a question of adjournment), shall be presented to the President of the United States; and before the same shall take effect, shall be approved by him, or being disapproved by him, shall be repassed by two-thirds of the Senate and House of Representatives, according to the rules and limitations prescribed in the case of a bill.

I.   THEY MUST BE SUBMITTED TO THE PRESIDENT. — Those resolutions, which are intended to have the effect of laws, need also the President's signature, like bills. The mere fact that they are called resolutions instead of bills, does not change the method of their going into effect. Were it not for this provision, Congress might try to elude the President's veto by passing an order or resolution, which should have the effect of law. The courts would probably decide that such action was unconstitutional, because an evasion of the President's veto power. But this clause of the Constitution settles the question beyond controversy.

But when a resolution is not intended to have the force of law, but only to express the opinion of one or both Houses, it does not need the President's signature. This is obvious in the case of a resolution of either House alone.

When both Houses together pass a resolution not intended to have the force of law, such a resolution is called a *concurrent resolution*, not a *joint resolution*, and it is not signed by the President.

II. Congressional action which need not be submitted to the President.

Any action of one House alone or both Houses together, which does not have the effect of law, does not need to be submitted to the President. The following proceedings do not need the President's signature, or a legal substitute for it:

I. *Any action of one House separately*, such as,

1. Anything affecting the *organization* of either House. These concern only that House, and are therefore determined by it alone. (*a*) Thus each House is the judge of the elections, qualifications and returns of its own members (Art. 1, Sec. 5, Clause 1). No other power can interfere with this right. Neither the President, nor the other House nor the courts have anything to do with this question. Each House can pass any orders, resolutions or votes upon any question as to who are lawfully entitled to sit as its members. The decision is final, whether right or wrong, and it can only be reversed by some other action of the same House.

(*b*) Each House can elect its own *officers*, except that the Vice President of the United States is President of the Senate (I, 3, 4). This right belongs to each House by itself, and no other power can lawfully interfere with it.

2. Any resolution expressing the *opinion* of one House. Any society, political convention, or public meeting may express its opinion by resolutions. And either House of Congress has the same right to express its opinions by resolutions. Such a resolution has no legal force, and does not require the assent of the other House or of the President.

3. An impeachment by the House, or the trial of an impeachment by the Senate, or any orders or resolutions relating to them, do not need the President's signature. In this case the two Houses are not acting as legislative bodies, but as judicial bodies, the House of Representatives as a public prosecutor and the Senate as a court. As their actions in this case are not in the nature of laws, they do not need the President's signature.

II. Certain resolutions of both Houses, which do not have the effect of laws, do not need the President's signature.

1. A resolution proposing an amendment to the Constitution does not need the President's signature. Such a resolution does not amend the Constitution, but only proposes an amendment. It is the action of the States, through legislatures or conventions, that actually amends the Constitution (see page 249).

2. A resolution which is in the nature of an agreement between the two Houses to do something, does not need the President's signature. Such a concurrent resolution has no binding force, except the honor of the two Houses. Each House still can do as it pleases. It is bound by no law. As such a resolution is not a law, it does not need the President's signature.

3. In brief, it may be said that any action of Congress which is in the nature of a *law*, must be submitted to the President for his approval, and any action which is not in the nature of a *law*, does not need to be so submitted.

SECTION 8.

POWERS OF CONGRESS.

ANALYSIS OF THIS SECTION.

(*And other powers of Congress granted in other parts of this Constitution.*)

<table>
<tr><td rowspan="30">POWERS OF CONGRESS.</td><td colspan="2">I. GENERAL STATEMENT. — All legislative powers granted by the Constitution are vested in Congress.............</td><td>I, 2</td></tr>
<tr><td rowspan="4">II. FINANCIAL POWERS ....</td><td>1. To lay and collect taxes, duties and excises......................</td><td>I, 8, 1</td></tr>
<tr><td>2. To pay the debts of the U. S......</td><td>I, 8, 1</td></tr>
<tr><td>3. To provide for the common defense and general welfare.............</td><td>I, 8, 1</td></tr>
<tr><td>4. To borrow money on the credit of the U. S.........................</td><td>I, 8, 2</td></tr>
<tr><td rowspan="12">III. COMMERCIAL POWERS ....</td><td>1. To regulate foreign commerce ....</td><td>I, 8, 3</td></tr>
<tr><td>2. To regulate domestic commerce ..</td><td>I, 8, 3</td></tr>
<tr><td>3. To establish uniform bankrupt laws..............................</td><td>I, 8, 4</td></tr>
<tr><td>4. To coin money ....</td><td>I, 8, 5</td></tr>
<tr><td>5. To regulate the value of foreign coins........... ....</td><td>I, 8, 5</td></tr>
<tr><td>6. To fix the standard of weights and measures................. ....</td><td>I, 8, 5</td></tr>
<tr><td>7. To provide for the punishment of counterfeiting...................</td><td>I, 8, 6</td></tr>
<tr><td>8. To establish post offices and post roads ....</td><td>I, 8, 7</td></tr>
<tr><td>9. To grant patents and copyrights..</td><td>I, 8, 8</td></tr>
<tr><td>10. To prohibit the slave trade after 1808.............................</td><td>I, 9, 1</td></tr>
<tr><td>11. To tax the slave trade before that date ....</td><td>I, 9, 1</td></tr>
<tr><td>12. To allow States to levy duties.....</td><td>I, 10, 2</td></tr>
</table>

POWERS OF CONGRESS.

IV. War Powers..

1. To declare war .... I, 8, 11
2. To send out privateers......... ... I, 8, 11
3. To make rules concerning captures on land or sea.................... I, 8, 11
4. To raise and support armies...... I, 8, 12
5. To provide and maintain a navy.. I, 8, 13
6. To make rules for the army and navy .... I, 8, 14
7. To provide for calling forth the militia .... I, 8, 15
8. To provide for organizing, arming and disciplining the militia..... I, 8, 16
9. To suspend the writ of *habeas corpus* in case of rebellion or invasion .... I, 9, 2
10. To allow States to keep armies and navies .... I, 10, 3
11. To allow States to make treaties or compacts. .... I, 10, 3
12. To allow States to engage in war.. I, 10, 3

V. Powers relating to Congress.

1. To apportion Representatives, I, 2, 3, and Am. XIV
2. To reduce the representation of States which abridge the number of voters................... Am. XIV, 2
3. To regulate the elections for Senators and Representatives I, 4, 1
4. To fix the time of the annual meeting .... I, 4, 2
5. To adjourn.................. .... I, 5, 4
6. To fix the salaries of Senators and Representatives .... I, 6, 1

VI. Powers relating to the President ......

1. To fix the day of choosing Presidential electors, and of their meeting to choose a President II, 1, 4
2. To canvass the returns of a Presidential election.............. Am. XII
3. To determine what officer shall act as President, when there is no President or Vice President .... II, 1, 6
4. To fix the salary of the President and other executive officers.. II, 1, 7
5. To regulate the civil service.... II, 2, 2

VII. Powers relating to the Judiciary.

1. To fix the salaries of U. S. Judges .... III, 1
2. To regulate the appellate jurisdiction of the Supreme Court, III, 2, 2

POWERS OF CONGRESS.

VII. Powers relating to the Judiciary, con.

3. To establish inferior courts,   I, 8, 9, and III, 1
4. To fix the place of trials for crimes committed outside of any State.................... III, 2, 3
5. To declare the punishment of treason. .... III, 3, 2

VIII. Powers relating to the jurisdiction of the U. S..

1. To define and punish piracies and felonies on the high seas, I, 8, 10
2. To define and punish offenses against the law of nations... I, 8, 10
3. To exercise exclusive legislation in the District of Columbia .... I, 8, 17
4. To exercise exclusive legislation in forts, arsenals and dockyards .... I, 8, 17
5. To govern the territory of the U. S........................... IV, 3, 2

IX. Powers relating to the States

1. To admit new States .... IV, 3, 1
2. To guarantee to every State a republican form of government........ .... IV, 4
3. To prescribe the manner of proving the public records of one State in another State.... IV, 1
4. To allow States to collect duties, I, 10, 2
5. To allow States to keep armies and navies, make treaties and engage in war .... I, 10, 2
6. To submit proposed amendments to the States.......... V

X. Miscellaneous powers........

1. To allow U. S. officers to accept presents or titles from foreign powers .... I, 9, 8
2. To remove rebel disabilities.... Am. XIV, 3
3. To enforce the provisions of Am's XIII, XIV and XV ....

XI. General powers....

1. To make all laws needed to make these powers effective. I, 8, 18
2. To make all laws needed to carry into effect all other powers vested in any part of the government .... I, 8, 18

SECTION 8.

POWERS OF CONGRESS.

I. THE POWERS OF CONGRESS ARE LEGISLATIVE POWERS.

Thus far this Article has treated of the *organization* of Congress. This section and the next treats of the *legislation* of Congress. Congress is the law-making power of the government, and any laws which the Federal government is authorized to make, may be made by Congress. The United States government can only make laws through Congress. And therefore the powers of law-making given in this section are expressly given to Congress, and the restrictions upon legislation by the United States, are expressly imposed upon Congress, as the legislative department of the government.

The powers of Congress are all legislative powers. Congress has all the legislative power of the Federal government, except as limited by the President's veto, and has no powers except legislative powers.

II. CONCURRENT POWERS OF STATE LEGISLATURES.

The States can make laws on those subjects given in this section or elsewhere, on which Congress can make laws, with these two exceptions: 1. States cannot legislate on subjects forbidden them by this Constitution. 2. State laws must give way to United States laws on all other subjects.

III. THESE LEGISLATIVE POWERS ARE SUBJECT TO THE PRESIDENT'S VETO.

As these powers are all powers to make laws, they are of course subject to the President's veto, as explained in the last section. There are some things Congress can do without the President, but nothing in the way of legislation.

CLAUSE 1.

TAXATION.

The Congress shall have power to lay and collect taxes, duties, imposts
and excises, to pay the debts and provide for the common defense and
general welfare of the United States; but all duties, imposts and excises
shall be uniform throughout the United States.

I. THE POWER OF TAXATION INHERENT IN GOVERN-
MENT. — Taxation of some kind is necessary to all government. The labor of government, like all other labor,
is expensive, and sometimes is very expensive. In war,
especially, the expenses of government become enormous.

All governments exercise the power of taxation as a
necessary part of their sovereignty. And if this Constitution had not expressly given this power, it still
would have been implied in the fact of a government.

Under the Articles of Confederation the sovereignty
was in the several States, and therefore the power of
taxation was left to each State separately. The United
States was not a nation, but a confederation of nations.
Congress under the Confederation was not the legislative department of a national government, but an
assembly of delegates from allied governments, to consult together for the common good. They could not
tax, but they could ask the States to tax, and the States
could tax or not as they pleased.

But this Constitution made us a nation, with a national government. For that government the power
of taxation is necessary, and is given in this clause.

II. THE POWER OF TAXATION RESIDES IN THE REPRE-
SENTATIVES OF THE PEOPLE. — In despotic or aristo-
cratic governments the power of taxation is not in the
hands of those who pay taxes. But in republics or

limited monarchies the people, or their representatives, have the power of taxation. When those who pay the taxes themselves levy them, taxes are more justly collected and more wisely used. There is no power of the government which the people watch more closely than the power of raising and expending the public funds.

III. THE STATES MAY ALSO LEVY TAXES. — The fact that the United States exercises the right of taxation, does not preclude the States from also levying taxes, nor does it forbid them authorizing cities, counties, towns, villages and school districts from levying taxes for their own purposes. But no State may levy duties on imports or exports for its own revenue. (Section 10.)

IV. METHODS OF TAXATION.— The following analysis gives all the methods of taxation named in the Constitution:

$$
\text{TAXES..}
\begin{cases}
\text{DIRECT} \dots \begin{cases} \text{Property tax.} \\ \text{Poll tax.} \end{cases} \\[2ex]
\text{INDIRECT} \dots \begin{cases} \text{Duties.} \\ \text{Imposts.} \\ \text{Excises.} \end{cases}
\end{cases}
$$

Taxes are direct or indirect; *direct taxes* are those which are paid directly by the tax payer to the government; *indirect taxes* are those which are paid directly by the merchant or manufacturer on his goods, but which are paid indirectly by those who buy those goods. Indirect taxes are easier for the government to collect, because people do not stop to think how much goes to the government of what they pay for goods.

For this reason the United States government has used indirect taxation almost entirely.

V. DIRECT TAXES. — The Constitution provides that direct taxes shall be laid upon the States according to their representative population (see I, 2, 3, and I, 9, 4). This was one of the compromises between the Northern and Southern States. The representative population is now, since slavery has been abolished, the same as the actual population, excluding uncivilized Indians. Only five direct taxes have been collected by the Federal government — in 1798, 1813, 1815, 1816, and 1862. But the States raise most of their taxes by direct taxation.

Direct taxes may be upon property or upon persons. Direct taxes upon property are levied by taking a certain per cent. of the assessed valuation of the property taxed. But when a direct property tax is levied by the United States, the per cent. will vary in the ratio of the population to the wealth of the several States. The amount to be raised is apportioned among the States according to their population, but within each State it will be apportioned according to property. The effect of this is to tax the property of the newer and poorer States, more than that of the older and richer ones. If the government raised many direct taxes, this would be an injustice to be redressed.

The Supreme Court has decided that an income tax, although paid directly by the tax payer, is not a direct tax within the meaning of the Constitution. (I, 2, 3.)

A direct tax upon persons is called a poll tax or capitation tax. In that case, each person liable to the tax is called on to pay an equal amount.

VI. DUTIES. — A duty is a tax on the importation or exportation of goods. Export duties are probably forbidden by the Constitution (I, 9, 5). Duties on imports are (*a*) specific duties or (*b*) ad valorem duties. A *specific* duty is one upon the weight or measure of goods; an *ad valorem* duty is one upon their value.

VII. THE TARIFF QUESTION.

The rate of duties is called a tariff. A *prohibitory tariff* is one which puts the duties on one or more articles so high that it does not pay to import them. A *protective tariff* is one high enough to make it profitable to manufacture or raise in this country articles thus protected. A *revenue tariff* is one high enough and yet not too high to yield a good revenue to the government. *Free trade* exists where there is no tariff.

The tariff question has been one of the great political questions on which parties have divided; and it is likely to be a prominent political issue for many years to come. No party wishes free trade, and none wishes a prohibitory tariff. The contest is between a high protective tariff and a revenue tariff. On this question people generally divide according to their real or supposed interests. As a rule, the agricultural sections of the country favor a revenue tariff, the manufacturing sections a protective tariff, and the commercial centers stand neutral.

The collection of duties is in charge of the Bureau of Customs, which is a part of the Treasury Department. Duties are collected at the *custom houses* located at the various *ports of entry*, by officers called custom house officers.

VIII. INTERNAL REVENUES.—The word *imposts* is used vaguely in the Constitution for any kind of indirect tax, and is intended to cover any indirect tax that any one could claim is not covered by the words *duties* and *excises*.

Excises are taxes levied on person who manufacture, or articles manufactured, in this country. The chief sources of revenue now from excises is the tax on liquors and tobacco, and the licenses required for carrying on certain kinds of business.

All these kinds of indirect taxes are called now *internal revenue*. Their collection is in the charge of the Bureau of Internal Revenue, which is a part of the Treasury Department.

IX. UNIFORMITY OF TAXATION.—Indirect taxes must be the same throughout the country. It is plain that this is the only fair way of taxation. Direct taxes, as we have seen, are not uniform throughout the country. But the indirect taxes, from which the United States gets most of its revenue, are uniform. The same duties are charged at one port of entry as at another, and the same excises are charged in one State as another.

X. THE OBJECTS OF TAXATION.— This section limits the power of Congress to tax the people to these three objects: (*a*) to pay the debts of the United States, (*b*) to provide for the common defense, and (*c*) to provide for the general welfare. Congress has no right to tax the people except for these three objects, and only enough to accomplish these objects. The general welfare is a vague expression, which allows a wide margin for the discretion of Congress as to what things are needed for the general welfare. But the public money cannot lawfully be squandered as it is in monarchies for the luxury and pride of a king and his court. It cannot be expended for the sole benefit of one State to the exclusion of the rest. It cannot be used for any thing that obviously does not provide for the common defense or for the general welfare.

CLAUSE 2.

THE POWER TO BORROW.

To borrow money on the credit of the United States.

I. THE PUBLIC DEBT. — This clause gives Congress the power to borrow. No other department of the government can borrow money except as authorized by law to do so. Sometimes in times of great emergency during war, the Secretary of the Treasury has borrowed money; but these acts were unlawful, and were only made lawful by a law passed afterwards.

In time of peace, the regular revenues ought to pay all expenses of the government. But no taxation which the people could afford to pay would be enough to carry on a great war without borrowing money. During the Civil War the expenses of the government were over two million dollars a day. A large part of this necessarily had to be borrowed.

II. CLASSIFICATION OF THE PUBLIC DEBT.

The debt of the United States is in three forms: (*a*) bonds; (*b*) treasury notes; (*c*) floating debt.

The greater part of the debt is in bonds. Of these there are two kinds, *registered* bonds and *coupon* bonds. The *registered bonds* are called so because a register of each bond is kept in the United States Treasury, with the name and residence of the holder of the bond. It is thus safe against thieves, because no one except the person who owns it can collect it or the interest on it from the government. If the holder of such a bond wishes to sell it, he must give notice to the proper officers at Washington, and have the bond transferred on the books to the person to whom he sells it.

The *coupon bonds* are not thus registered at Washington, and thus are as liable to be stolen as any other property. They are named from the coupons or little slips of paper attached to them, each of which represents the interest on that bond for six months. As these become due, they may be cut off and sold at any broker's office or bank. The government will pay the bonds or coupons, when they are due, to any person who presents them. The government bonds that are now outstanding nearly all bear interest at the rate of four, four and a half, or five per cent., payable semi-annually.

Treasury notes, commonly called "greenbacks," are promises to pay money on demand. As they are made a legal tender for debts, they circulate as money. Although the notes are promises to pay on demand, they circulated from 1862 till 1879 without being paid by the government.

The floating debt consists of salaries due, interest accruing, bills of contractors not yet paid, and the like. This debt is never very large, and is kept paid up as promptly as possible.

III. PAYMENT OF THE DEBT.

The public debt is being gradually paid up, and that much faster than the public debt of other nations. Because of this, the credit of the United States is as good as that of any nation in the world ex-

F

cept England, and we are able to borrow money at low rates of interest. As the national debt is constantly being reduced, it is not worth while to give it here. By watching the newspapers early in January and July each year, the semi-annual statement of the debt can be found for that date.

CLAUSE 3.

THE POWER OVER COMMERCE.

To regulate commerce with foreign nations, and among the several States, and with the Indian tribes.

I. PREVIOUS HISTORY. — Before the Revolution, Great Britain regulated the commerce of the colonies with each other, with the home country and with the rest of the world. During the war and until this Constitution was adopted, each State regulated its own commerce in its own way. Each State tried to favor its own commerce at the expense of the rest, and the result was that the commerce of all was hampered, and local jealousies were greatly increased. If this power of regulating commerce had not been given to the general government, there can be little doubt that these commercial rivalries would have broken up the Union eventually. It was wise, therefore, to give the power of regulating commerce to Congress.

II. STATE POWERS OF REGULATING COMMERCE. — The States have no power over the subject of commerce except,

1. Commerce within the State; or

2. Such duties on commerce as Congress may allow (I, 10, 2 and 3), and these must be uniform in all the States (I, 9, 6); or

3. By inspection laws.

The States have no power over commerce within their

boundaries, except that which is wholly within their boundaries. For instance, commerce on the Erie canal is wholly within the State of New York, and the New York legislature and not Congress is the proper body to deal with it. But the Hudson river is partly in New York and partly in New Jersey, and the two bodies have each jurisdiction on that river. Commerce between New York and Albany on that river is in the jurisdiction of the State of New York. But commerce between New York and Jersey City is under the jurisdiction of the United States.

Inspection laws are intended to prevent frauds in the sale of goods. Inspectors are appointed in many States who inspect goods offered for sale, and see that they are of the proper weight or measure and of the right quality. These inspectors are generally paid by fees, which, of course, are really the same as duties on the goods inspected. A State might, under the name of inspection fees, impose heavy duties on goods coming from other States or countries. To prevent this, the Constitution (I, 10, 2) provides (*a*) that the net produce of such imposts shall be paid into the United States treasury, and (*b*) that inspection laws shall always be subject to the revision of Congress.

III. COMMERCE WITH FOREIGN NATIONS. — Congress has power to *regulate* commerce with foreign nations. But Congress has not power to *prohibit* commerce for any length of time. One Congress laid an embargo on all foreign commerce, forbidding it as a reprisal for the action of European powers. The measure aroused bitter political feeling, and was repealed in a little over a year. It is not likely that any such embargo will ever be laid on our commerce again. Congress has the right to so regulate foreign commerce as to raise a

revenue from it, or to favor our own commerce or manufactures, or to retaliate injuries or reciprocate benefits
derived from the commercial laws of other nations, and
the right to regulate commerce has been used in all these
ways.[1]

There is one way in which foreign commerce may be
regulated without an act of Congress. A treaty made
by the President and confirmed by the Senate, may
regulate commerce between the United States and the
power with which the treaty is made. Such a treaty
annuls any act of Congress in conflict with it, and cannot be repealed by act of Congress (see page 254). Such
commercial treaties are a part of the supreme law of
the land, and are superior to any act of Congress.

IV. COMMERCE BETWEEN THE STATES. — Congress
has power to regulate commerce among the several
States. In the exercise of this power, Congress has
wisely made all commerce within the United States free.
A merchant can travel from State to State without being stopped by vexatious duties at the border of each
State. Freight and passengers are carried past State
boundaries without hindrance. For all the purposes of
commerce this great territory is a unit. The only regulations that have been prescribed are such as are needed
for the safety of ships and steamboats.

Railroads have thus far been left under the control of
the several States, but there is no doubt that Congress
could control the whole subject of railroads, if it chose.
The only possible exception would be in the case of
those railroads which are wholly within one State.

---

[1] "In the practice of the government, the commercial power has been
applied to embargoes, non-intercourse, non-importation, coasting trade,
fisheries, navigation, seamen, privileges of American and foreign ships,
quarantine, pilotage, wrecks, light-houses, buoys, beacons; obstructions in
bays, sounds, rivers and creeks; inroads of the ocean, and many other
kindred subjects; and doubtless, includes salvage, policies of insurance,
bills of exchange, and all maritime contracts, and the designation of ports
of entry and delivery." — *Farrar's Manual of the Constitution*, p. 328.

The control of these would perhaps be still in the hands of the State in which they are.

V. COMMERCE WITH THE INDIAN TRIBES. — Congress has sole control of commerce with the Indian tribes. These tribes are not foreign nations, nor are they composed of citizens. They are subject peoples; and as such they are under the control of the Federal government. Commerce, like all other relations with them, is under the control of the general government. Even if one of these tribes is located within the boundaries of a State, the State has nothing to do with it. The United States alone controls all relations with it.

CLAUSE 4.

NATURALIZATION AND BANKRUPTCY.

To establish an uniform rule of naturalization, and uniform laws on the subject of bankruptcies throughout the United States.

I. REASON FOR THIS CLAUSE. — Naturalization is the process by which a foreigner becomes a citizen. The power of naturalization is one of the attributes of sovereignty. As long as the States were held to be sovereign, it was proper that they should have the power of naturalization, as they did under the Articles of Confederation. But when this Constitution was framed to make us one nation, this power of naturalization was taken from the State legislatures and given to Congress. Some practical abuses had arisen from the States requiring different times of residence. A foreigner who thought the time required in one State too long, had only to move to a neighboring State to be naturalized in a much shorter time. It was, therefore, provided that the rule of naturalization should be uniform.

II. WHAT IS CITIZENSHIP. — A citizen is a member

of the body politic.   All the citizens together make up the nation.   All persons who are not citizens are aliens.

A common mistake is to suppose that citizens are the same as voters.   As a fact, most citizens are not voters, and not all voters are citizens.   Women and children are not voters, but are citizens, if otherwise qualified. And in several States men can vote who are not citizens of the United States, but who have only declared their intention to become citizens.   The student should carefully distinguish between citizens and voters.

III. WHO ARE CITIZENS. — By the Fourteenth Amendment citizenship is defined thus:

" All persons born or naturalized in the United States, and subject to the jurisdiction thereof, are citizens of the United States and of the State wherein they reside."

The phrase, " and subject to the jurisdiction thereof," was meant to shut out from citizenship those Indians who obey their tribal customs, instead of the laws of the United States.

Those Indians who, by permission of Congress, have left their tribes, and are subject to the United States laws, are citizens.

There are thus two ways in which any one may become a citizen:

1. By birthright.
2. By naturalization.

A nation is like a family in this respect, for there are two ways in which a person may become a member of a given family — by birthright and adoption.   Naturalization makes any one a citizen of a given nation in the same way in which adoption makes any one a member of a given family.   Citizens of the United States, then, may be either natural born citizens or naturalized citizens.

IV. NATURAL-BORN CITIZENS. — This phrase is used
in Article II, section 1, where it is provided that the
President of the United States shall be a natural-born
citizen.   A natural-born citizen is not necessarily a
native of the United States. Members of Indian tribes
are natives, but are not natural-born citizens. And there
are some natural-born citizens who are not natives of
the United States, but were born in other countries.
There are two conditions required to make a natural-born
citizen — parentage and place of birth. A child born
of American parents in any place under American jur-
isdiction· is unquestionably a natural-born American
citizen. But where the parentage and birthplace do not
agree, there is a case of doubtful citizenship which is
decided by the choice of the person himself, when he
comes to years of manhood.

Any person born of an American father, in a place
subject to the jurisdiction of a foreign nation, may be
a natural-born American citizen, if he claims that privilege when he arrives at the proper age. So, also, any
person born of a foreign father in any place subject to
the jurisdiction of the United States, may be a natural-
born American citizen, if he choose. In these doubtful
cases the person may choose the country of his father
or the country of his birth. So that a person may be a
natural-born citizen of the United States, without being
a *native* of the United States.

The places outside the United States which are subject to the jurisdiction of the United States, are
(*a*) United States men-of-war anywhere. (*b*) Ships
bearing the American flag, while on the high seas, but
not in a foreign port. (*c*) Places purchased for naval
stations. (*d*) The houses in which American ambassadors in foreign lands reside. This extends also to the

persons and families of these ambassadors and their subordinate officers. So that a child born to any of them in a foreign country is considered to be born under the jurisdiction of this country (see also page 211). This extends to consuls in heathen or Mohammedan lands, but not to consuls in Christian'lands.

So also the children of foreign ambassadors or their subordinates born in this country are not natural-born citizens.

V. NATURALIZED CITIZENS. — Persons have been naturalized in each of the following ways:

1. *Under the naturalization law of the United States.* For this, two steps are necessary:

(*a*) The foreigner who wishes to be naturalized must "declare his intention to become a citizen of the United States." He can do this at any time after coming to this country, the very day he lands if he pleases. It must be before the Clerk of some United States or State court, who gives him a certificate, which is popularly called his "first papers."

This declaration of intention is the first step to citizenship, and entitles the person taking it to certain privileges. It entitles him to protection in foreign countries. It entitles him to take up a homestead of 160 acres of land. It entitles him in several States to vote, if otherwise qualified, and to hold most offices.

(*b*) But in order to become a full citizen, he must take another step, which can only be done during a term of some United States or State court, and in open court. Before taking this step, he must have resided in the United States five years, and it must be at least two years after he took out his first papers, and he must have sustained a good moral character during that time, and been "attached to the Constitution of the

United States, and well disposed to the good order and happiness of the same." [1]

All this having been satisfactorily proved, he renounces all allegiance to any foreign power, and swears allegiance to the United States, and receives a certificate of naturalization. This completes his naturalization, and is popularly called " taking out his second papers." He is thus entitled to all the privileges of a citizen, except being elected President or Vice President.

2. *By treaty or annexation.* When the United States annexed Texas, the citizens of that commonwealth were made citizens of the United States, by the act of annexation, by which Texas was made a State in the Union. The same was the case with every addition of territory made by treaty with France or Spain. Their free inhabitants, except wild Indians, became citizens at once.

3. *Members of Indian tribes* may be made citizens by act of Congress, on leaving their tribal relations and coming under the jurisdiction of the United States.

4. *Slaves are not citizens.* When the slaves in the South were freed, as the result of our civil war, the act that made them freemen made them citizens. But to make assurance doubly sure, the Fourteenth Amendment was passed, which made them citizens, if they were not already.

VI. NATURALIZATION OF WOMEN AND CHILDREN. — Women and children may be naturalized in the following manner: 1. When a man is naturalized in any of the ways named above, it naturalizes his family also. The family which is naturalized consists of his wife and his children who are under twenty-one years old, but not of other persons who may be living in the family.

---

[1] During our civil war, some special privileges in regard to naturalization were given to foreigners who enlisted in our army. These are omitted as of no importance now.

If a foreigner has declared his intention to become a citizen and dies before becoming a citizen, his widow and minor children may go on with the naturalization at the proper time, in his place.

2. If a foreigner comes to this country when he is under eighteen years of age, and resides here five years, he may take out his first and second papers at the same time, but he must be at least twenty-one, and must have resided here five years, when he is thus naturalized.

3. A woman who is over twenty-one, and who is not married at the time, may be naturalized on the same conditions and in the same way as a man. Several women have been thus naturalized in order to take up and acquire titles to homesteads.

4. A woman not a citizen becomes a citizen on marrying a citizen.

VII. BANKRUPTCY. — A person who is unable to pay his debts is an insolvent person. A bankrupt is an insolvent person, who has been declared to be such by the proper legal authority. A bankrupt law is a law under which an insolvent person may give up to his creditors voluntarily, or be compelled by them to give up, all his property which is liable for debt, and may then be freed from the rest of his debts. The objects of such a law are to divide the property of a bankrupt fairly among all his creditors as far as it goes, and to give the bankrupt a chance to begin business again, free from his old debts.

Congress has power to pass a uniform bankruptcy law. It must be *uniform;* that is, it must apply alike to all parts of the United States. As long as Congress does not exercise this power, the States have the right to pass such laws; but when the United States has a bankrupt law, it supersedes all State laws upon the subject.

the States have the right to pass such laws; but when the United States has such a law, it supersedes all State bankrupt laws, and this law is executed by United States courts and officers. State laws on this subject are often called insolvency laws.

CLAUSE 5.

COINAGE AND WEIGHTS AND MEASURES.

To coin money, regulate the value thereof, and of foreign coin, and fix the standard of weights and measures.

I. THE POWER OF COINAGE. — The power to coin money is an attribute of sovereignty, and naturally belongs to the United States as a sovereign power. The States have no right to coin money (I, 10, 1). Much less have cities, counties, or villages, or private individuals or corporations. Only the United States can coin money, and then only by act of Congress. No officer of the United States can coin money except as authorized to do so by act of Congress.

II. UNITED STATES MONEY. — Money is coined in the United States in the mints at Philadelphia, San Francisco, Carson and Denver. The three latter places have been made mints because they are in the gold and silver districts of California, Nevada and Colorado.

Money has been coined from gold, silver, copper and nickel. The gold coins of the United States are now the dollar piece, the quarter eagle or two and a half dollar piece, the three dollar piece, the half eagle or five dollar piece, the eagle or ten dollar piece, and the double eagle or twenty dollar piece. The silver coins of the United States are now the trade dollar, the dollar, the half dollar, the quarter dollar, and the dime. The minor coins are made of copper or nickel, and are

a five cent piece, a three cent piece, a two cent piece
and a one cent piece.

III. TREASURY NOTES AND BANK BILLS. — Some
persons claim that treasury notes, or " greenbacks" are
money.   In popular language they are often called
money, but in reality they are only promises to pay
money. The government has the right to issue them,
and perhaps also to make them a legal tender for debts,
so that they circulate the same as money; but that does
not make them money. They are the same as bank notes,
except that it is the government and not a private bank
which issues them. If the student will read the words
printed on one of the greenbacks, he will see that they
do not profess to be money, but only promises to pay,
or "bills of credit" (I, 10, 1). The *currency* of a
country is composed of everything that circulates as
money, and is received in payment of debts in ordinary
business transactions. In this country the currency is
composed of (*a*) coin, (*b*) treasury notes, (*c*) bank
notes, (*d*) bank drafts and bills of exchange, (*e*) checks
drawn by individuals on banks where they have deposits.
Treasury notes are thus a part of the currency, but are
not money.

IV. FOREIGN COINS. — Congress has regulated the
value of foreign coins, so far as the rate at which they
shall be taken for taxes and duties. But there is now
no law attempting to regulate the value of foreign coins
in the payment of debts. People may take foreign
coins in business dealings, if they choose, but they are
not obliged to by law.

V. THE STANDARD OF WEIGHTS AND MEASURES. —
Congress has never exercised the power to fix the standard of weights and measures, but has left the subject to
the State legislatures. This standard, however, is, with

slight exceptions, the same in all the States, so that we have the advantages of uniformity.

Congress has adopted a standard of weights to be used in the mints in coining money, but has not required this to be used elsewhere.

Congress has also enacted that the metric system of weights and measures shall be lawful but not obligatory. The object of this is to make people familiar with this system, which will probably sometime be adopted by all civilized nations, so as make all weights and measures throughout the world the same.

CLAUSE 6.

COUNTERFEITING.

To provide for the punishment of counterfeiting the securities and current coin of the United States.

Under the power conferred by this clause, the United States punishes the counterfeiting of its coins, bonds, notes, stamps, and other securities. The punishment is by fine and imprisonment in various degrees.

CLAUSE 7.

POST OFFICES AND POST ROADS.

To establish post offices and post roads.

I. VALUE OF THE POST OFFICE. — This is the power of the general government which most concerns the daily life of our citizens. Every time we receive or send a letter, or postal card, or newspaper, we touch the machinery of the United States government. We thus have friendly and business intercourse with distant people, or get periodical literature far cheaper and more certainly than we should be able to if the government

did not manage the post office. For one cent we can
send a short note to any person in the United States;
for three cents we can send a long letter. It is plain
that for the States to have each its own postal system
would lead to endless confusion and delay. The power
over post offices and post roads is therefore given, by
this clause, to the United States.

II. MANAGEMENT OF THE POST OFFICES.

The Postmaster General has general charge of the postal business of the United States. Besides the assistants and clerks required in the Department at Washington, there are many thousand
persons constantly employed in the postal service of the United
States. In every city and village of the United States, and in
some country places far from towns, post offices are established,
each in charge of a postmaster, with as many assistants as he may
need. Of the postmasters, about 1,600 holding the most important
offices, in which the pay is one thousand dollars or more, are appointed by the President, with the consent of the Senate. The
rest, over 40,000 in number, are appointed by the Postmaster General.

In addition to these, every considerable railroad has a system of
mail cars, which are really traveling post offices, which receive and
distribute mail as the train passes from one end of the railroad to
the other. By this, all the delay of sorting out mail at distributing
post offices is saved, and a letter now travels as quickly to its des-
tination as a passenger does.

In cities of 20,000 population or more, the mail is carried to people's doors by carriers, and no one is obliged to go to the post office
for his mail, if he has it directed to his street and number.

III. THE POST OFFICE AS A BANK.

There is danger in sending money through the mail, that it may
be stolen by some one of the many persons who handle each letter.
One way of guarding against this is by *registering* a letter containing money or valuables. For a small fee the letter is registered,
and its progress traced till it reaches the person to whom it is sent.

But a better method of sending money is by *money orders*. A
money order is the same as a draft of one bank on another; only in
this case it is the draft of one postmaster on another. The fee is

small, and there is no risk in sending money in this way. But the government will not take great risks; it sells no money order over fifty dollars. For a larger sum than this one should go to a bank for a draft

IV. FOREIGN POSTAGE.

By postal treaties with other countries we now have mail communication with all civilized nations. A letter can be mailed at any post office in the United States to almost any part of the world, and a money order can now be bought at a money order office in the United States to Canada and to many parts of Europe.

V. POST ROADS.—Congress has authority to *establish* post roads.

Generally it has simply *used* roads already established by the States. But it has established some highways and railroads under the authority of this section. The principal highway thus established, was the Cumberland road from the Potomac to the Ohio river, and the principal railroads thus established are the Union and Central Pacific, together making one line, and the Southern Pacific and the Northern Pacific Railroads. These roads were none of them built by the United States directly, but by incorporated companies, which were assisted by the United States with money and bonds. They were built under the authority and with the assistance of the United States, as post roads and military roads.

CLAUSE 8.

COPYRIGHTS AND PATENTS.

To promote the progress of science and useful arts, by securing for limited times to authors and inventors the exclusive right to their respective writings and discoveries.

I. COPYRIGHTS.— A copyright secures to an author the exclusive right to publish and sell his writings.

The progress of science and literature is greatly promoted by giving this privilege to authors. Most people cannot afford to write merely for fame, and unless they can be at least paid for their time, they cannot write much. A copyright law, by giving them the control of their writings, is an encouragement to authors.

The United States copyright law has created an American literature since this Constitution was adopted. A large part of this literature would never have been written, if there had been no United States copyright law.

A copyright is given for twenty-eight years, and can be renewed for fourteen years more. It may be sold or inherited, like other property. This book is copy-righted; see the next page after the title page.

II. PATENTS.— A patent secures to an inventor the exclusive right to manufacture and sell a new inven-tion. The liberal patent laws of the United States have encouraged very greatly the progress of the useful arts. The natural ingenuity of the American people has been so stimulated by the rewards of successful inventors, that the United States to-day leads the world in the manufacture of labor-saving machinery. At every World's Fair, American inventions and manufactures take a large share of the prizes in this line. Among the important inventions of Americans, are the tele-graph, the steamboat, the cotton gin, the sewing ma-chine, the reaper, the threshing machine, the sleeping car, the telephone, the phonograph.

Besides these great inventions, thousands of lesser ones, and thousands of improvements upon machines invented elsewhere, help to show the inventiveness of the American mind, and the value of our patent laws.

A *caveat* is given for one year to any inventor who wishes to secure his invention, but who needs time to perfect it before patenting. A *patent* is given only to inventions really new, or to improvements on old inventions. A patent is given for seventeen years, and may be extended for seven years more by the patent office. Congress by special law has sometimes extended the term of certain patents still further.[1]

Patents may be sold or inherited, like other property. Every article which is patented must have the word "patented," with the date of the patent, affixed to it in some way.

CLAUSE 9.

UNITED STATES COURTS.

To constitute tribunals inferior to the Supreme Court.

I. SUPREME COURT. — A Supreme Court of the United States is provided for in Article III, section I. But Congress fixes the number of the judges, their salaries, and their duties, except as provided by the Constitution.

II. INFERIOR TRIBUNALS. — By this clause Congress has power to organize inferior courts. This power has been used to organize the following courts:

1. United States circuit courts.
2. United States district courts.
3. A court of claims.
4. A supreme court of the District of Columbia.
5. Territorial courts in each organized territory.

The power to organize these courts implies also the power to determine the powers of each court, within the limits of the Constitution. This power also Congress has frequently exercised.

---

[1] But the exercise of this power is very poor policy, because those inventors who need the benefit of an extension of a patent are the very ones who are not powerful enough to secure it; and those who can afford to lobby through Congress a special law extending their patents, have become rich enough not to need it. The result in such cases is to give a monopoly of a useful invention for a long time to people who do not need it and to whom it is not in justice due.

G

CLAUSE 10.

CRIMES AT SEA.

To define and punish piracies and felonies committed on the high seas, and offenses against the law of nations.

I. PIRACY. — Piracy is robbery at sea. By the general consent of Christian nations, a pirate is a common enemy and an outlaw. A pirate is not entitled to the protection of the country of which he is a citizen, but may be taken by the forces of any other nation as well and punished. The universal punishment for piracy is death.

In addition, the United States and some other nations have made the slave-trade piracy, and punish it with death. As this is not agreed to by all nations, slave traders do not commit a crime against the law of nations, but only against the law of their own nation. An American slave-trader can be tried only by the courts of his own country; while an ordinary pirate, although American, could be executed by any power which captured him, with or without trial.

II. FELONIES ON THE HIGH SEAS. — Crimes are either *felonies* or *misdemeanors*. If the penalty attached to them be death, or imprisonment in a state prison, they are felonies; otherwise they are misdemeanors.

The high seas, are those waters of the ocean outside the jurisdiction of any particular State. Generally this extends to low-water mark. This is the line that divides the jurisdiction of the United States from that of those States which border on the ocean. But so far as it concerns other nations, the jurisdiction of the United States extends to three miles from low-water mark, including all bays and gulfs.

As between the different nations of the world, the high seas, that is, the ocean beyond three miles from shore, are neutral ground, and free to all, to traverse, but not owned by any nation. The jurisdiction of each nation extends (*a*) to its merchant vessels while on the high seas, but not in foreign ports, and (*b*) to its ships of war everywhere, in port or on the high seas. And felonies committed by American citizens anywhere beyond low-water mark and outside the jurisdiction of another nation, are punishable by United States law and not by State law.

III. OFFENSES AGAINST THE LAW OF NATIONS. — The law of nations, or *international law*, consists of those rules which Christian States acknowledge in their relation with each other.

To secure the observance of these rules by American citizens, laws are necessary. Our government is responsible for its conduct and for the conduct of its citizens towards other nations or their subjects. A single person could involve us in difficulties and perhaps in war with some foreign nations, if we had no laws to secure the observance of the Law of Nations by our citizens.

For instance, during our Civil War the English government allowed Confederate privateers to be fitted out in English ports to prey on our commerce. When our government demanded reparation for this breach of the Law of Nations, it was offered as an excuse that the English law was not such that they could prevent those privateers being fitted out.

Our answer was, that it was the business of England to have such laws that she could fulfill her duties to other nations; that it was not our fault that her laws were not what they should be; and that we could not take that as an excuse. The Tribunal of Arbitration to which the dispute was referred, decided that we were right, and condemned England to pay a heavy indemnity for our losses by those privateers.

Now the same principle applies to the United States. It is the business of our government to obey the law of nations and to make our citizens obey it. And it is no excuse that we have no laws by which we can enforce this. It is our business to have such laws, and to enforce them.

Congress, therefore, very properly has the power to make laws respecting offenses against the law of nations, and this subject is very properly not left to the States.

CLAUSE 11.

THE WAR POWER.

To declare war, grant letters of marque and reprisal, and make rules concerning captures on land and water.

I. THE POWER TO DECLARE WAR. — The power to make war and peace is one of the highest attributes of sovereignty. Even under the Articles of Confederation the general government had the power to make war and peace. The only question that could arise is, whether this power should be legislative or executive. In this Constitution it is divided. The power to declare war is given to Congress, but the power to make treaties, which includes the power to make peace, is given to the President with the consent of the Senate.

A declaration of war is not necessary for a war. Acts of hostility are enough, and with Indian tribes, fighting begins generally without any formal declaration of war. So also in the case of our Civil War, there was no regular declaration of war. The war was begun by the rebels, and the government defended itself.

II. PRIVATEERING. — Privateers are those private armed vessels which are engaged in authorized war. They are distinguished from a regular navy because they are fighting for the sake of plunder and are only controlled by their commissions, while vessels of the regular navy sail under the orders of their own government, and in command of responsible officers.

Privateers must always have a commission from their own government to show that they are not pirates. The commission is called a " letter of marque and reprisal."

Marque means boundary, and *reprisal* means retaliation. A letter of marque and reprisal is thus a commission to a private vessel to go beyond the boundary of its own nation and seize the vessels of a certain nation in retaliation for wrongs done by that nation.

To issue letters of marque and reprisal is an act of war. It may be done without other acts of war, as in the case of our hostilities against France in 1798, in which letters of marque and reprisal were issued, but war was not regularly entered upon by either side.

Or it may be done as a part of a regular war, as was the case in our war of 1812, with England.[1]

III. PRIZES. — Congress can make rules respecting captures on land or sea. This is a necessary incident

[1] Privateering is a remnant of piracy, as Franklin says: "The practice of robbing merchants on the high seas, is a remnant of the ancient piracy. Though it be accidentally beneficial to particular persons, it is far from being profitable to all engaged in it, or to the nation that authorizes it."

Privateering is not exactly piracy now, under the regulations of modern warfare; but it is a guerrilla warfare at sea.

The tendency of international law now is to discourage, and if possible abolish, privateering. Several of the leading nations of Europe, at the treaty of Paris in 1856, agreed to abolish privateering, as between each other, and have since induced other powers to unite in that agreement. The United States refused to agree to abolish privateering, unless the further step should also be taken, to forbid all seizures of private property at sea, except contraband of war. Steps have been taken by several powers looking toward that result.

And it will not be many years before the United States, in common with all Christian nations, will bind itself to abolish all privateering, and all seizures of private property at sea. When that time comes, this clause of the Constitution will become obsolete.

of the war power. This power, however, is limited by the recognized rules of international law, and by special treaties which we have made with several nations.

When ships are captured at sea, either by men-of-war or by privateers, they are brought into some American port and tried by a United States district court, sitting as a prize court. All questions, regarding the lawfulness of the capture and the share of the prize to be paid to each sailor, are also settled by the court according to United States laws. It is usual to divide the proceeds of a captured ship among the officers and men of the men-of-war or privateers which make the capture.

Captures may also be made on land of certain kinds of property according to the regular rules of war. In this case the proceeds of the captures go to the United States and not to the soldiers making the capture. Questions in regard to the lawfulness of these captures will go before a United States court, and be decided according to the laws of the United States and the recognized rules of war.

IV. CAPTURES AT SEA.

In war, those nations which are engaged in it are called *belligerents*, and all others *neutrals*. The treatment of neutral ships and of neutral goods on an enemy's ships has been growing milder during this century. The question is still in process of being settled by the nations of Europe and America. There is little doubt but that the rule adopted by many nations (Treaty of Paris, 1856) will ultimately be adopted by all, and thus become a part of international law. This rule is that neutral ships with their cargoes (whether these are neutral or not), and neutral goods in an enemy's ships, are exempt from capture with two exceptions: (a) where they are attempting to run a blockade of an enemy's port, and (b) when they are contraband of war. The abolition of privateering goes along with this (see page 101).

It is possible that the powers of Europe may finally agree to the proposal of the United States to go still further and exempt all pri-

vate property at sea from seizure, whether it belongs to a neutral
or a belligerent. If this should ever be agreed upon, then war at
sea will be confined to ships of war, and merchants will not be interfered with by war, except to prevent the trade in contraband
goods or in case of a blockade. If this should ever be the case, this
clause of the Constitution would, of course, be limited in its effect to
these two cases. In the interest of humanity, we may hope that the
civilized nations of the world will adopt these milder rules of naval
warfare. But the United States is as yet only bound by international law to observe these rules:

1. Neutral goods in neutral ships are exempt.

2. Neutral goods in enemy's ships are also exempt.

3. But enemy's goods in neutral ships are liable to seizure.

4. Contraband goods, that is, arms or articles that directly help
to carry on war, can be seized in neutral ships as well as in enemy's
ships. In frequent cases, the ships carrying contraband may also
be seized.

5. Neutral ships attempting to run a blockade, may be seized.

6. And the ships and goods, private or public, belonging to a
nation at war with us, may be seized, either by our ships of war, or
by our privateers bearing a lawful commission.

V. Captures on Land.

The rule on land is, that the property of neutrals is exempt from
seizure or destruction, except so far as a state of war naturally puts
it at hazard. It will not be intentionally captured or destroyed by
a belligerent. But all the property of the enemy, both public and
private, is liable to seizure. But in practice this is so modified that
private property is only taken when it is needed for the operations
of our army, or it is desired to prevent its use by the others.

For instance, an army will take any provisions it needs, and any
horses and wagons, wherever it can find them. It will capture or
destroy all arms, ammunition and military stores of the enemy.
And on a retreat, it will destroy railroads and bridges to hinder the
advance of the enemy.

CLAUSE 12.

THE REGULAR ARMY.

To raise and support armies, but no appropriation of money to that use
shall be for a longer term than two years.

I. THE ARMY. — War calls for armies. One of the
great curses of Europe is the burden of enormous standing armies in every nation. The expense of supporting
them is very great, and adds greatly to the taxation;
large numbers of men are withdrawn from active
industry at the sacrifice to themselves and to the
nation of what they could otherwise earn. And the
presence of a large army is a constant temptation to
use it in war, and a constant temptation to ambitious
generals or politicians to usurp authority.

From this curse we are freed in this country. The
ocean separates us from any foe we need fear. A standing army is only needed to fight the Indian tribes, and
to provide trained officers in case of war. We have a
small standing army in time of peace. When war
comes, we can easily increase our army by volunteering
or by conscription, and on the return of peace, disband
these forces again. This has been the constant policy
of our government.[1]

II. APPROPRIATIONS FOR THE ARMY. — No appropriation can be made by Congress for more than two years.
If Congress could make an appropriation for many
years in advance, the party temporarily in power might
fix a large standing army on the country for many
years. As it is, the people can at any time, through

---

[1] " Avoid the necessity of those over-grown military establishments, which
under any form of government are inauspicious to liberty, and which are to
be regarded as particularly hostile to republican liberty."— *Washington's
Farewell Address.*

their representatives in Congress, reduce the army or abolish it altogether. In practice, Congress makes appropriations for the army from year to year.

III. THE COMMAND OF THE ARMY. — The President is commander-in-chief of the army. (Art. I, Sec. 2.) The general direction of all business pertaining to the army is in the War Department, at the head of which is the Secretary of War. But the immediate command of the army is in the General; and all orders of the President or of the Secretary of War are transmitted to him to be carried out.

IV. THE ORGANIZATION OF THE ARMY.

In the army the unit of organization is the company. When full, a company consists of three commissioned officers, and about one hundred enlisted men. But a company often is much smaller. In time of peace the companies are reduced in size, and filled up again when the army needs to be enlarged. Thus we increase or diminish our regular army simply by filling up the companies or allowing them to be reduced, without changing the number of companies and regiments. Of the enlisted men in a company, from nine to thirteen are non-commissioned officers, a First Sergeant, four other Sergeants, and from four to eight Corporals. These non-commissioned officers are appointed from the best of the men.

The commissioned officers of a company are a Captain, a First Lieutenant and a Second Lieutenant. The highest commissioned officer who is able to serve commands the company. If in battle all the commissioned officers are disabled, then the highest non-commissioned officer able to serve, takes command. But in any other case, a commissioned officer from some other company takes command temporarily. Captains and Lieutenants are called *line officers*, and all higher officers are called *field officers*.

A regiment of infantry is composed of ten companies, a regiment of cavalry or artillery of twelve. The officers are a Colonel, a Lieutenant Colonel, and in an infantry regiment one Major, but in a cavalry or artillery regiment three Majors, each of whom commands a battalion of four companies. The highest of these able to serve commands the regiment, and if all are disabled, the senior Captain (the Captain who has held that rank longest) takes command tem-

porarily.   In that case the Captain leaves his company in charge of
the next highest officer.   So also in a cavalry or artillery regiment,
if a Major has to command a regiment, the senior Captain of that
battalion commands the battalion temporarily.

Each regiment has also an Adjutant and several non-commissioned officers and clerks.   Surgeons and chaplains are assigned to
regiments or to detachments of various sizes to suit the needs of the
service.

A Brigade is composed of from three to five regiments, together
with one or more batteries (that is companies) of artillery, and is
commanded by a Brigadier General or by the Senior Colonel.

A Division is composed of from three to five brigades, and is
commanded by a Major General or by the Senior Brigadier General.

An Army Corps is composed of several divisions, and is usually
commanded by a Major General.

The whole Army of the United States is commanded by a General (W. T. Sherman) and Lieutenant General (P. H. Sheridan).

There are various departments attached to the Army, each with
its corps of officers.

1. The Adjutant General's Department.
2. The Inspector General's Department.
3. The Bureau of Military Justice.
4. The Signal Service.
5. The Quartermaster's Department.
6. The Subsistence Department.
7. The Medical Department.
8. The Pay Department.
9. The Corps of Engineers.
10. The Ordnance Department.
11. And several Post Chaplains.

During our Civil War, a large number of militia and volunteers
were called into the service.   These were organized substantially as
given above, except that each regiment, brigade, division and army
corps had its own staff, instead of the staff being organized into
departments, as above stated.

The following table shows the various ranks of commissioned
officers in the Army, with the corresponding rank of naval officers:

Army.	Navy.
1. General.	Admiral.
2. Lieutenant-General.	Vice-Admiral.
3. Major-General.	Rear-Admiral.
4. Brigadier-General.	Commodore.
5. Colonel.	Captain.
6. Lieutenant-Colonel.	Commander.
7. Major.	Lieutenant-Commander.
8. Captain.	Lieutenant.
9. First Lieutenant.	Master.
10. Second Lieutenant.	Ensign.

Within these grades, promotions are usually made by seniority; that is, when a vacancy occurs, it is filled by promoting the officer who stands next in rank,[1] which is determined by seniority of commission; that is, the officer who has held that rank the longest ranks first, the next next, and so on.

But in time of war, promotions are frequently made for merit, without regard to seniority. Most officers of the regular army are educated at the United States Military Academy, at West Point, New York.

CLAUSE 13.

THE NAVY.

To provide and maintain a navy.

I. OUR NAVY. — A navy cannot be raised as easily as an army, and it is necessary to have a considerable navy in order to protect our commerce in all parts of the world. A navy is of more use in time of peace than an army is, and of less use, generally, in war. It is better, therefore, to keep a regular navy, and not to depend upon a volunteer navy in case of war, as we do upon a volunteer army. For the same reason appropriations for a longer time are not forbidden. They may be necessary in building ships.

---

[1] For the insignia of these various ranks, see Webster's Unabridged Dictionary.

II. The command of the navy. — The President is Commander-in-Chief of the navy as well as of the army of the United States (Art. II, Sec. 2). The general direction of all business relating to the navy is in the Navy Department, at the head of which is the Secretary of the Navy.

III. The organization of the navy. — In the navy the unit of organization is the ship.

Vessels in the United States navy are arranged in four rates according to size, besides iron-clad vessels, torpedo boats and tugs. Vessels of the first or second rate are generally commanded by Captains, those of the third rate by Commanders, and those of the fourth rate by Lieutenant Commanders. Each vessel has also a number of officers and men according to its size. A squadron of several vessels is commanded by a Rear Admiral or a Commodore.

The whole navy of the United States is under the general command of an Admiral and a Vice Admiral.

There is also a Marine Corps in connection with the navy. Marines are soldiers who serve on board ships or in navy yards. Their organization is similar to that of the army, as far as their small numbers allow.

Most officers of the navy are educated at the United States Naval Academy at Annapolis, Md. For the rank of naval officers see page 107.

CLAUSE 14.

ARMY AND NAVY REGULATIONS.

To make rules for the government and regulation of the land and naval forces.

I. The power to make rules. — The power to make war, and to organize armies and navies, implies also the power to rule these armies. Congress therefore has the power to make rules for the government of the army and navy. These rules together are called *military law* and *naval law*. These must not be confused with *martial law*. Military law and naval law do not govern civilians, but only soldiers and sailors. Martial law is the government by an army of a part of this or any other country held by our armies, while war is going on. Military law is the government *of* armies; martial law is the government *by* armies.

II. THE ARMY AND NAVY REGULATIONS. — Congress has made rules for the government of the army and navy, called the Army Regulations and the Navy Regulations. These prescribe the duties of every officer, soldier or sailor, and provide punishments for every offense. For trifling offenses the officer in command may reprimand, or put under arrest without trial. But no such arrest can be longer than ten days. All serious offenses must be tried by Court Martial. A Court Martial is organized regularly, and proceeds according to regular rules, giving the accused a fair trial, but one more summary than in a civil court.

Soldiers and sailors can be punished for disobeying orders, as well as for what would be crimes in the case of ordinary citizens. And officers can also be punished for conduct unbecoming a gentleman.[1] Punishments may extend even so far as death. The President has power to pardon, or to reduce the punishment to a lighter one. Every officer, soldier and sailor must swear allegiance to the United States, and promise obedience to the rules of the army or navy, as the case may be. Every officer must subscribe to these rules, and every soldier or sailor must have them read to him.

---

[1] Officers have been severely punished for such offenses as refusing to pay their debts, slandering the wife of a brother officer, etc.

CLAUSE 15.

THE POWER TO CALL OUT THE MILITIA.

To provide for calling forth the militia to execute the laws of the Union, suppress insurrections and repel invasions.

I. WHO ARE THE MILITIA?—The militia are citizen soldiers. The regular army is composed of men whose business is to be soldiers, and who do nothing else. The militia are citizens who are liable to be called away from their regular business to serve as soldiers for a short time. By act of Congress, all male citizens, and those who have declared their intention to become citizens, between the ages of twenty and forty-five, constitute the national forces, and are liable to perform military duty when called out by the President. These constitute the unorganized militia, and are not ready for service till called out, officered, armed and drilled. The organized militia are those men who have been formed into companies and regiments by authority of State or United States laws, and are officered, armed and drilled, and ready to be called out at any time.

II. CALLING OUT THE MILITIA.— The militia may be called out for three things: (a) to execute the laws of the United States, (b) to suppress insurrections, and (c) to repel invasions. Each State may also call out its own militia for similar purposes. The President alone can call out the militia of the United States, and he may call out any number at his discretion, and from all the States or from some only, as may be most convenient. He calls on the Governor of each State for a certain number of militia, and it is then the duty of the Governors of the States called on, each to call out that number of militia. If the States do not furnish their militia as called for, the government will draft men enough to make up the number.

The militia have been called out under this clause only on three occasions:

In the Whisky Rebellion of 1794, the militia of four neighboring States were called out to enforce the laws. In the War of 1812, the militia were again called out to repel invasion, and in the Civil War the militia were again called out to suppress insurrection.

III. VOLUNTEERS.— Under Clause 12, the government has always maintained a small standing army. At several times the government has also accepted the services of volunteer companies or regiments for longer or shorter times. These volunteers are not a part of the regular army nor are they called out as militia. All our great wars have been fought chiefly by the aid of volunteers; and in most of our Indian wars volunteers have served beside the regular soldiers.

CLAUSE 16.

THE POWER TO ORGANIZE THE MILITIA.

To provide for organizing, arming and disciplining the militia, and for governing such part of them as may be employed in the service of the United States, reserving to the States respectively, the appointment of the officers, and the authority of training the militia according to the discipline prescribed by Congress.

I. STATE AND UNITED STATES POWERS OVER THE MILITIA. — The States may have their own militia, subject to their own laws, and many of them do have such militia. (See Amend. II.)

The militia of each State are organized under the laws of that State. But the United States may at any time prescribe regulations for organizing, arming and drilling the militia. But the States carry out these regulations. When the States furnish militia to the United States, they usually do it by regiments, with officers appointed by the State. These regiments are mustered into the United States service, and are then organized into brigades, divisions and army corps by the United States, the President appointing the officers of the brigades, divisions and army corps.

When volunteers or militia are mustered into the service of the United States, they are subject to the Army Regulations like the regular soldiers.

II. THE VALUE OF CITIZEN SOLDIERS. — The United States does not depend for its defense upon professional soldiers, who make a business of war, but upon the courage and patriotism of all its citizens. As we are free from any serious danger of foreign invasion, we do not even need to have our citizens trained in the use of arms and in military manœuvers. And therefore we have paid little attention to the organization and training of our militia, perhaps too little attention. But our Civil War showed what a nation of citizens untrained in war can do in time of need. In four years, over two and a half million men were mustered into the armies of the United States, and nearly all as militia or volunteers. The navy of the United States may be increased in time of war by volunteering, but not by calling out the militia or by drafting.

CLAUSE 17.

THE POWER OF EXCLUSIVE LEGISLATION.

To exercise exclusive legislation in all cases whatsoever, over such district (not exceeding ten miles square) as may, by cession of particular States, and the acceptance of Congress, become the seat of government of the United States, and to exercise like authority over all places purchased by the consent of the legislature of the State in which the same shall be, for the erection of forts, magazines, arsenals, dockyards, and other needful buildings.

I. THE EXTENT OF THIS POWER. — Within the boundaries of the States, Congress exercises only a limited power of legislation. It can legislate only on those subjects granted in this section or in other parts of the Constitution. Other subjects are either reserved to the States to legislate on or are forbidden to both State and United States governments.

But in certain places the United States can exercise all the authority which it can exercise in the States, and also all the authority which a State can exercise. These places are:

1. The District of Columbia.
2. Forts, magazines, arsenals and dockyards in which the jurisdiction has been ceded to the United States.
3. Territories. (See IV, 3, 2.)
4. On board United States men-of-war anywhere. (See page 99.)
5. On board United States merchant vessels when at sea. (See page 99.)
6. In the tide waters of the coast, so far as they are not under the jurisdiction of the several States. (See page 98.)

Over these places the United States exercises exclusive jurisdiction, and Congress has therefore the exclusive power of legislation there.

II. THE DISTRICT OF COLUMBIA. — The States of Maryland and Virginia ceded to the United States in 1790, a tract of country just ten miles square (or a hundred square miles in area). This was named the District of Columbia, and in 1800 the seat of government was moved there. In 1846, that part of the District of Columbia lying southwest of the Potomac, which had been given by Virginia, was ceded back to Virginia. The District of Columbia now contains sixty-six square miles.

H

The city of Washington, in the District of Columbia, is the Capital of the United States. There was no city or village at which the capital was located, but the city of Washington was created to be the capital. Its name was given it to perpetuate the memory of the greatest American, who was "first in war, first in peace, and first in the hearts of his countrymen." It is not far from his own home, at Mount Vernon, where he is buried.

III. TAXATION WITHOUT REPRESENTATION. — The District of Columbia can be taxed by Congress, but it is not entitled to represention in Congress, nor can its people vote for Presidential electors. This inequality could only be obviated by ceding the District back to Maryland or erecting it into a separate State. And this ought not to be done, because the United States needs to have absolute control of its capital.

IV. WHY CONGRESS HAS EXCLUSIVE JURISDICTION.— The government of the United States should be supreme at its capital if anywhere. If the capital of the United States were within any of the States, it would be subject to the mixed jurisdiction of the State and of the United States, and this would lead to endless complications and difficulties.[1]

V. FORTS, NAVY YARDS AND ARSENALS. — The United States can also have jurisdiction over the places

[1] An illustration of the troubles that would arise if the capital were within a State, was furnished at the close of the Revolutionary war, when a small body of troops mutinied because they had not been paid, and marched into Philadelphia to demand their pay of Congress. As there were no legal troops near, Congress had to call on Pennsylvania for militia or police to defend them against the mutineers. This the government of Pennsylvania weakly hesitated to do. Thereupon Congress removed to Trenton, in New Jersey, for safety. Should such an occasion happen in Washington now, the President could at once call out every able-bodied man in the District to defend the government, without waiting for the slow movements of State governments to furnish him militia. As it is, all questions of jurisdiction are avoided. In the District of Columbia there is but one jurisdiction, and that belongs to the United States.

needed for forts, arsenals, navy yards and other public buildings. But the consent of the legislature of the State in which these buildings are situated, must first be obtained.

In giving this consent, State legislatures have generally reserved the right to serve all State processes, civil and criminal, in these places. The object of this is, that these places may not be a sanctuary for criminals, who otherwise could not be arrested by State authority if they escaped into these places.

We must distinguish between the *property* of the United States and the *jurisdiction* of the United States. Forts, arsenals and navy yards are the property of the United States and are also in its jurisdiction. In the District of Columbia, the United States has property only in the public buildings and grounds; but it has jurisdiction over all the District. In the case of public lands unsold, within a state, the United States has property, but has no more jurisdiction than anywhere else in the State. When the United States owns property, it owns it as a private individual does, except that it cannot be taxed by a State.

CLAUSE 18.

INCIDENTAL POWERS.

To make all laws which shall be necessary and proper for carrying into execution the foregoing powers, and all other powers vested by this Constitution in the Government of the United States, or in any department or officer thereof.

I. THESE POWERS INCIDENTAL. — This clause gives Congress the power not only to pass such laws as have been expressly named in this section, but any laws which may be necessary and proper for carrying into execution these express powers, and also any laws which may be necessary and proper for carrying into execution any other powers vested by the Constitution in any part of the government. For instance, the power in Clause 7, to establish post offices and post roads, is a power expressly granted to Congress. But in order to carry this power into execution, it is necessary and proper to protect the mail. Congress has therefore assumed under this clause the additional power to pass laws punishing robbery of the mails, and requiring all persons who handle the mail in any way to be under oath, and requiring postmasters to give bonds. Congress has, also, under this clause, created a Post Office Department, with some sixty thousand post offices and postmasters. But in carrying out Article II, Sec. 2, Congress has by law vested the appointment of these officers partly in the President with the consent of the Senate, and partly in the Postmaster General.

II. WHY INCIDENTAL POWERS ARE GRANTED. — The powers granted to Congress by this clause are incidental or implied powers, not expressly given by any part of the Constitution. This clause was opposed by a large party led by Patrick Henry, for fear that Congress should find an excuse in it to override the rights of the States, and the Tenth Amendment was passed to quiet them. But experience has shown that the States still retain all the rights that they need, and that the Federal government has not grown into a despotism because of this clause.

The framers of the Constitution claimed that this clause only asserted in words what would have been implied in any case. They claimed that it was only common sense that a government should be able to do what it was established on purpose to do. And they claimed that it was a sound rule of law, admitted by all judges, that when a power was granted, liberty to do all that was needed to carry it into effect was also granted (see Amend. X). Experience has shown that the very political parties which wished to limit the power of Congress and the President, have been when in power the very ones to do things not expressly granted in the Constitution. They were more sensible in their practice than in their theories. This Constitution creates a real national government, and this government must have national powers. Some of these needful powers can be foreseen, and are named in this section and elsewhere. But it was impossible to see all the emergencies that might arise, and therefore this general power is also given.

III. WHAT LAWS CONGRESS MAY PASS. — Congress has a right to make any laws, (1) which are expressly authorized by the Constitution; (2) or which are implied in the express powers given to Congress, and necessary to carry them out; (3) or which are necessary to carry out any powers vested in the United States, or in any United States officer; (4) or which are necessary for the common defense or the general welfare. The enacting clause gives the power to the government to provide for the common defense, and to promote the general welfare.

But Congress cannot make laws on subjects, (1) which are expressly prohibited to Congress; (2) or which are expressly reserved to the States; (3) or which have not been granted to either the States or National government.

IV. POWERS EXERCISED UNDER THIS CLAUSE.
The following powers are some of those which have been exercised by Congress under this clause:

1. The slave trade has been prohibited. The Constitution pro-

vides that Congress shall not prohibit it before 1808 (Art. I, sec. 9). The necessary implication is that it can after that date.

2. The writ of *habeas corpus* has been suspended in time of war. The Constitution provides that that writ shall not be suspended except in case of rebellion or invasion (Art. I, sec. 9). The necessary implication is that it may be suspended in that case.

3. Congress has erected light houses, as a power implied in the right to regulate commerce.

4. The United States has acquired territory by purchase and by conquest, and has governed that territory or formed states out of it. No express authority is given in the Constitution for this. When President Jefferson bought Louisiana, he is reported to have said that he stretched the Constitution till it cracked. But he forgot that Congress could do anything necessary for the defense and welfare of the nation. Texas was also annexed, and other great additions to our territory have been made by conquest and purchase under the same power.

5. The United States punishes offenses committed on board ships of war, even in port, and by persons not in the military or naval service. The reason is, that a ship of war is by the law of nations always in the jurisdiction of the nation to which it belongs.

6. All persons in the United States service are exempt from State control while engaged in their duties as officers or employees of the United States. Congress has not even made any law on this subject, but the Supreme Court has decided that this is a necessary incident of the general sovereignty of the United States.

And the following implied powers have been exercised by Congress, but have been opposed as unconstitutional by powerful political parties:

1. National banks have been created.
2. Paper money has been issued by the government as a war measure.
3. International improvements have been made, such as roads and canals, and making rivers navigable.
4. An embargo was laid on all commerce once only.
5. Most of the "reconstruction measures" at the close of the Civil war.

Of the great political parties, the Federalists, the Whigs, and the Republicans (the present party), have been inclined to give the national government as much power as possible under this clause. And the anti-Federalists and the Republicans (the old party) and the Democrats have been inclined to give it as little power as possible.

V. ADDITIONAL POWERS GIVEN TO CONGRESS IN OTHER PARTS OF THIS CONSTITUTION.

In addition to the powers named in this section, many other powers are either expressly given to Congress, or plainly implied in other parts of the Constitution.[1] A list of these powers is given below. These are all legislative powers, and require the action of the President unless otherwise specified.

A. POWERS RELATING TO CONGRESS. — 1. *The power to apportion Representatives* among the several States according to their population, and to fix the number of Representatives, giving at least one to each State, and not more than one to every thirty thousand population (I, 2, 3), and *the power to reduce the representation of a State* for denying the right of suffrage to male citizens over twenty-one, except for crime or treason (Amendment XIV, 2).

2. *The power to regulate elections for Senators and Representatives*, in regard to the time, place and manner of holding such elections, except as to the place of choosing Senators (I, 4, 1).

3. *The power to fix the time of the annual meeting of Congress* (I, 4, 2).

4. *The power to adjourn.* This is not done by law but by a concurrent resolution, and does not require the action of the President. But either House alone may by resolution adjourn for not more than three days at a time. The power to adjourn includes the power to adjourn to some particular time or place. But neither House alone can change the place of sitting.

5. *The power to fix the salary of Senators and Representatives*, together with the salary of all officers and employees of either House (I, 6, 1).

B. POWERS RELATING TO THE EXECUTIVE. — 1. *The power to fix the day of choosing Presidential Electors, and of their choosing President and Vice President* (II, 1, 4), with the limitation that the day shall be uniform throughout the United States.

2. *The power to canvass the votes of the President and Vice*

---

[1] As these are discussed in their proper places, a brief mention only is here given to each.

President (Amendment XII). This is the power implied in the words, "The votes shall then be counted." Congress has assumed the power under these words to canvass the votes and determine what votes shall be received, and what thrown out. The right of Congress to act as a canvassing board has been disputed; but the practice is now firmly established.

3. *The power to determine what officer shall act as President when there is no President or Vice President* (II, 1, 6.) Such officer is an acting President only, and holds only till the disability of the President or Vice President is removed, or a President can be elected.

4. *The power to fix the salary of the President*, but not to increase or diminish it during his term of office (II, 1, 7.)

5. *The power to regulate the civil service of the United States* (II, 2, 2.) This includes the power to establish or abolish offices, and to fix salaries and duties of officers, and to regulate the manner of appointment of inferior officers.

6. *The power to control the reception of titles and presents by officers of the United States* (I, 9, 7). No officer of the United States can accept any title or present from any foreign king or state, except with the consent of Congress.

C. POWERS RELATING TO THE COURTS. — 1. *The power to fix the salaries of judges* of the Supreme Court and of all other United States courts (III, 1, 1).

2. *The power to regulate the appellate jurisdiction of the Supreme Court* (III, 2, 2). The original jurisdiction of the Supreme Court is fixed in the Constitution (III, 2, 2).

3. *The power to regulate the jurisdiction of inferior courts.* A power implied in the power to organize inferior courts (I, 8, 9, and III, 1).

4. *The power to fix the place of trial for crimes committed outside of any State* (III, 2, 3).

5. *The power to declare the punishment for treason*, but under the limitation that no attainder of treason shall work corruption of blood or forfeiture, except during the life of the person attainted (III, 3, 2).

6. *The power to forbid jury trials* in lawsuits, where twenty dollars or less is involved (Amendment VII).

D. POWERS RELATING TO THE STATES.—1. *The power to allow States to levy duties*, but the net produce of such duties shall be paid into the United States treasury, and the State laws on that subject shall be subject to the revision and control of Congress (I, 10, 2).

2. *The power to allow or forbid States to keep armies and navies in* time of peace (I, 10, 2).

3. *The power to allow or forbid States to make compacts* with other States or with foreign powers (I, 10, 2).

4. *The power to allow or forbid States to engage in war* (I, 10, 2).

5. *The power to prescribe* the manner of proving the public records of one State in another. This must be by general law (IV, 1).

6. *The power to admit new States into the Union,* with the limitation that no new State shall be formed within the boundaries of another State, or by the junction of two States or parts of States, without the consent of the legislatures of the States concerned.

7. *The power to guarantee each State a republican form of government* (IV, 4).

8. *The power to propose amendments to the Constitution,* which become parts of the Constitution by ratification of three-fourths of the States (V). For this the President's signature is not required.

E. LEGISLATIVE POWERS.— 1. *The power to prohibit the slave trade after 1808* (I, 9, 1).

2. *The power to suspend the writ of habeas corpus* when in cases of rebellion or invasion the public safety may require it (I, 9, 2).

3. *The power to make all appropriations* of money from the treasury. This implies also the power to investigate all expenditures of money by any department of the government (I, 9, 6).

4. *The power to govern the territory of the United States,* and to dispose of the public land and other property belonging to the United States (IV, 3, 2).

5. *The power to enforce the provisions of Amendments XIII, XIV, and XV,* by appropriate legislation (Amendments XIII, 2; XIV, 5; XV, 2).

SECTION 9.

PROHIBITIONS ON CONGRESS.

ANALYSIS OF THIS SECTION.

(And other prohibitions on Congress in other parts of this Constitution.)

PROHIBITIONS ON CONGRESS.

I. FINANCIAL ...
1. To draw money from the treasury otherwise than by an appropriation bill.............. .... I, 9, 6
2. To make appropriations for the army for more than two years.. I, 8, 12
3. To levy direct taxes except in proportion to population...... I, 9, 4
4. To appropriate money without publishing accounts........ .. I, 9, 6
5. To question the validity of the public debt .... Am. XIV
6. To pay rebel debts or claims for slaves .... Am. XIV

II. COMMERCIAL..
1. To prohibit the slave trade before 1808............................ I, 9, 1
2. To levy export duties............ I, 9, 5
3. To discriminate against the commerce of particular States .... I, 9, 6

III. RELATING TO U. S. OFFICERS
1. To increase or diminish the President's salary during his term of office........................ II, 1, 7
2. To diminish the salary of U. S. Judges during their continuance in office .... III, 1, 1
3. To impose religious tests for office.......................... VI, 3

IV. RELATING TO THE STATES.
1. To erect new States out of parts of States without the consent of the States concerned....... IV, 3, 2
2. To exercise powers reserved for the States .... Am. X

PROHIBITIONS ON CONGRESS.

V. RELATING TO PERSONAL LIBERTY....

1.	To suspend writ of *habeas corpus* except in war	I, 9, 2
2.	To pass a bill of attainder.......	I, 9, 3
3.	To pass an *ex post facto* law....	I, 9, 3
4.	To erect a titled aristocracy	I, 9, 8
5.	To deny the right of trial by jury,	III, 2, 3
6.	To make anything treason except rebellion	III, 3, 1
7.	To make an attainder of treason work corruption of blood or forfeiture except for life...	III, 3, 2
8.	To establish or prohibit religion.	Am. I
9.	To abridge the freedom of speech and of the press..........	Am. I
10.	To abridge the right of assembly and petition.......	Am. I
11.	To suppress the militia	Am. II
12	To quarter soldiers, except in war	Am. III
13.	To authorize unreasonable scarches and scizures	Am. II
14.	To refuse a fair trial to accused persons............. ....Am's	V and VI
15.	To take private property for public use without just compensation	Am. V
16.	To refuse trial by jury in important civil suits	Am. VII
17.	To impose excessive bail, fines and punishments..............	Am. XIII
18.	To deny other personal rights not enumerated	Am. IX
19.	To establish slavery or serfdom	Am. XIII
20.	To deny negroes the right to vote,	Am. XV

CLAUSE 1.

THE SLAVE TRADE.

The migration or importation of such persons as any of the States now existing shall think proper to admit, shall not be prohibited by the Congress prior to the year one thousand eight hundred and eight, but a tax or duty may be imposed on such importation, not exceeding ten dollars for each person.

THE SLAVE TRADE. — The United States has the honor of being the first nation to take steps to abolish the African slave trade. When this Constitution was

adopted, ten States out of the thirteen had already prohibited the slave trade.　But North Carolina, South
Carolina and Georgia insisted on some guarantee that
their slave trade should not be disturbed.　It was finally
compromised by this clause, which gave them twenty
years in which to import negroes from Africa.

The slave trade *to* foreign countries was prohibited in
1794, and the importation of slaves was prohibited in
1807, to take effect January 1, 1808, the very first day
when it was constitutional to do so. .

Great Britain abolished the slave trade in 1807, a few
days after our act was passed.

The framers of the Constitution were ashamed to use
the words "slave" or "slavery," and therefore used the
word "persons" instead.

Slavery is now abolished by the thirteenth amendment, and of course the slave trade with it is thus prohibited by the Constitution.

CLAUSE 2.

THE WRIT OF HABEAS CORPUS.

The privilege of the writ of habeas corpus shall not be suspended, unless
when in cases of rebellion or invasion the public safety may require it.

I.　OBJECT OF THE WRIT. — The writ of *habeas corpus* is intended to release any person illegally imprisoned.　Any person who is imprisoned without proper
warrant or indictment, can sue out a writ of *habeas corpus*, before any judge or court commissioner.　Unless
the officer who has him in charge can show a legal warrant or other authority, the prisoner is discharged.
The writ of *habeas corpus* is a guarantee of personal liberty, against unjust imprisonment by officers.

The words "habeas corpus" are the first two words
of the old Latin form of the writ, from which the writ
is named.

II. Suspension of the writ. — When the writ of *habeas corpus* is suspended, this safeguard against arbitrary and illegal arrest is laid aside for the time being. To suspend the writ of *habeas corpus*, means to give government officers power to arrest and imprison any one without a regular warrant or indictment.

The writ can only be suspended when the public safety requires it, in case of rebellion or invasion. Martial law then takes the place, partly or wholly, of civil law (see page 270). Persons are then arrested, tried and punished by martial law, and no writ of *habeas corpus* can save them. This is a necessity of war, when the public safety overrides all other considerations.

III. Disputed questions.

1. *Who has power to suspend the writ?* All agree that Congress has the power. But it is claimed by many that no one else has. The question whether the President or other executive officers have the right to suspend the writ, has never been decided by the courts. As a fact, the writ has been suspended several times by commanding generals and by the President.

2. *Where can the writ be suspended?* Only in that part of the country actually involved in the war. During the Civil War a man named Mulligan was arrested for treasonable conspiracy in Indiana, tried by a court martial and condemned to be executed. But the Supreme Court released him on a writ of *habeas corpus*, on the ground that Indiana was not the seat of war, and therefore martial law could not lawfully be proclaimed there. His offense was one to be tried by the civil courts, and liable to a less punishment than that of death.

CLAUSE 3.

BILLS OF ATTAINDER AND EX POST FACTO LAWS.

No bill of attainder or ex post facto law shall be passed.

I. Bills of attainder. — *A bill of attainder* is a law inflicting punishment without trial. It was a common practice in England, some centuries ago, for Parliament to pass bills of attainder. They answered all the ends of impeachment and much more. It was usual in such bills to prescribe the punishment of death, confiscation of property, deprivation of all honor and titles, and corruption of blood, so that the descendants could not inherit property through the person attainted.

Such an act is an easy means of revenge upon political opponents, and is generally used for that end. It gives the accused no regular trial. It punishes for acts that are not prohibited by law, it gives the accused little or no means of defense, and it punishes his family as well as himself. The power to pass bills of attainder is therefore wisely forbidden (*a*) to Congress, and (*b*) to the State legislatures (section 10).

Persons who offend against the law may still be tried in the courts, and political offenses committed by public officers may be tried by impeachment, under careful limitations.

This wise provision of our Constitution has taken the sting out of our political contests.

II.   EX POST FACTO LAWS. — *An ex post facto* law is one which punishes not only those who may afterwards break it, but those who have already done anything contrary to it, or one which adds a greater punishment to crimes already committed. This applies only to criminal laws and not to civil laws. A civil law may be retrospective, and not violate this clause of the Constitution. It is plainly unjust to punish any one for breaking a law which was not in existence when he did the act. This is also forbidden to the States as well as to the United States (section 10).

CLAUSE 4.

DIRECT TAXES.

No capitation, or other direct tax shall be laid, unless in proportion to the census or enumeration hereinbefore directed to be taken.

DIRECT TAXES IN PROPORTION TO POPULATION. — A capitation tax is a poll tax; a fixed sum on each person liable to it, without regard to his wealth or poverty.

According to section 2 of this Article, the representative population was to be made up by excluding wild Indians, and counting only three-fifths of the slaves, but counting all the free population. But by the Fourteenth Amendment, the representative population consists of the whole number of persons in each State, excluding uncivilized Indians. This clause provides that all direct taxes must be levied on the State in proportion to this representative population. No poll tax has ever been levied by the United States, and only a few direct taxes.

CLAUSE 5.

EXPORT DUTIES.

No tax or duty shall be laid on articles exported from any State.

I. EXPORT DUTIES FORBIDDEN. — *Export duties* are taxes laid on articles carried out of the country. It is the practice in many countries to tax both imports and exports. If exports are taxed, their price will be raised, and the products raised or manufactured in this country cannot be so profitably sold in foreign countries, and perhaps cannot compete at all with the same products from foreign countries. An export duty usually tends to discourage home production. But import duties may be used so as to encourage home production, or at least not to harm it. For this reason, export duties are forbidden by this section.

II.   A DISPUTED QUESTION — ARE ALL EXPORT DUTIES FORBIDDEN BY THIS CLAUSE?

Probably they are. But it is claimed by some that the intention of this clause is to prevent a discrimination against any one or more States, by export duties levied in those States alone. They claim that an export duty levied equally throughout the Union is not forbidden by this clause.

The courts have never been called upon to decide this case. But in all probability, they would decide any export duty whatever to be unconstitutional. For an export duty on any one article is a tax upon the productions of a few States for the benefit of the rest. Thus, an export duty on cotton would be a tax upon the productions of the Gulf States; an export duty on wheat and beef would be a tax on the productions of the Interior States, and an export duty on manufactured goods would be a tax on the industry of the Eastern and Middle States.

CLAUSE 6.

COMMERCIAL RESTRICTIONS.

No preference shall be given by any regulation of commerce or revenue to the ports of one State over those of another; nor shall vessels bound to or from one State, be obliged to enter, clear, or pay duties in another.

COMMERCIAL RESTRICTIONS FORBIDDEN. — This clause makes commerce entirely free between the States, and makes unlawful any preference of the commerce of one State over that of another. To "enter" a port is to land the whole or a part of the cargo there; to "clear from" a port is to take in the whole or a part of the cargo there.

While we were British colonies, the British government had put all sorts of restrictions on the commerce of the colonies, in order to favor British merchants at the expense of the colonies, and this was one cause of the Revolutionary War. This clause prevents any such restrictions or distinctions between the States.

CLAUSE 7.

APPROPRIATIONS AND ACCOUNTS.

No money shall be drawn from the treasury, but in consequence of appropriations made by law; and a regular statement and account of the receipts and expenditures of all public money shall be published from time to time.

APPROPRIATIONS AND ACCOUNTS REQUIRED. — This is to prevent frauds on the treasury. It does not prevent all frauds; but it makes them much more difficult. A fraud now is liable to be detected, not only by the executive officers, but also by Congress and by the people, for

1. No money can be paid out except on an appropriation passed in the form of a law.

2. And all accounts of the government must be published for the information of the people.

Appropriations are voted by Congress each winter for the year ending June 30. The head of each Department furnishes an estimate of what will be needed in his department for the ensuing year. These estimates must go into details, and show how much is needed for each item of expense. These estimates are carefully considered in each House of Congress, and are frequently cut down. A separate appropriation bill is generally made for each branch of the service. These appropriation bills usually originate in the House of Representatives. They are frequently amended in the Senate, and they may be vetoed by the President.

The account of the receipts and expenditures of the government are published every year in the form of a report of the Secretary of the Treasury.

I

CLAUSE 8.

TITLES OF NOBILITY.

No title of nobility shall be granted by the United States; and no person holding an office of profit or trust under them, shall, without the consent of the Congress, accept of any present, emolument, office, or title of any kind whatever, from any king, prince, or foreign State.

I. No TITLES GRANTED BY CONGRESS.— One of the fundamental principles of our government is, that all men are equal before the law. We cannot have a titled aristocracy without violating this principle. It is true that we cannot regulate social intercourse and make people treat one another as equals in society. Color, ancestry, office, wealth, and culture, will always create social distinctions. But before the law, every citizen of the United States is equal with every other. No titles of nobility give a few citizens an invidious distinction above the rest.

II. FOREIGN TITLES, OFFICES AND PRESENTS.— This clause also prohibits United States officers from accepting titles, offices or presents from foreign nations. These might easily become bribes to officers to betray their country. Such things have frequently been done in the history of other republics, and have periled their liberties. In case such a present is not meant as a bribe, it is easy to secure the consent of Congress to its being received.

It is a usual courtesy of sovereigns to exchange presents. When the President receives such a present from a foreign sovereign, it is not meant for him as an individual, but for him as the head of our nation for the time being. Such presents are accepted, and kept as the property of the United States. If courtesy requires a present in return, it is voted by Congress.

III.　What is not prohibited by this clause.—
1. Officers of the several States are not prohibited by
this Constitution from receiving titles and presents from
foreign powers; but they are generally prohibited by
the State Constitutions.　2. Citizens of the United
States who do not hold office are not prohibited from
accepting titles, offices or presents from foreign sovereigns.　And several Americans have accepted office
and received honors in foreign countries.　These honors
have been either for services rendered to those countries
or for services rendered to the cause of science.

An amendment was proposed by Congress in 1811, to
prevent citizens of the United States taking titles,
offices or presents from foreign sovereigns, but it has
never been ratified by the State legislatures. (See page
251).

IV.　Additional prohibitions on Congress.
Besides the things prohibited in this section, the following things
are expressly prohibited to Congress in other parts of the Constitution:

1. To make any appropriation of money for the army for a longer
term than two years.　(I, 8, 12.)

2. To increase or diminish the salary of the President during the
period for which he is elected.　(II, 1, 7.)

3. To diminish the salary of judges during their continuance in
office.　(III, 1.)

4. To make an attainder of treason work corruption of blood or
forfeiture except during the life of the person attainted.　(III, 3, 2.)

5. To erect new States out of parts of States without the consent
of the States concerned.　(IV, 3, 2.)

6. To impose religious tests for office.　(VI, 3.)

7. To make any law respecting an establishment of religion, or
prohibiting the free exercise thereof, or abridging the freedom of
speech or of the press, or the right of the people peaceably to
assemble and to petition the government for a redress of grievances.
(Am. I.)

8. To make laws infringing any of the personal rights guaranteed

in the first eight amendments. In all these amendments, except the first, Congress is not mentioned by name. The intention is to forbid not only Congress, but every branch of the government, legislative, executive and judicial, from infringing these rights.

9. To exercise powers not given it by the Constitution expressly or by implication.   (Am. X.)

10. To re-establish slavery.   (Am. XIII.)

11. To question the validity of the public debt.   (Am. XIV.)

12. To pay rebel debts or claims for slaves.   (Am. XIV.)

13. To deny or abridge the right of citizens of the United States to vote on account of race, color, or previous condition of servitude. (Am. XV.)

SECTION 10.

PROHIBITIONS ON THE STATES.

ANALYSIS OF THIS SECTION.

(And of other prohibitions, expressed or implied in the Constitution.)

PROHIBITIONS ON THE STATES.

I. ABSOLUTE

1. To make alliances............. I, 10, 2
2. To send out privateers .... I, 10, 2
3. To coin money .... I, 10, 2
4. To issue paper money, or make anything but gold or silver legal tender................. I, 10, 2
5. To pass bills of attainder ..... I, 10, 2
6. To pass *ex post facto* laws.... I, 10, 2
7. To pass laws impairing the obligation of contracts .... I, 10, 2
8. To grant titles of nobility..... I, 10, 2
9. To deny the citizens of other States the privileges of citizens........................ IV, 2, 1
10. To refuse to give up persons charged with crime in other States .... IV, 2, 1
11. To refuse to give up runaway slaves .... IV, 2, 2
12. To re-establish slavery........ Am. XIII
13. To abridge the privileges or immunities of citizens of the United States .... Am. XIV
14. To deprive any person of life, liberty, or property, without due process of law.......... Am. XIV, 1
15. To deny any person within its jurisdiction the equal protection of the laws........... Am. XIV, 1
16. To fill offices with unpardoned rebels .... Am. XIV, 3
17. To assume the rebel debt or claims for the loss of slaves. Am. XIV, 4
18. To deny negroes the right to vote .... Am. XV

II. IMPLIED

19. To interfere with the exercise of any authority belonging to the U. S.......
20. To interfere with the property of the U. S. by taxation or otherwise.........
21. To lower the value of U. S. property by taxation .....

Decisions of the Supreme Court

PROHIBITIONS ON THE STATES.	III. CONDITIONAL.	1. To levy duties on imports and exports	I, 10, 2
		2. To impose tonnage duties	I, 10, 2
		3. To keep a standing army or navy	I, 10, 2
		4. To make agreements or compacts with other States or foreign powers	I, 10, 2
		5. To engage in war	I, 10, 2

CLAUSE 1.

ABSOLUTE PROHIBITIONS.

No State shall enter into any treaty, alliance, or confederation; grant letters of marque and reprisal; coin money; emit bills of credit; make anything but gold and silver coin a tender in payment of debts; pass any bill of attainder, ex post facto law, or law impairing the obligation of contracts, or grant any title of nobility.

I. To MAKE ALLIANCES.—The States are forbidden to enter into any treaty, alliance, or confederation. The power to make treaties is a sovereign power, and is rightly reserved for the United States. If the States could make separate treaties and alliances, there would soon be an end to the Union. The way would be open for foreign intrigues. Some States would ally themselves with one nation, and some with another; and when these foreign nations were at war with one another, they would be drawn into the war on opposite sides. It would be to the interest of foreign nations to foment every sectional difference; and we should have a civil war on our hands every few years, even if we did not split into three or four separate nations.

II. To ISSUE LETTERS OF MARQUE AND REPRISAL.—If a State could authorize privateers it could easily involve us in difficulties or war with foreign nations. Under the Articles of Confederation, each State could issue letters of marque and reprisal. But it is here wisely prohibited to the separate States.

III. To COIN MONEY.— The power to coin money is given to the United States in section 8, and is here taken from the States. It is an attribute of sovereignty, by all nations reserved for the sovereign power. That sovereign power in this country is the United States, not the several States.

Another reason is to secure a uniform currency all over the United States. If each State could coin money there might be as many different sets of coins as there were States, and there would be certain to be several different sets. Such a state of things would be very inconvenient for business. Therefore the power to coin money is reserved to the United States, and prohibited to the several States.

IV. To ISSUE PAPER MONEY.— To " emit bills of credit " means to issue paper money. The same reasons that make it best to prohibit State coinage, also make it best to prohibit State paper money.

Another reason is that paper money is so easily made, and so liable to inflation, and therefore to depreciate in value, that the power to issue is a dangerous power to give a government. Recent experience had shown the framers of the Constitution the dangers of paper money. During the Revolutionary War the United States issued great quantities of paper money, which rapidly fell to almost nothing in value and was never redeemed. This, perhaps, was necessary to raise money in war. But the States after the war issued great amounts of paper money, which they could not redeem. To prevent this in the future, this clause was inserted in the Constitution.

No State can issue paper money, whether it is made a legal tender or not; but State bonds are not to be · considered as paper money. But a State could, until

1863, charter banks which should issue paper money, which people could take or not as they chose. Since then the United States has assumed its prerogative on this subject. It has taxed the old State banks out of existence; it has created a system of National banks; and it has issued paper money, as a war measure, and made it a legal tender. The supreme court has decided that the United States cannot constitutionally issue paper money, except as a war measure.

V. To MAKE ANYTHING BUT GOLD OR SILVER LEGAL TENDER.— A legal tender is anything which must be accepted in payment of debts, when offered. The pres·ent paper money of the United States is such a legal tender. This power of making something besides gold and silver a legal tender, is a part of the power of con-trolling the currency which is forbidden to the States.

But the States have the power to make gold and sil-ver legal tender, to any amount. And a State could make the silver coin of the United States, which is worth considerably less than gold, a legal tender to any amount, even though by the United States law it is legal tender only in small amounts.

VI. To PASS BILLS OF ATTAINDER AND EX POST FACTO LAWS.— Bills of attainder and ex post facto laws are forbidden to the States as well as to the United States, so that such unjust laws can no more be passed anywhere in this country. (See page 126.)

VII. To PASS LAWS IMPAIRING THE OBLIGATION OF CONTRACTS.— The States are forbidden to break con-tracts by law, but the United States can do it, and has done it. For instance, in the case of a bankrupt law, a State bankrupt law will operate only upon contracts made by its citizens after the law was passed. But a

United States bankrupt law will release the bankrupt from the legal obligation for debts made before the law was passed as well as afterwards.

But a contract which is for an immoral purpose, or which involves an immoral consideration, is never valid, and may always be broken. The obligation of these contracts is not impaired by the law annulling them, for they never had any obligation.

And a State may prescribe under what conditions a contract shall be made, so as to cover future contracts, but not past ones. Thus a State may say what forms deeds and mortgages must have in order to be valid, but this will only be binding in regard to deeds and mortgages executed after the law was passed.

These words of the Constitution thus reserve to the United States the power of impairing the obligation of contracts, and forbids it to a State.

VIII. CHARTERS OF CORPORATIONS.

Two famous decisions of the United States Supreme Court have defined the power of States over the charters of corporations. In the celebrated case of Dartmouth College against Woodward, in which Daniel Webster appeared for the College, that court decided that charters are in the nature of contracts between the State and the corporation chartered, and therefore that such charters cannot be repealed or amended by the State without the consent of the corporation. Such corporations are therefore practically perpetual.

But a recent decision of the Supreme Court in regard to the railroad laws of some Western States, allows the State the right to control railroad companies in the exercise of their chartered powers, so far as these are public franchises. A railroad company, because it has a charter, is not for that reason freed from any obligation to the public which a private person would have who transported passengers and freight (as he might do with a hack and dray). All common carriers, that is, persons or companies who make a business of carrying passengers or freight, can be controlled in their charges and their methods of management, when it is for the public good, and railroad companies are not exempted from this State control because they have been chartered by the State.

An additional reason exists in the case of railroads. The State exercise‹ for them the right of eminent domain, and allows the railroad to take the land needed for its track and buildings with or without the consent of the owners of the land. As the State thus gives a railroad a public franchise for the public good, it is fair that the same law of the public good should be exercised to prevent extortion or mismanagement of a railroad so as to injure the public.

Nor could a State legislature, by a charter to a railroad company, give up its right to control the tariff and the management of the railroads. That is a right inherent in the people, which the legislature, as the representatives of the people, can exercise for them, but which they cannot sell or give away.

This right of the State to control corporations does not extend further than to the good of the public in general. But as far as the action of a corporation affects only its own members, and does not conflict with existing State laws, or with public policy, the State will not interfere. For instance, within these limits a State cannot interfere with the internal government of a church, or of a secret society, or of a literary association, or any other voluntary organization. It can protect them in their property, and prevent their meetings being disturbed, but will leave them to manage their internal affairs according to their own rules.

IX. To GRANT TITLES OF NOBILITY.— The States as well as the United States are forbidden to grant any titles of nobility. If this is forbidden to the United States, it certainly ought to be forbidden to the States.

As a historical fact, it may be interesting to know that no American titles of nobility have ever been granted, except in the famously foolish constitution drawn up for Carolina by the philosopher John Locke. These titles soon died out, and no others have ever been created. Persons have come to this country who held titles in foreign lands, and have even acquired citizenship here; and American citizens have been honored with titles abroad. But since our independence, no title of nobility has ever been made or recognized by our laws. Those who are nobles in foreign lands, here are simple citizens.

CLAUSE 2.

CONDITIONAL PROHIBITIONS.

No State shall, without the consent of the Congress, lay any imposts or duties on imports or exports, except what may be absolutely necessary for executing its inspection laws; and the net produce of all duties and imposts, laid by any State on imports or exports, shall be for the use of the treasury of the United States; and all such laws shall be subject to the revision and control of the Congress.

No State shall, without the consent of Congress, lay any duty of tonnage, keep troops or ships of war in time of peace, enter into any agreement or compact with another State, or with a foreign power, or engage in war, unless actually invaded, or in such imminent danger as will not admit of delay.

I. To LAY DUTIES ON IMPORTS AND EXPORTS.— Compare this with Section 8, Clause 1. If States could lay taxes as they pleased on imports and exports, it would lead to much injustice of one State toward the commerce of another, and much jealousy and rivalry between States.

The Constitution intends to give the United States the complete control over foreign commerce and commerce between the States. It would have been simpler to have forbidden the States absolutely from laying duties on exports or imports. But the convention meant to leave it open to Congress if they chose to let the States appoint revenue officers and collect duties under United States laws. The States had been collecting duties for themselves. And it might be convenient for a time to still leave it to the States, only making the duties uniform and paying the net revenue from duties into the United States treasury.

But Congress at once assumed the power of laying duties, and has never consented since to give up any part of that power to the States. The States have never collected duties under this clause, and probably never will.

But the States may pass inspection laws to secure good measure in goods offered for sale, or to prevent goods dangerous to health being sold. And they may charge fees for the inspection; enough to pay the expenses of the inspector, and no more.

II.   To IMPOSE TONNAGE DUTIES.— Duties of tonnage are duties on ships according to the amount of freight they can carry. The tonnage is the amount of freight they can carry; thus a ship of a hundred tons burden is one that can carry a hundred tons of freight. A tonnage duty is a duty on commerce, and it is put under the control of Congress like all that relates to commerce. The consent of Congress is necessary before a State can lay a tonnage.

III.   To KEEP A STANDING ARMY OR NAVY.— No State can keep an army or navy in time of peace, without the consent of Congress. The national government usually will reserve that right to itself. But should an extraordinary occasion arise, Congress has the power to authorize a State or States to keep troops or ships of war in time of peace. In time of war, it may be very necessary for a State to raise an army or a navy for its own defense and that of other States. In that case the consent of Congress need not be asked for.

It is not intended by the words " keep troops " to prevent States organizing and arming their militia in time of peace, as well as war.[1] It is a standing army that is forbidden.

IV.   To MAKE AGREEMENTS AND COMPACTS. — How do the agreements and compacts named here differ from the treaties, alliances and confederations named in the

---

[1] Compare Section 8, Clause 16, of this Article, and Amendment II.

first clause of this section? In the one case, a State is prohibited absolutely from making them; in the other case, it is only required to gain the consent of Congress.

The natural interpretation is, that these compacts and agreements refer only to such business transactions as States sometimes must have, as well as private individuals; while treaties, alliances and confederations refer to political agreements. The latter are absolutely forbidden to the States.

No State can hold any *political* relations whatever, except as a member of the Union. It cannot have any political relations with other States or with foreign nations. That is all reserved for the United States. But a State may have *business* relations with other States, or with foreign powers. But as these could easily pass into political relations, the power is reserved to the United States to control these business relations. Examples of business relations between the States are, " questions of boundary, interests in land situated in the territory of each other, and other internal regulations for the mutual comfort and convenience of States bordering on each other. Such compacts have been made since the adoption of the Constitution." (Story.)

The consent of Congress to such compacts need not be expressed. It may be inferred from the legislation of Congress on the subject.[1]

V. To ENGAGE IN WAR. — A State may engage in war, if actually invaded or threatened with invasion; and as the necessity would be pressing, it would not be needful to wait for the United States authorities; but the State could defend itself at once with all the force at its command. But unless in self-defense, a State cannot make war, but must wait the decision of the United

---

[1] Virginia *vs.* West Virginia, 11 Wall. 39.

States government. If Congress should ever authorize one or more States to engage in war, it would not be a State war, but a United States war. There is no way in which some of the States can get into a war, defensive or offensive, without involving the rest in it too. If a State is invaded, it is also the United States which is invaded, and not only the State but the United States which will resent the invasion. If a State goes to war, the United States is responsible for it, and must either uphold it, or put a stop to the war at once. The Constitution thus gives each State the right of self-defense, but reserves all other powers of war to the United States.

VI. Other prohibitions on the states.— In other parts of the Constitution, the States are prohibited from the following things:

1. To deny the citizens of another State the privileges of a citizen. This is implied in Art. IV, Sec. 2, Clause 1.

2. To refuse to give up persons charged with crime in other States. This is implied in Art. IV, Sec. 2, Clause 1.

3. To refuse to give up a person held to service in another State. This is implied in Art. IV, Sec. 2, Clause 2. As slavery is now abolished, this provision is now practically obsolete.

4. To re-establish slavery. (Amendment XIII.)

5. To abridge the privileges or immunities of citizens of the United States. (Amendment XIV, Clause 1.)

6. To deprive any person of life, liberty or property without due process of law. (Amendment XIV, Clause 1.)

7. To deny any person within its jurisdiction the equal protection of the laws. (Amendment XIV, Clause 1.)

8. To fill offices with unpardoned rebels. (Amendment XIV, Clause 3.)

9. To assume the rebel debt or claims for the loss of slaves. (Amendment XIV, Clause 4.)

10. To deny the right of citizens of the United States to vote on account of race, color or previous condition of servitude. (Amendment XV.)

The Supreme Court has also decided that the following powers are denied to the States, by implication:

1. To interfere with the exercise of any authority belonging to the United States.

2. To interfere with the property of the United States by taxation or otherwise.   .

3. To lower the value of United States bonds or paper money by taxation.

ARTICLE II.

THE EXECUTIVE DEPARTMENT.

"As for an absolute monarchy, as it is called (that is to say, when the whole state is wholly subject to the will of one person, namely, the king), it seems to many to be unnatural that one man should have the entire rule over his fellow citizens, when the state consists of equals. * * * And for this reason it is as much a man's duty to submit to command, as to assume it, and this also by rotation; for this is law, for order is law; *and it is more proper that the law should govern than any one of the citizens.* Upon the same principle, if it is advantageous to place the supreme power in some particular persons, *they should be appointed to be only guardians and servants of the laws.*"— Aristotle, Politics, Book III, ch. 16.

I. The executive department carries out the laws.— As the legislative department of the government is to make the laws, so the executive department of the government is to carry out and enforce the laws. In making laws we need deliberation, and the combined wisdom of many. In executing the laws we need the decision and force which a single will can give. Therefore, as the legislative power is vested in a Congress of two houses, each composed of many persons, representing all parts of the country and all interests, so the executive power is vested in one person, assisted by many others under his direction.

The chief executive of this country is not called king or emperor, because that would imply that he inherited his place as of right. He is called simply President.

II. The executive power is made distinct from and independent of the legislative.— Under the Confederation, Congress when in session was the executive as well as the legislative department of the government, and when Congress was not in session, a committee of Congress was the executive. It was found by experience that the legislative and executive powers could not be combined profitably. Besides the general weakness of the government under the Confederation, there was a special weakness of *action*. Congress could pass laws and resolutions, but it could not put them into effect. So keenly was this felt, that no opposition was made in the Constitutional Convention to an executive distinct from and independent of Congress. We thus returned to the usual form of representative governments, a government in which the power that makes the laws and the power that executes them are kept distinct from and independent of each other. This was the form of the English government, and of the colonial governments.

In the case of those States which during and after the Revolution made their executives dependent on their legislatures, experience had shown the same defect as in the Confederation. And these States also soon returned to the typical form of representative government — a government consisting of three distinct parts, legislative, executive and judicial, each independent of the other.

IV. THE EXECUTIVE POWER IS VESTED IN ONE MAN.— The essential thing in a good executive is energy of action. This can only be secured by putting power and responsibility in the hands of one man. No council or committee will act with such decision, steadfastness, secrecy, activity and dispatch as one competent man will do.

Where several persons are associated together in any governing body, there are sure to be differences of opin-

K

ions and party spirit, and there are apt to be personal jealousies and secret intrigues. These are fatal to any prompt or decisive action, which is the very thing needed in an executive. The experience of the Confederation taught the framers of the Constitution that it is safer to put the executive power in the hands of one man than to vest it in a council. The experience of all civilized governments confirms this.

V. THE EXECUTIVE IS MADE RESPONSIBLE TO THE PEOPLE. — An irresponsible, unlimited executive is a despotism. The executive ought to have power, but not irresponsible or unlimited power. If the President could not be called to account for his actions, he would be able to do what he pleased, and usurp power in one way or another, until he became Monarch of a kingdom instead of President of a republic.

The President is limited in his powers by this Constitution, which defines his duties. Should he overstep that limit, or otherwise grossly betray the trust confided in him by the people, he could be impeached and removed from office.

But he is held responsible to the people in a far more effectual way by being elected for a limited term. The fact of election gives the people an opportunity to have such a President as the majority of them wish. Even if they should be deceived in their choice, or if the President, after his election, should be led astray by some foolish policy, or some ambitious design, he cannot do much mischief, or get many persons to help him in any very foolish or dangerous designs in the short time he has to rule.

On the other hand, the hope of re-election will lead a President to perform the duties of his office, and to carry out the wishes of the people as faithfully as he can. Thus the executive is limited and made responsible:

1. By the fear of impeachment.
2. By being the choice of the nation.
3. By his term of office being short.
4. By his hope of re-election.

VI. ALL EXECUTIVE OFFICERS ARE AGENTS OF THE PRESIDENT.

The executive power is vested in the President. But of course it is impossible for him to do everything himself. Nearly all the work of the executive department is done by officers of various kinds. As these officers are appointed by the President, or by other officers whom he appoints, and as they may be removed at pleasure,[1] they are for all practical purposes his agents or clerks, and what they do he may be said to do. For instance, the act of collecting the custom duties is an executive act. The President, however, cannot collect those duties himself in all the ports of the United States. But he appoints the Collector of Customs and his chief assistant in each port, who, with the assistance of clerks working under their direction, collect the customs. But as these officers are responsible to the President for the faithful performance of their duties, and can be removed by him, it is really the President who collects the customs. If there is corruption and mismanagement in the New York Custom House, for instance, it is the President's duty to see that it is stopped, by removing the guilty officers; and if he does not do so, he makes himself responsible for the corruption. So also with every branch of the service. The executive *power* is vested in the President, but that power is carried into effect by the various executive officers.

But these officers are not merely agents of the President; they are agents of the people. The executive power is entrusted to the President to be used for the public good, and according to law. These officers are not merely subject to the President; they are also subject to the law; and therefore, in some degree, to the law-making body. Congress controls the subordinate executive officers in the following ways:

1. Congress creates by law the offices which they fill.

---

[1] For the limitations on the President's power of appointment and removal, see pages 185–190.

2. Congress can abolish any of these offices by law, and thus indirectly remove an officer.

3. These officers are paid by appropriations made by act of Congress, which may be withheld, and the officers thus be compelled to resign, for lack of pay.

4. Congress, or either House, can appoint an investigating committee, who will examine into the conduct of any officers of the government, and publish the results to the people; thus if reform is needed, rousing public sentiment to demand a reform.

5. Congress, or either House, can pass a resolution requesting the President to remove certain officers.

6. In cases of flagrant misconduct, if the President should refuse to remove the guilty official, the House of Representatives can impeach him; and, if found guilty by the Senate, he will be removed from office.

In one or more of these ways, Congress can, to a large extent, prevent or punish corruption or treason in office. If the President should undertake to carry out some foolish or ambitious project, he would need the assistance of many officials to do it. But Congress can always interfere with any such designs, by some of the methods named above. In addition to this, the Senate has also a share in the President's appointments, as we shall see.

SECTION 1.

ORGANIZATION.

ANALYSIS OF THIS SECTION.

THE PRESIDENT.

I. TERM OF OFFICE — four years .... II, 1, 1

II. QUALIFICA-TIONS ....
- (a.) Age — 35 years....................... II, 1, 5
- (b.) Citizenship — natural born citizen. II, 1, 5
- (c.) Residence — 14 years in the U. S... II, 1, 5

III. ELECTION..

1. *Presidential electors* .....
- (a.) Number equal to the Senators and Representatives of each State. II, 1, 2
- (b.) Chosen as legislature of each State directs......... II, 1, 2
- (c.) Congressmen and U. S. officers disqualified .... II, 1, 2

2. *Time of choosing electors.*
- (a.) Fixed by Congress .... II, 1, 4
- (b.) Uniform through the U. S......... II, 1, 4

3. *Time of their meeting* ....
- (a.) Fixed by Congress .... II, 1, 4
- (b.) Uniform through the U. S......... II, 1, 4

4. *Election of electors* .....
- (a.) Meet in respective States... Am. XII
- (b.) Vote by ballot Am. XII
- (c.) Separately for President and Vice President ... Am. XII
- (d.) Both cannot be of the same State as themselves........ Am. XII
- (e.) A majority elects........ Am. XII
- (f.) They vote but once. .... Am. XII

THE PRESIDENT.

III. ELECTION..

5. *Canvassing the returns* .....
- (a.) Returns sent to President of Senate.... Am. XII
- (b.) Opened in presence of Congress .... Am. XII
- (c.) And counted.. Am. XII

6. *Election by House of Representatives* ....
- (a.) Only in case no person has a majority of the electoral votes .... Am. XII
- (b.) Must choose among the three highest Am. XII
- (c.) By ballot...... Am. XII
- (d.) Each State has one vote..... Am. XII
- (e.) Quorum—two-thirds of the States ... ... Am. XII
- (f.) Majority of all the States necessary to a choice ..... Am. XII

IV. SALARY ...
- (a.) Fixed by law .... II, 1, 7
- (b.) Not increased or diminished during his term of office.................. II, 1, 7
- (c.) No other emolument. .... II, 1, 7

V. OATH OF OFFICE... II, 1, 8

VI. REMOVABLE
- (a.) For high crimes and misdemeanors II, 4
- (b.) On impeachment by House of Representatives .... I, 2, 5
- (c.). And conviction by the Senate...... I, 3, 7

VII. DUTIES. (See Sections 2 and 3.)

VIII. VACANCIES
- (a.) Filled by Vice President, if there be one............................... II, 1, 6
- (b.) Or by such officer as Congress has by law appointed .... II, 1, 6

THE VICE PRESIDENT.

- I. TERM OF OFFICE — same as President .... II, 1, 1
- II. QUALIFICATIONS — same as President.................... Am. XII
- III. ELECTION ..
  - 1. Same as President.................... Am. XII
  - EXCEPT —
  - 2. *Election by Senate* ......
    - (a.) Only in case no person has a majority of the electoral votes .... Am. XII
    - (b.) Must choose between the two highest.. Am. XII
    - (c.) Quorum— two-thirds of whole number of Senators.......... Am. XII
    - (d.) Majority of all the Senators needed to elect......... Am. XII
- IV. OATH OF OFFICE.. VI, 3
- V. REMOVABLE — same as President........................ II, 4
- VI. DUTIES ....
  - 1. As President of the Senate with casting vote .... I, 3, 4
  - 2. Become President in case of vacancy. II, 1, 6
- VII. VACANCIES — not filled....................... .... II, 1, 6

CLAUSE 1.

IN WHOM VESTED.

The executive power shall be vested in a President of the United States of America. He shall hold his office during the term of four years, and together with the Vice President, chosen for the same term, be elected as follows.

I. TERM OF OFFICE. — The President's term of office is four years. This is twice as long as that of a Representative, and two-thirds as long as that of a Senator. The term of office of President, Vice President, Representatives and Senators begins and ends on the fourth of March in the odd years (except when a vacancy is filled). On the fourth of March, at noon, in every odd year, the terms of office of all Representatives and of one-third of the Senators come to an end, and the terms of office of their successors begin. Every other odd year, on the fourth of March, at noon, the terms of office of the President and Vice President also come to an end, and the terms of office of their successors begin. As the election for President and Vice President takes place every leap year, this term of office begins on the fourth of March in the year next following each leap year. With this clue, the student can easily remember the years of each Presidential term, except where cut short by death.

II. RE-ELECTION OF THE PRESIDENT. — The letter of the Constitution does not forbid the re-election of a President any number of times. But it has become a well understood custom, though never formally enacted, that the President may be re-elected once, but no more. This custom was begun by Washington when he declined a third term, on the ground that two terms are enough for a President. It was confirmed by the action of Jefferson in also declining a third term, and by the constant practice of the country since then. Some Presidents have wished a third term, but the people have refused to grant it. It may now be considered a settled part of the unwritten Constitution, that a President may be elected twice, but no more.

III. THE VICE PRESIDENT. — The Vice President is elected for two purposes:

1. To fill the place of President, when there is a vacancy in that office.

2. To preside over the Senate meanwhile. When the Vice President becomes President, he does not preside over the Senate.

Four cases have occurred in which the Vice President has become President. At the death of President Harrison, Vice President Tyler became President; at the death of President Taylor, Vice President Fillmore became President; at the death of President Lincoln, Vice President Johnson became President; at the death of President Garfield, Vice President Arthur became President. No case has occurred in which the Vice President has become President for any other reason than the death of the President

CLAUSE 2.

PRESIDENTIAL ELECTORS.

Each State shall appoint, in such manner as the legislature thereof may direct, a number of electors, equal to the whole number of Senators and Representatives to which the State may be entitled in the Congress; but no Senator or Representative, or person holding an office of trust or profit under the United States, shall be appointed an elector.

I. THE PRESIDENT ELECTED INDIRECTLY. — In the Constitutional Convention, it was first voted that the President should be elected by Congress. But on further consideration, the plan was adopted of electing him by presidential electors. The Convention did not intend that the President should be elected by the people. They thought that the chief of the nation ought not to be elected by the passions and prejudices that often control a popular election; but by the calm judgment of a few of the best men of each State.

The idea was a fine one in theory; but in practice it did not work as its authors expected it would. In actual practice the President is elected by the people indirectly. The electors are always pledged beforehand to vote for certain persons for President and Vice President; and they are only so chosen because they are so

pledged.   The presidential electors have never failed to
vote for the candidate of their party.[1]

II.   APPOINTMENT OF PRESIDENTIAL ELECTORS.—The
manner of choosing presidential electors is left to the
several States.   The following different methods have
been followed in some or all of the States:

1. They have been chosen by the State legislature.
This was the usual method at first.

2. They have been chosen in several States by the
people voting by districts.   This is the fairest method,
and represents the will of the people most accurately.
Under this plan, a State will generally choose some of
its electors from one party and some from the other,
while under either of the other plans, the party which
has a majority, however small, in the State, will carry
all the electoral votes of the State.

3. They are now chosen in all the States by vote of
the people on a general ticket.   Whichever party carries the State, has all the electoral votes of the State.[2]

III.   QUALIFICATIONS OF PRESIDENTIAL ELECTORS.—
Only one qualification is prescribed.   No Senator or
Representative, or any United States officer, can be a
presidential elector.   This was intended to keep the
electors as free as possible from personal interests in the
result of the election.   But as electors now are only
machines to cast certain votes, this provision is of no
practical importance.   It has been evaded in various
ways.

---

[1] Except in the case of the death of Horace Greeley, who died after the
electors were appointed, and before they met.   In that case the Democratic
electors voted for several different persons, according to their own individual
preferences.

[2] The case has happened, where there were three or more parties, that two
have combined in a State against a third on an electoral ticket divided between the two parties.   That is the only way in which the vote of a State
has been divided under the present practice.

IV. NUMBER OF PRESIDENTIAL ELECTORS. — This is the same as the number of Senators and Representatives to which the State is entitled in Congress. The small States thus have a greater voice in the election of President than their population would entitle them to.

CLAUSE 3.

ELECTION OF PRESIDENT AND VICE PRESIDENT.

TWELFTH AMENDMENT.

The electors shall meet in their respective States and vote by ballot for President and Vice President, one of whom, at least, shall not be an inhabitant of the same State with themselves; they shall name in their ballots the person voted for as President, and in distinct ballots the person voted for as Vice President, and they shall make distinct lists of all persons voted for as President, and of all persons voted for as Vice President, and of the number of votes for each; which lists they shall sign and certify, and transmit sealed to the seat of government of the United States, directed to the President of the Senate. The President of the Senate shall, in the presence of the Senate and House of Representatives, open all the certificates, and the votes shall then be counted; the person having the greatest number of votes for President shall be the President, if such number be a majority of the whole number of electors appointed; and if no person have such majority, then from the persons having the highest numbers not exceeding three on the list of those voted for as President, the house of Representatives shall choose immediately, by ballot, the President. But in choosing the President, the votes shall be taken by States, the representation from each State having one vote; a quorum for this purpose shall consist of a member or members from two-thirds of the States, and a majority of all the States shall be necessary to a choice. And if the House of Representatives shall not choose a President whenever the right of choice shall devolve upon them, before the fourth day of March, next following, then the Vice President shall act as President, as in the case of the death or other constitutional disability of the President.

The person having the greatest number of votes as Vice President, shall be the Vice President, if such number be a majority of the whole number of electors appointed, and if no person have a majority, then from the two highest numbers on the list, the Senate shall choose the Vice President; a quorum for the purpose shall consist of two-thirds of the whole number of Senators, and a majority of the whole number shall be necessary to a choice. But no person constitutionally ineligible to the office of President shall be eligible to that of Vice President of the United States.

A. *The First Process.*

I. ELECTION BY THE ELECTORS. — The presidential electors thus chosen, elect a President and Vice President, if they can, under the following restrictions:

1. They meet in their respective States. They do not all meet in one place. They meet in their own States, and usually at the State capitals. The object of this is to prevent bargaining for votes, which would be easy if they all met in the same place. Vacancies in the College of Electors in any State are filled in such way as that State has prescribed by law. This is done in many States by the electors themselves. If a vacancy exists by reason of death, absence, or ineligibility of an elector, the College of Electors select some one to fill the vacancy, and then proceed to vote for President and Vice President.

2. They vote by ballot. The vote by ballot is frequently used in elections in the United States, for the purpose of allowing the voter to conceal his vote, and thus to be more independent. It is used for that purpose here. But as the presidential electors have ceased to be independent voters, and as every one knows how they will vote, long before they meet, this provision is practically useless.

3. They ballot for President and Vice President separately. This prevents any mistakes or confusion in voting.

4. Only one of these can live in the same State with themselves. This is to prevent both President and Vice President being from the same State. They have usually been not only from different States, but from different sections of the country.

5. A majority of the electors is required to elect. A majority is more than half of the whole number of

votes. A candidate may have the largest number of votes and not have a majority, and thus fail to be elected by the electors.

6. The electors vote but once. This follows from their meeting in different places. Before the invention of the telegraph, it would have been impossible to have even got the news of the result in time to vote a second time, if there was no election the first time. And even now, it would be quite inconvenient for thirty-eight sets of men, meeting in thirty-eight different places, to keep on voting and announcing the results of the ballot. The electors must therefore elect a President or Vice President on the first ballot, or not at all.

II. COUNTING THE VOTES.— The votes thus cast are counted as follows:

1. The electors in each State make a list of all persons voted for by them for President and a list of all persons voted for by them for Vice President. They sign these lists and certify that they are genuine. All the electors in each State sign and certify these lists.

2. Three sets of these lists exactly alike are made out, of which one is sent to the President of the Senate by mail, another by special messenger, and the third is delivered to the judge of the United States district court for the district in which the electors meet. If the President of the Senate fails to receive the certificates of election from any State by the first Wednesday in January, he is authorized to send a special messenger for the certificate in the hands of the District Judge.

3. The President of the Senate, who may or may not be the Vice President (I, 3; 4 and 5), presides over a joint convention of the Senate and House of Representatives. In their presence he opens the certificates, which are read by clerks, and the votes for each candi-

date are added up and announced by tellers appointed from each House. No provision is made for the case of a disputed election of presidential electors in any State. This fact led to the contested presidential election of 1876.

4. If any candidate for President is found to have a majority of all the electoral votes cast for President, he is thereupon declared elected. And if any candidate for Vice President is found to have a majority of all the electoral votes cast for Vice President, he is declared elected Vice President. If in either case no one has a majority, there is no election by the electors.

B. *Second Process.*

III. ELECTION OF PRESIDENT BY THE HOUSE OF REPRESENTATIVES. — When the presidential electors fail to elect a President, the right of election goes to the House of Representatives under the following conditions:

1. No candidate can be voted for except the three who received the highest number of votes for President.

2. The vote is by ballot.

3. The vote is by States, each State having one vote. The vote of each State is given as the majority of the members from that State who are present may direct. If the vote of a State is equally divided, that fact is reported, and the vote of that State is not given to any candidate.

4. A quorum for the purpose of voting for a President must consist of a member or members from two-thirds of the States. A quorum for ordinary purposes consists of a majority of the members elected.

5. A majority of all the States is necessary to a choice. If a State is divided, its vote helps to prevent an election. Thus in 1801, when the election was thrown into the

House of Representatives, there were sixteen States; of these, eight voted for Jefferson, six for Burr, and two were divided. There was therefore no election. Thirty-five times the House voted with the same result. On the thirty-sixth ballot, some members from the two divided States who had voted for Burr, purposely left the room. The members from those States who remained could then give a majority in each for Jefferson, so that he had ten States and Burr six, and Jefferson was elected.

6. The House must proceed at once to elect a President. If they fail to elect before the fourth of March, then the Vice President just elected becomes President. The reasons for this are, that the President's term of office must begin on the fourth of March, and that the House of Representatives ceases to exist on the same day, and the new House comes into power.

IV. ELECTION OF VICE PRESIDENT BY THE SENATE.— When the presidential electors fail to elect a Vice President, the choice devolves upon the Senate, under the following conditions:

1. No candidate can be voted for except the two who received the highest number of votes for Vice President. This ensures a speedy election.

2. A quorum to elect a Vice President is two-thirds of the whole number of Senators.

3. A majority of all the Senators is necessary to a choice. It is not merely a majority of all present, but a majority of all.

V. THE OLD METHOD OF ELECTING PRESIDENT AND VICE PRESIDENT.

When the Constitution was first adopted, it prescribed a method of electing President and Vice President, somewhat different from the one now in use. The new method was adopted by an amendment to the Constitution in 1804, in consequence of the danger to the country shown in the disputed election of 1801. The Constitution originally read as follows:

> The electors shall meet in their respective States, and vote by ballot for two persons, of whom one at least shall not be an inhabitant of the same State with themselves. And they shall make a list of all the persons voted for, and of the number of votes for each; which list they shall sign and certify, and transmit, sealed, to the seat of the government of the United States, directed to the President of the Senate. The President of the Senate shall, in the presence of the Senate and House of Representatives, open all the certificates, and the votes shall then be counted. The person having the greatest number of votes shall be the President, if such number be a majority of the whole number of electors appointed; and if there be more than one who have such a majority, and have an equal number of votes, then the House of Representatives shall immediately choose by ballot one of them President, and if no person have a majority, then from the five highest on the list the said House shall in like manner choose the President. But in choosing the President, the votes shall be taken by States, the representation from each State having one vote; a quorum for this purpose shall consist of a member or members from two-thirds of the States, and a majority of all the States shall be necessary to a choice. In every case, after the choice of the President, the person having the greatest number of votes of the electors, shall be the Vice President. But if there should remain two or more who have equal votes, the Senate shall choose from them by ballot the Vice President.

The following is an analysis of this method of election, with a comparison with the method now in use:

A. *First Process.*

ELECTION BY THE ELECTORS.—The electors having been chosen in such way as the several States have prescribed, proceed to elect a President and Vice President, if they can, under the following conditions:

1. They meet in their respective States. This provision is still retained.

2. They vote by ballot. This provision is still retained.

3. They vote for two persons. They did not designate which of the two they wished to be President and which Vice President. This was a fatal defect, as the election of 1801 showed. The majority of the electors wished Jefferson to be President and Burr Vice President, but both received the same number of votes, and Burr came near being elected President by the House of Represent-

atives. This defect is remedied in the amended mode of electing President and Vice President.

4. A majority was required, then as now, to elect a President. But as each elector had two votes, the majority required was not a majority of all the votes, but a majority of all the electors. But a majority was not required to elect a Vice President. The person having the second highest number of votes was in any case to be Vice President.

COUNTING THE VOTES.—No change has been made in this.

B. *Second Process.*

ELECTION OF PRESIDENT.—If no person had a majority of all the electoral votes, or if two had a majority and both had the same number, then the House of Representatives proceeded to choose a President under the following conditions:

1. If two candidates each were voted for by a majority of all the electors, and had the same number of votes, then the House must choose between these two. This was the case in the celebrated election of 1801. This case would be impossible as the Constitution now stands, and therefore is not provided for.

2. If no candidate was voted for by a majority of the electors, then the House must choose from the five highest on the list. This is now changed to the three highest.

3. The vote was by ballot, then as now.

4. The vote was by States, then as now.

5. The quorum remains the same.

6. A majority of all the States was necessary to a choice, then as now.

7. The House was required to proceed to an election immediately. This has not been changed.

8. No provision was made for the case of the House of Representatives failing to elect before the fourth of March. The election of 1801 showed this to be necessary. It is now provided for.

ELECTION OF VICE PRESIDENT. — Under the old plan, it would be unlikely that the Senate would ever be called on to elect a Vice President. After the President was elected, either by the electors or by the House of Representatives, the candidate who stood equal or next highest on the list became Vice President, whether he had a majority of electoral votes or not. The only case in which the Senate would be called on to select a Vice President, would have

K

been when two stood next on the list to the President-elect, and both had the same number of electoral votes. In that case the Senate was to choose between these two by ballot.

As the Vice President is now voted for separately from the President, it is provided that a majority of electoral votes is necessary to elect a Vice President; that if no person has a majority, the Senate elect by ballot from the two highest; that a quorum shall consist of two-thirds of the Senators, and a majority of all the Senators shall be necessary to a choice.

The essential difference between the old plan and the new is, that under the old plan each elector voted for two persons, without saying which one he wished for President or Vice President, while under the present plan each elector votes for two persons, distinctly naming one for President and the other for Vice President. All the other changes are such as are made necessary to carry out this change.

Under the old plan, the President was several times of one political party, and the Vice President of the other party. But under the present plan, that could only occur in case the presidential electors failed to elect, and the Senate and House of Representatives were controlled by opposite parties.

VI. THE DISPUTED ELECTION OF 1876.

Just as the disputed election in 1801 called the attention of the country to one defect in the Constitutional provision for the election of President and Vice President and led to the twelfth amendment, so another disputed election called the attention of the country to another defect, and will probably lead to another amendment of the Constitution.

No provision is made in the Constitution for the case of a disputed election in a State. It was intended that the certificate of the proper officer in each State should attest the election of the electors, and that their certificate should attest their own vote. An extraordinary case arose in 1877, when Hayes and Tilden, the rival candidates, each had a certificate of election from a set of electors in several States. As the Senate and House were controlled by opposite parties, neither would yield. Just before the time for counting the votes, an extraordinary tribunal was created, consisting of five Senators, five Representatives, and five Judges of the Supreme Court, to whose decision these contested cases were referred. All of them were decided in favor of Hayes, and he was declared elected President by one majority.

It was claimed by one side that the Constitution gave the President of the Senate the right to decide which were the legal electoral votes. And it was claimed by the other side that Congress or either House could refuse to receive the vote of any State, where there was a dispute in regard to it. Both these claims were preposterous. The fact is, the Constitution is defective at this point, in not providing for the contingency, and it should be amended.

VII.　LIST OF THE PRESIDENTS:

Inaug-urated.	Name.	State.	By what party elected.
1789	George Washington	Virginia	All parties.
1793	George Washington	Virginia	All parties.
1797	John Adams	Massachusetts	Federalist.
1801	Thomas Jefferson	Virginia	Republican.
1805	Thomas Jefferson	Virginia	Republican.
1809	James Madison	Virginia	Republican.
1813	James Madison	Virginia	Republican.
1817	James Monroe	Virginia	Republican.
1821	James Monroe	Virginia	Republican.
1825	John Quincy Adams	Massachusetts	Republican.
1829	Andrew Jackson	Tennessee	Democrat.
1833	Andrew Jackson	Tennessee	Democrat.
1837	Martin Van Buren	New York	Democrat.
1841 {	William Henry Harrison	Ohio	Whig.
	John Tyler	Virginia	Whig.
1845	James K. Polk	Tennessee	Democrat.
1849 {	Zachary Taylor	Louisiana	Whig.
1850 {	Millard Fillmore	New York	Whig.
1853	Franklin Pierce	New Hampshire.	Democrat.
1857	James Buchanan	Pennsylvania	Democrat.
1861	Abraham Lincoln	Illinois	Republican.
1865 {	Abraham Lincoln	Illinois	Republican.
	Andrew Johnson	Tennessee	Republican.
1869	Ulysses S. Grant	Illinois	Republican.
1873	Ulysses S. Grant	Illinois	Republican.
1877	Rutherford B. Hayes	Ohio	Republican.
1881 {	James A. Garfield	Ohio	Republican.
	Chester A. Arthur	New York	Republican.

It will be seen from the above that Virginia has furnished five Presidents (one of whom, however, was elected Vice President), Tennessee three (one elected as Vice President), Massachusetts two, Illinois two, Ohio three, New York three (two elected as Vice President), Louisiana one, New Hampshire one and Pennsylvania one.

The Presidents from Virginia have served eight terms and a fractional term, those from Illinois three terms and a fractional term, those from Tennessee three terms and a fractional term, and the rest a less time.

After Washington's two administrations, which were not partisan, though Washington himself was a Federalist, the Federalists carried one presidential election, the old Republicans seven, the Democrats six, the Whigs two, and the present Republican party six.

NOTE.— HISTORY OF THE PRESIDENTIAL ELECTIONS.— The following is a brief history of the presidential elections:

1. At the first Presidential election, George Washington was elected President unanimously. John Adams had the next highest number of electoral votes and was elected Vice President. The other votes were scattered. Parties were not yet fully defined. Both Washington and Adams were Federalists, that is, in favor of giving more power to the Federal government than the Republicans, afterwards called Democrats, wished to give. But Washington governed in an unpartisan way, choosing his cabinet from both parties.

2. Washington was elected unanimously. Adams was elected Vice President, as a Federalist candidate.

3. Adams was elected President, and Jefferson Vice President. This election had the peculiar feature of electing the chief of the opposing parties one to each of the two highest offices. This was possible under the old method of electing the President, but would not be possible now.

4. To prevent such a result again, the electors of each party concentrated their votes on two candidates. The result was that Jefferson and Burr, the Republican (or Democratic) candidate, each received 73 votes, which was a majority of all the electors. It was well known that the Republican electors wished Jefferson as President. The election went to the House of Representatives, who were obliged to choose between these two. The Republicans in the House voted for Jefferson, and the Federalists for Burr, in order to embarrass and divide the Republicans. For thirty-five successive ballots, eight States voted for Jefferson, six for Burr, and two were divided. Jefferson was finally elected President, and Burr Vice President. This election showed a great defect in the Constitution, which was remedied by the Twelfth Amendment.

5. Jefferson was re-elected President, and George Clinton Vice President, by the Republicans (or Democrats) under the new method.

6. Madison was elected President, and George Clinton was re-elected Vice President, by the Republicans (or Democrats).

7. Madison was re-elected President, and Elbridge Gerry was elected Vice President, by the Republicans (or Democrats).

8. The successful termination of the war with England, in spite of the opposition of the Federalists, completely destroyed them as a party, and James Monroe was elected President, and Daniel Tompkins Vice President, by the Republicans (or Democrats), by a large majority.

9. They were re-elected almost unanimously. This was called " the era of good feeling," when the old party issues had passed away and new issues had not yet come up.

10. There were four tickets in the field. Calhoun was elected Vice President by the electors. No one was elected President by the electors, but Jackson had the largest popular vote. The House of Representatives elected J. Q. Adams President, on the first ballot. He was the last President elected by the old Republican party.

11. Jackson was elected President, and Calhoun Vice President, by the Democratic party.

12. Jackson was re-elected President, with Van Buren as Vice President.

13. Van Buren was elected President by the Democrats, and R. M. Johnson Vice President, the election going to the Senate.

14. Harrison and Tyler were elected by the Whig party. But Harrison died just one month after he was inaugurated, and Tyler, who became the President, soon left the Whig party for the Democratic.

15. Polk and Dallas were elected by the Democrats.

16. Taylor and Fillmore were elected by the Whigs. President Taylor died after serving one year and four months, and Fillmore became President.

17. Pierce and King were elected by the Democrats. But King died before being sworn in as Vice President.

18. Buchanan and Breckenridge were elected by the Democrats.

19. Lincoln and Hamlin were elected by the Republican party (not to be confused with the old Republican party, who were the predecessors of the Democrats), and the Southern States seceded in consequence.

2'. Lincoln was re-elected, with Andrew Johnson as Vice President. The States engaged in secession did not vote. But Lincoln was assassinated one month and ten days after his second inauguration, and Andrew Johnson then became President, and like Tyler went over to the Democratic party.

21. Grant and Colfax were elected by the Republican party. Virginia, Mississippi and Texas did not vote.

22. Grant was re-elected with Wilson, by the Republican party. Arkansas, Georgia and Louisiana were excluded from the count for irregularities in the election.

23. This Presidential election was the most exciting on record. The votes of South Carolina, Florida, Louisiana and Oregon were in dispute. If any one of them were counted for the Democratic candidates, they would be elected. As the Senate was Republican and the House Democratic, they could not agree in regard to which set of certificates from either of these States should be counted. A compromise was at last effected by creating an extraordinary commission, to consist of five Senators (three Republicans and two Democrats), five Representatives (three Democrats and two Republicans), and five Judges of the Supreme Court (two Republicans and two Democrats, and the fifth to be chosen by the other four). The decisions of this commission were to be binding unless reversed by a vote of both Houses. This electoral commission, by a vote of eight to seven, admitted the certificates from the Republican electors of all the States in dispute, and thus gave the election to Hayes and Wheeler by one electoral vote. The count was not completed by Congress until March 3. This disputed election showed the need of a change in the manner of electing the President, or at least in the manner of counting the vote.

24. Garfield and Arthur were elected by the Republican party. Garfield was assassinated July 2, and died September 19, 1881, living only seven months of his term. Arthur became President.

CLAUSE 4.

TIME OF THESE ELECTIONS.

The Congress may determine the time of choosing the electors, and the day on which they shall give their votes; which day shall be the same throughout the United States.

TIME OF PRESIDENTIAL ELECTIONS. — Congress has determined the time of these elections by law. The following table will aid the memory:

1. *Election of Electors*, the Tuesday after the first Monday of November (in each leap year), the day on which Representatives are also chosen.

2. *Electors vote for President and Vice President*, the first Wednesday in December.

3. The President of the Senate sends for missing returns the first Wednesday in January.

4. The votes are counted the second Wednesday in February, and thereafter till a President is elected, but not longer than till the fourth of March. The same dates hold for the Senate in electing a Vice President.

6. The President is inaugurated the fourth of March. If that falls on Sunday, he is inaugurated on the fifth.

CLAUSE 5.

QUALIFICATIONS OF PRESIDENT AND VICE PRESIDENT.

No person except a natural-born citizen, or a citizen of the United States, at the time of the adoption of this Constitution, shall be eligible to the office of President; neither shall any person be eligible to that office, who shall not have attained to the age of thirty-five years, and been fourteen years a resident within the United States.

I. CITIZENSHIP. — The President must be a natural-born citizen of the United States. The President must be a citizen by inheritance, not by adoption. He cannot be a naturalized citizen; but it is possible that a person born out of the United States might be President. The child of American parents born in foreign lands, would be 'a natural-born American citizen, but not a native-born citizen (see page 87).

Naturalized citizens, who were citizens at the time the Constitution was adopted, were made eligible to the office of President. But none of that class are now alive, and none have ever been elected President. This provision is therefore now practically obsolete.

II. AGE AND RESIDENCE.— The President must be at least thirty-five years old.

He must have resided within the United States at least fourteen years. This residence need not have been immediately before his election, but may have been at any time previously. Persons have been elected President soon after a return from an embassy to some other country. The object of this provision was to prevent any person who had recently been naturalized from being elected President, soon after the Constitution was adopted. This would also cover the case of natural-born citizens who had spent nearly all their lives abroad. A sufficient residence is required to make the candidate for the presidency familiar with the institutions of the country he aspires to govern.

III. QUALIFICATIONS OF VICE PRESIDENT. — The Vice President must have the same qualifications as the President, because he may become President.

IV. A TABLE OF QUALIFICATIONS.— The following
table will aid the student's memory:

	AGE.	CITIZENSHIP.	RESIDENCE.
President..............	35	Natural-born citizen.	Fourteen years in the United States.
Vice President.......	35	Natural-born citizen.	Fourteen years in the United States.
Senator	30	Nine years a citizen.	In the State from which chosen.
Representative	25	Seven years a citizen.	In the State from which chosen.

The following is a table of additional particulars:

	TERM OF OFFICE.	HOW ELECTED.	VACANCIES, How FILLED.
President.........	4 years...	By electors......	By Vice President.
Vice President....	4 years...	By electors.......	Not Filled.
Senator	6 years...	By State Legislatures	By Governor or State Legislature.
Representative ...	2 years...	By the people....	By the people of the District.

CLAUSE 6.

VACANCIES.

In case of the removal of the President from office, or of his death, resignation, or inability to discharge the powers and duties of the said office,
the same shall devolve on the Vice President, and the Congress may by
law provide for the case of removal, death, resignation or inability, both
of the President and Vice President, declaring what officer shall then act
as President, and such officer shall act accordingly, until the disability
be removed, or a President shall be elected.

I. VACANCIES IN THE PRESIDENCY, HOW MADE.— The
office of President may become vacant by death, by his
removal on impeachment, by his resignation, or by such
disability as insanity, or extreme and long continued

sickness. It may also be vacant in case of the failure of both the presidential electors and of the House of Representatives to elect a President before the fourth of March. (Clause 3.)

The absence of the President from Washington does not create a vacancy. Presidents have performed many official duties at a distance from the capital.

When the President is impeached, there is no vacancy. When Andrew Johnson was impeached, he held his office, and as the Senate acquitted him, no vacancy occurred.

II. VACANCIES IN THE PRESIDENCY, HOW FILLED. — When a vacancy exists, and there is a Vice President, he fills that vacancy, unless he also is incapacitated in some way. If the President should be only disabled from performing the duties of his office by insanity or sickness, the Vice President would act as President for the time being, until the disability cease. But when the vacancy is a permanent one, the Vice President becomes President. Only three vacancies in the office of President have occurred, in each case by the death of the President, and in each case the Vice President has succeeded to the office of President.

III. VACANCIES IN THE VICE PRESIDENCY. — The office of Vice President may become vacant by his death or resignation, by his removal on impeachment, or by his promotion to the office of President. When a vacancy occurs it is not filled. But the duties of the Vice President as President of the Senate are performed by the President *pro tempore* of the Senate.

IV. VACANCIES IN BOTH PRESIDENCY AND VICE PRESIDENCY. — The Constitution leaves it to Congress to provide for the case of a vacancy in the office of both President and Vice President. Congress has provided that in case of such double vacancy, the President of the Senate, and if there be no President of the Senate, then the Speaker of the House of Representatives, shall act as President, until the disability be removed or a new President be elected. In that case a special election must be held the next fall, and a President must be elected to fill the unexpired term, unless it is the last year of the term. This case has never arisen.

When the Vice President becomes President on the death, removal or resignation of the President, he holds the office for the whole of the unexpired term. But if the President of the Senate or the Speaker of the House of Representatives fill a vacancy, he would be only Acting President, and he would only hold the office of President until a special election could be held. But if the vacancy occur in the last year of the President's term, the Acting President holds the office for the remainder of the term.

V. DISPUTED QUESTION.

Would the absence of the President from the United States create a vacancy? The case has never occurred, and therefore no positive answer can be given. But most of the States have provided that the absence of the Governor from the State creates a vacancy in the office during his absence, and that the Lieutenant-Governor shall act as Governor during his absence from the State; and this would lead us to suppose that if the case should ever arise, it would be decided that the absence of the President from the United States creates a temporary vacancy.

CLAUSE 7.

SALARY.

The President shall, at stated times, receive for his services a compensation which shall be neither increased nor diminished during the period for which he shall have been elected, and he shall not receive within that period any other emolument from the United States, or any of them.

THE SALARY OF THE PRESIDENT.— The salary of the President was twenty-five thousand dollars until 1873, when it was raised to fifty thousand dollars. Besides this, the United States has built a house called the White House, and keeps it furnished for the President's use. He also has special appropriations for any special expenses. He is expected to spend full as much as he receives. No executive of any country as large as this receives so small a salary.

The salary of the Vice President was first five thousand, then eight thousand, then ten thousand, and is now eight thousand a year.

The reason for neither increasing nor diminishing the salary of the President during his term is to make him more independent of Congress. This was evaded when President Grant's salary was raised for his second term, before his first term had ended, but after he had been elected for a second term.

CLAUSE 8.

OATH OF OFFICE.

Before he enter on the execution of his office, he shall take the following oath or affirmation: "I do solemnly swear (or affirm) that I will faithfully execute the office of President of the United States, and will, to the best of my ability, preserve, protect and defend the Constitution of the United States."

I. THE OATH OF OFFICE. — The oath of office may be administered to the President by any Judge; but the practice is to have the Chief Justice of the Supreme Court perform this duty. The Chief Justice of the Supreme Court is the highest officer who can administer an oath, and ranks next to the President.

The President's oath of office contains two pledges:

1. To faithfully perform the office of President of the United States.

2. To the best of his ability to preserve, protect and defend the Constitution of the United States.

The oath is a very simple oath as compared with many oaths of office. It embraces only the two most essential points. If the President has conscientious scruples against taking an oath, he can affirm instead of swearing.

II. INAUGURATION OF THE PRESIDENT. — The President is inaugurated on the fourth of March, at noon. Besides other ceremonies, the oath of office is administered, and the President delivers an inaugural address. The fourth of March, 1877, came on Sunday. It was a legal question whether the President's term in that case ended on the fourth or fifth of March. The difficulty was avoided by President Hayes taking the oath of office in private on the fourth, and again in connection with the inaugural ceremonies on the fifth, and by President Grant doing no official acts after noon of the fourth of March.

In the three cases when the Vice President became President, he took the oath of office, but there were no public inaugural ceremonies.

SECTION 2.

POWERS AND DUTIES OF THE PRESIDENT.

ANALYSIS OF THIS SECTION.

(And of other executive powers in the Constitution.)

POWERS AND DUTIES OF THE PRESIDENT.

I. POWERS HELD JOINTLY WITH THE SENATE.
1. To make treaties .... II, 2, 2
2. To appoint and remove officers.. II, 2, 2

II. POWERS HELD JOINTLY WITH CONGRESS ...
1. Over legislation
   - (a.) By the veto I, 7, 2, 3
   - (b.) By his messages..... II, 3
2. Protection of States .... II, 4
3. To decide between rival State governments .... IV, 4
4. To protect the Union against rebellion or invasion (implied)..

III. SOLE POWERS
1. Commander-in-Chief .... II, 2, 1
2. Cabinet...................... II, 2, 1
3. Pardon and reprieves .... II, 2, 1
4. Temporary appointments .... II, 2, 3
5. Appointment of inferior officers, II, 2, 2
6. Messages to Congress .... II, 3
7. Convening and adjourning Congress .... II, 3
8. Receiving Ambassadors .... II, 3
9. Executing the laws.... .... II, 3
10. Commissioning officers .... II, 3

IV. PROHIBITIONS ON ALL EXECUTIVE OFFICERS.........
1. Cannot suspend the writ of *habeas corpus* except in war time........................... I, 9, 2
2. Cannot draw money from the Treasury except as appropriated by law .... I, 9, 6
3. Cannot receive offices or presents from foreign powers without the consent of Congress.. I, 9, 7
4. Bound by oath to support the Constitution and fulfill duties of office... .... VI, 3
5. Cannot infringe rights guaranteed in Amendments.......... I-X

CLAUSE 1.

SOME SOLE POWERS OF THE PRESIDENT.

The President shall be commander-in-chief of the army and navy of the United States, and of the militia of the several States, when called into the actual service of the United States; he may require the opinion, in writing, of the principal officer in each of the executive departments, upon any subject relating to the duties of their respective offices, and he shall have power to grant reprieves and pardons for offenses against the United States, except in cases of impeachment.

A. *Commander-in-Chief.*

I. THE REASON FOR THIS POWER. — In order to execute the laws of the United States, and to protect the nation from invasion or insurrection, it is necessary that the President should have charge of a military force. In almost all governments the chief executive officer is commander-in-chief, and in creating a chief executive for the United States, it was natural and necessary that he should have command of the army and navy. These forces are subject to the general rules made by act of Congress (I, 8, 14), are supported by appropriations made by Congress (I, 8, 12), and can be reduced in number, reorganized, or abolished altogether by Congress (I, 8, 12). So that the President cannot well use these forces for very harmful purposes.

II. WHAT MILITARY FORCES ARE UNDER HIS COMMAND. — The military forces under his command are the regular army, the regular navy, a volunteer army and navy, whenever these are authorized by Congress, and the militia of the several States when called into the United States service. All these forces are under the command of the President, subject to the powers of Congress named above. But the militia of any State are under the command of the President only when actually in the service of the United States.   Otherwise they are under the command of the governors of their respective States.

III. The president need not command in person. — The President may command the army in person, or he may put one or more military officers in command to carry on military operations under his general directions.   The latter has always been the case. The President has never actually taken the field in person; but he has appointed officers to command, with certain general instructions, which they were to carry out as best they could with the means at their command.

The President has the right to make additional rules for the army and navy, so far as they do not conflict with those established by law.

B. *The Cabinet.*

I. Executive departments. — This clause by implication provides for executive departments.   These have been established by law, and increased in number from time to time.   The head of each department is called a secretary.   These departments again are divided into bureaus, each with its officers and employes.

The numbers, titles, and compensation of these officers are fixed by law.   The principal officers are appointed by the President, with the advice and consent of the Senate, and can be removed at pleasure. The clerks and employes in each department are appointed by the chief of that department, and can be removed at pleasure.

These departments are all subject to the President, and must carry out his orders.   The executive power is vested in the President, and he is responsible for its exercise.

The names of these executive departments, and the
titles of the head of each, are given in the following
table:[1]

DEPARTMENTS.	SECRETARIES.
Department of State	Secretary of State.
Treasury Department	Secretary of the Treasury.
War Department	Secretary of War.
Department of the Navy	Secretary of the Navy.
Department of the Interior	Secretary of the Interior.
Post Office Department	Post Master General.
Department of Justice	Attorney General.

II. THE CABINET. — President Washington began
the practice of consulting the heads of departments separately or together, orally or in writing, about all
important matters, thus making an informal Cabinet.
President Jefferson began the practice of holding regular Cabinet meetings, a practice which has been kept up
by all Presidents since. President Hayes added the
Vice President to the Cabinet. This practice of holding
Cabinet meetings, and of consulting with them on all
important matters, is not binding on the President. He
can do it or not, as he chooses. But it is so great a
help to him in the management of his office, that it is
not likely that any President will ever dispense with it.

A Cabinet meeting is not so much in the nature of a
legislature as of a council of war. The President takes
the opinions of his Cabinet, but he is not bound by
them. Still, as they are his political friends, and generally his personal friends, a wise President is usually
guided by them to a great extent.

The Cabinet meetings are usually secret. The con-
sultations are not published. They are therefore much
freer than they could be if they were public or were to

[1] There is a so-called Department of Agriculture, but as the chief is called a
commissioner, and does not belong to the Cabinet, it is not given in the list
above. It is properly a bureau instead of a department.

be published. The things which the Cabinet advise the President to do, are of course known when he does them, and often are told to the public before they are put in action, though sometimes they are kept secret for a time.

III. REPORTS OF HEADS OF DEPARTMENTS. — It has become the custom for the heads of departments and for the heads of important bureaus to prepare full reports to the President, which he transmits to Congress with his annual message. Most Americans must have seen these reports, for they are printed every year by thousands and scattered over the country.

The President sometimes calls for written reports or opinions at other times. The Attorney-General, as the law officer of the Government, is frequently called upon for an opinion in writing as to the lawfulness of certain courses of action. The reports or opinions in writing which the President can require, must be upon a subject relating to the duties of the Secretary's office. Thus the President would call on the Secretary of State for an opinion upon our relations with any foreign power, or upon the Secretary of the Treasury for an opinion on a financial question, and so on.

IV. ORGANIZATION OF THE DEPARTMENTS. — The executive departments are each divided into bureaus, with their chiefs and a force of clerks, copyists and messengers, etc.

THE DEPARTMENT OF STATE.

The chief of this department is called the Secretary of State. His duties are:

1. *Domestic.*— He keeps the originals of the Constitution and of all laws and public documents. He keeps the great seal of the United States, and seals all commissions to office, all proclamations of the President, and all copies of papers and records in his office.

L

2. *Foreign.*— He keeps the originals of all treaties, and all correspondence with foreign powers, conducts all such correspondence, issues warrants for the extradition of criminals to foreign powers, and issues passports to citizens of the United States who wish to travel abroad.

In this department there is an Assistant Secretary of State, appointed by the President with the consent of the Senate, and many clerks. There are three bureaus in this department, each with a chief and a force of clerks. They are:

    1. The Diplomatic Bureau.
    2. The Consular Bureau.
    3. The Domestic Bureau.

Connected with the Department of State are the Diplomatic Service and the Consular Service.

THE DIPLOMATIC SERVICE.

To every country with which we have diplomatic relations we send a foreign minister. Those sent to the most important countries are called Ministers Plenipotentiary; those sent to less important countries are called Ministers Resident. The duties of both classes are the same. Most Ministers have Secretaries of Legation. In the absence of the Minister, the Secretary of Legation transacts all business for him.

THE CONSULAR SERVICE.

Consuls have charge of our commercial relations. They guard the interests of our commerce, and the rights of seamen. In all countries not Christian, consuls have a great increase of power and duties. An American citizen in England is subject to English law; but an American citizen in Turkey or China is subject to American law, not Turkish or Chinese law. To administer American law in non-Christian lands, consuls have some judicial powers given them.

THE TREASURY DEPARTMENT.

The chief of this department is called the Secretary of the Treasury. He has charge of everything that relates to the revenues and expenditures of the United States.

This department has more work, and employs more clerks than any other. There are two Assistant Secretaries of the Treasury, and the following bureaus, each with a force of clerks:

BUREAUS.	CHIEFS.
Office of First Comptroller........	First Comptroller.
Office of Second Comptroller......	Second Comptroller.
Office of First Auditor...........	First Auditor.
Office of Second Auditor.........	Second Auditor.
Office of Third Auditor..........	Third Auditor.
Office of Fourth Auditor.........	Fourth Auditor.
Office of Fifth Auditor...........	Fifth Auditor.
Office of Sixth Auditor..........	Sixth Auditor.
Office of Treasurer..............	Treasurer of the United States.
Office of Commissioner of Customs,	Commissioner of Customs.
Bureau of Internal Revenue......	Commissioner of Internal Revenue.
Bureau of Statistics.............	Director of the Bureau of Statistics.
The Mint......................	Director of the Mint.
The Coast Survey...............	Superintendent of the Coast Survey.
Office of the Supervising Architect,	Supervising Architect.
Light House Board.............	Secretary of the Treasury (ex officio).

THE WAR DEPARTMENT.

This department has charge of all that relates to the Army. The officers in charge of Bureaus are army officers. The Secretary sometimes has been an army officer. The divisions of the department are as follows:

BUREAUS.	CHIEFS.
Office of Adjutant General	Adjutant General.
Office of Quartermaster General	Quartermaster General.
Office of Commissary General........	Commissary General.
Office of Paymaster General........	Paymaster General.
Office of Surgeon General...........	Surgeon General.
Office of Chief of Engineers.........	Chief of Engineers.
The Ordnance Office	Chief Ordnance Officer.
The Signal Office..................	Chief Signal Officer.
The Bureau of Military Justice	Judge Advocate General.

The Military Academy at West Point, N. Y., trains officers for the army, and is in charge of the War Department. One cadet is sent from each Congressional district, nominated by the Representative from that district, one from each Territory, nominated by the Delegate, and ten at large, appointed by the President. Each cadet pledges himself to serve at least five years in the army after he graduates.

DEPARTMENT OF THE NAVY.

This department has charge of all that relates to the Navy. The chief officers in this department are navy officers, detailed for that purpose. The Secretary of the Navy has sometimes been a navy officer. The work is divided thus:

BUREAUS.

The Bureau of Yards and Docks.
of Equipment and Recruiting.
of Navigation.
of Ordnance.
of Medicine and Surgery.
of Provisions and Clothing.
of Steam Engineering.
of Construction and Repairs.

The Naval Academy at Annapolis, Md., trains officers for the Navy. The cadets are appointed in the same way as for West Point.

DEPARTMENT OF THE INTERIOR.

This is the most miscellaneous department. Its duties can be best learned from the names of the bureaus into which it is divided. They are as follows:

BUREAUS.	CHIEFS.
The Patent Office.....	Commissioner of Patents.
The Pension Office....	Commissioner of Pensions.
The Land Office......	Commissioner of the General Land Office.
The Indian Bureau...	Commissioner of Indian Affairs.
The Census Bureau ...	Superintendent of the Census.
The Bureau of Education.	Commissioner of Education.

The Department of Agriculture (so called), whose chief is styled Commissioner of Agriculture, is nominally independent. Properly, it is a bureau in the Department of the Interior.

POST OFFICE DEPARTMENT.

This department has charge of all that relates to the post offices. It is divided as follows:

BUREAUS.	CHIEFS.
Appointment Office.	First Assistant Postmaster General.
Contract Office	Second Assistant Postmaster General.
Finance Office.	Third Assistant Postmaster General.
Money Order Office.	Superintendent of the Money Order System.
Foreign Mail Office.	Superintendent of the Foreign Mails.

DEPARTMENT OF JUSTICE.

This department has charge of the prosecution and defense of suits for or against the United States. All the District Attorneys and Marshals of the United States Courts act under the orders of this department. The department has several chief officers who correspond nearly to the assistant secretaries and chief of bureaus in the other departments. They are as follows:

Solicitor General.
Assistant Attorney General.
Assistant Attorney General at the Court of Claims.
Assistant Attorney General in the Department of the Interior.
Assistant Attorney General in the Post Office Department.
Solicitor of Internal Revenue.
Naval Solicitor.
Examiner of Claims.
Solicitor of the Treasury.
Assistant Solicitor of the Treasury.

C. The Pardoning Power.

I. REASONS FOR THIS POWER. — The experience of the world has shown that in administering justice, mistakes are sometimes made. Innocent persons are sometimes convicted of crimes by mistake, or by false witnesses, and guilty persons are sometimes sentenced to a punishment more severe than they deserve. Sometimes, also, a crime cannot be proved against a number of guilty persons, except by the testimony of one of their number, which testimony will not be given unless the witness is assured that he will not be punished for his share in the crime. For these reasons, all governments have allowed a pardoning power, and have almost always placed this power in the hands of the executive.

The pardoning power is liable to great abuses. The executive may refuse to pardon those who deserve to be pardoned, and may encourage crime by pardoning great criminals. Our Presidents have been inclined to be too easy, rather than too severe, in the exercise of this power. It has sometimes been proposed to give this power to the courts; but no serious attempt has yet been made in that direction.

II. Extent of the pardoning power. — 1. The President may pardon before trial and conviction as well as after.

2. He may grant a conditional pardon.

3. He may commute a sentence to one less severe.

4. He may remit fines, penalties and forfeitures imposed under the revenue laws.

5. He may stop a criminal proceeding carried on in the name of the United States, at any stage of the process, and order the Attorney General or District Attorney to enter a *nolle prosequi*.[1]

6. He can reprieve a condemned person; that is, suspend his punishment for a time. This power is rarely used except where a person is condemned to death.

7. He can issue a pardon to take effect at some future time.

---

[1] *Nolle prosequi* is a Latin phrase, meaning *not to wish to prosecute*. The effect of entering a *nolle prosequi* is to stop the case and release the accused. But the accused may be prosecuted again for the same offense at some future time, which would not be the case if he had been acquitted by the verdict of a jury.

8. His power extends to military as well as civil offenses.

III. LIMITATIONS ON THE PARDONING POWER. — 1. A pardon, reprieve or commutation must be accepted by the criminal, or it is void.

2. In cases of impeachment, the President has no official power. An impeachment is a political, and not a criminal, trial, and is directed against an executive or judicial officer for malfeasance in office. Besides, if the President were impeached, it would be obviously unfair to allow him to pardon himself.[1] Or if an officer appointed by the President was impeached for carrying out some ambitious design of the President, the President would be tempted to pardon him.

The President's power to pardon only extends to offenses against the United States. When offenses have been committed against a State, he has no power to pardon.

CLAUSE 2.

POWERS HELD JOINTLY WITH THE SENATE.

He shall have power, by and with the advice and consent of the Senate, to make treaties, provided two-thirds of the Senators present concur; and he shall nominate, and by and with the advice and consent of the Senate, shall appoint Ambassadors, other public Ministers and Consuls, Judges of the Supreme Court, and all other officers of the United States, whose appointments are not herein otherwise provided for, and which shall be established by law; but the Congress may by law vest the appointment for such inferior officers as they may think proper, in the President alone, in the courts of law or in the heads of departments.

A.   *The Treaty-making Power.*

I.   TREATY MAKING. — In monarchies the sovereign or his council have the sole power of making treaties and managing all the foreign relations of the govern-

---

[1] The case would be that supposed by the old negro in Washington, when President Johnson was impeac.ed by the House of Representatives. The negro said, "No use to impeach de President. He'll *veto* it sure."

ment. It is necessary often to conduct negotiations with other governments with secrecy and despatch, which could not be expected if the national legislature was to make treaties and manage foreign relations. But as this is a republic, the representatives of the people ought to have some voice in matters so important to the national welfare. Both objects are gained in our plan of making treaties. The negotiations preliminary to a treaty are conducted by the executive, as well as the ordinary correspondence with other governments. But no treaty is valid until the Senate, by a two-thirds majority, has assented to it. The Senate has several times exercised its right of rejecting a treaty proposed by the President.

II. A DISPUTED QUESTION.

It is still an open question whether the President and Senate can make a treaty involving the payment of money without the consent of the House of Representatives. The President and Senate cannot compel the House to vote an appropriation with which to pay any sum promised in the treaty, but they can bind the honor of the nation to fulfill a contract lawfully made with a foreign power. In such cases the House has never refused to vote the appropriation, but has done it under protest. The House of Representatives claims that it ought not to be expected to vote money for an object about which it has not been consulted. The question is still undecided.

III. KINDS OF TREATIES. — Treaties are of four kinds:

1. Treaties of peace, which close a war and formally declare its results.

2. Treaties of alliance, in which two or more nations agree to help each other for some common object. A treaty of alliance may be merely defensive, in which each agrees to help the other when attacked; or it may be offensive and defensive, in which the allies agree to carry on war against a common enemy.

3. Commercial treaties, in which two or more nations agree as to certain regulations of commerce between them.

4. Treaties to define and establish rules of international law. International law is to-day that body of customs and treaties which govern civilized nations in their relations with one another. These are constantly being changed and improved. On many disputed questions of international law, treaties have been made between a part of the civilized nations of the world, which are therefore law as between them, but not for the other nations.

B. *The Appointing Power.*

I. OFFICERS OF THE UNITED STATES ARE APPOINTED, NOT ELECTED. — The rule in the United States service is, that officers shall be appointed, not elected. Most State and county officers are now elected by the people. But at the time when the Constitution was adopted these officers were generally appointed. That is still the case in England. This Constitution follows the practice then prevalent. It is not likely that it will ever be changed, so as to elect United States officers by the people.

It should be remembered that Senators and Representatives are not *officers* of the United States, but *representatives* — the Senators of the States, and the Representatives of the people. The only United States officers who are elected are President and Vice President. All other officers of the United States are appointed in one way or another.

II. APPOINTMENTS IN CONCURRENCE WITH THE SENATE. — All the principal appointed officers of the United States are appointed by the President with the advice and consent of the Senate. For these officers the appointment of the President is either a mere nomination, or it is a temporary appointment. If the Senate is in session, an appointment by the President is only a nomination to the Senate. If the Senate refuses to confirm the nomination, the officer cannot be commissioned, and the President must appoint or nominate some one else, until he selects some one whom the Senate is willing to confirm. But in the recess of the Senate, the President can make a temporary appointment, which will hold good till the Senate meets (see next clause).

III. THE ACTION OF THE SENATE. — These appointments are considered by the Senate in secret session. They are usually referred to a committee, who inquire into them and report on some following day. Appointments by the President are often rejected by the Senate. There are only two cases in which the Senate is in the habit of confirming appointments at once without referring to a committee.

1. The President's Cabinet are almost invariably confirmed without hesitation, as a mark of courtesy to the President. The Cabinet are his advisers, and he ought not to be hampered in carrying out the duties of his office, by being deprived of the men he wishes to have for his advisers, or by having men he does not wish forced upon him.

2. When a Senator, or a person who has been a Senator, is named by the President for an office, the Senate is in the habit of confirming the nomination at once, as a mark of courtesy to a colleague.

IV. EXECUTIVE SESSIONS OF THE SENATE. — When the Senate considers a treaty or an appointment, it goes into an "executive session." This is so called because the business then transacted is not properly legislative business but executive business. These sessions are always secret. No one is allowed to be present but the members and officers of the Senate, and these are all pledged to secrecy in regard to the debates. The action taken is of course necessarily made public at once, except sometimes in case of treaties. But the debates and votes are kept secret. This is to give greater freedom to Senators in speaking and voting than they would have if their action was made public. Appointments are confirmed by a simple majority, but treaties require a two-thirds majority.

V. Appointments without the concurrence of the senate.— The Constitution provides that Congress may by law vest the appointment of inferior officers in the President alone, in the courts, or in the heads of departments.

This only applies to those inferior officers whose appointment is expressly given by law to one of those three powers. In all other cases, no matter how insignificant the office, the officer must be appointed by the President and Senate concurrently. By far the largest class of these officers are those postmasters whose salaries are less than one thousand dollars. These are over 50,000 in number, and are appointed by the Postmaster General.

VI. Removals.— The power to appoint, when unlimited, implies the power to remove. The question was settled in Washington's administration, that the President can remove all officers whom he can appoint, except judges, who hold for life.

This power was limited in 1866 and 1867 by two laws. The first provided that no officer in the military or naval service of the United States can be dismissed the service in time of peace, except on the sentence of a court martial.

The other law is the tenure-of-office act. Originally, this act so limited the President's power of removal that it was exactly equal to his power to appoint. That is, the President could not remove an officer except with the consent of the Senate; he could only suspend an officer until the Senate took action upon the case.

But this has since been amended, so that the President can now suspend an officer until the close of the next session of the Senate, and make a temporary appointment in his place (clause 3). If the Senate before the close of its session does not confirm the person or persons whom the President nominates for the vacancy, the old officer comes back again. But it should be noted that the President, if he is obstinate, can suspend him again and make another temporary appointment, and so on, till the Senate yields (see page 190).

VII. The appointment and removal of inferior officers.— The Constitution allows Congress by law to vest the appointment of inferior officers in the President alone, in the courts of law, or in the heads of departments. The object of this is to avoid taking up the time of the Senate or of the President with the appointment of a multitude of petty officers; and also to allow certain officers to be appointed by those most interested in them.

Congress has exercised this right. The chief classes of inferior officers who are appointed thus, are as follows:

1. All postmasters whose salaries are less than a thousand dollars a year are appointed by the Postmaster General.

2. Most of the clerks, messengers, etc., in the Departments at Washington, are appointed by the Secretary in whose Department they are. The chiefs of the Bureaus and a few of the most important officers in each

Department, are appointed by the President with the
consent of the Senate.

3. The clerks in the various Custom Houses are appointed by the Chief Collector in each Custom House.

4. The clerks of the United States Courts are appointed
by the Courts. In the cases of those inferior officers
for whose appointment the concurrence of the Senate
is not needed, it is also not needed for their removal.
The same power which appoints can also remove.

VIII. THE TENURE OF OFFICE. — This is now in
nearly all cases, except Judges and Clerks of Courts,
for four years unless sooner removed. Officers are frequently removed for political reasons, as well as for
unfitness. Officers are also frequently reappointed at
the end of their first term.

CLAUSE 3.

THE POWER TO APPOINT TEMPORARILY.

The President shall have power to fill up all vacancies that may happen
during the recess of the Senate, by granting commissions which shall
expire at the end of their next session.

I. TEMPORARY APPOINTMENTS. — The Constitution
provides that appointments to office (except some inferior ones) shall be by the joint action of the President
and Senate. But the Senate is not always in session,
and vacancies may occur when the Senate is not in
session. The Constitution provides that in such cases
the President alone may make an appointment to fill
the vacancy. The officer so appointed holds only till
the close of the next session of the Senate.

When a vacancy occurs during the recess of the
Senate, the President may (1) leave the office vacant till
the Senate meets, or (2) make a temporary appointment.

In many cases he is obliged to do the latter, because the office must have some one in it, so that public business may go on. In other cases, it is better to wait till the Senate meets, and thus be sure that the President's choice meets with the approval of the Senate. This is the case with Judges of the Supreme Court, and with officers of the army and navy in time of peace.

II. VACANCIES, HOW CAUSED. — Vacancies may be caused by death, by resignation, or by removal. The President can make a vacancy in an office by removing the officer holding it, and then fill the vacancy with some one he prefers. This, of course, can only be done in those offices over which he has the power of removal.

III. AN EVASION. — If a vacancy occurs or is made during the recess of the Senate, the President can appoint some one to fill it, and if the Senate refuses to confirm him, wait till the Senate adjourns, and then reappoint him, and so on. He can do this because the term for which he commissions the officer lasts till the end of the next session of the Senate. When they adjourn, that creates a vacancy in the office, which he has power to fill. This appointment lasts till the close of the next session, and so on. Thus, if a President is disposed to be obstinate, he can in almost any case defeat the will of the Senate. But as the President needs the co-operation of the Senate in many things, he will not usually try to provoke a contest over appointments.

IV. APPOINTMENT TO LIFE OFFICES. — If a vacancy occurs in a life office, such as a judge or officer of the army or navy, any appointment made by the President in the recess of the Senate could only be till the close of the next session of the Senate, and not for life. To make it for life, the Senate must confirm the appointment.

V. Civil service reform.

Originally the appointments to all the offices under the United States were expected to be for such a time as the officer was faithful and efficient, and it was not supposed that officers would be removed except for unfaithfulness and inefficiency. An exception was always made in the case of the Cabinet officers and Foreign Ministers. These officers were expected to carry out the President's political policy, and were therefore frequently changed. But all the inferior officers were expected to perform the duties of their office according to the orders given by their superior officers, without regard to their politics. During the first forty years of the republic, very few removals were made, and those only for good cause.

But President Jackson, in 1829, introduced a new practice, which has ever since been followed. He and his Cabinet officers removed from office all government officers who had been active in opposing his election, and filled their places with active partisans of his own. The practice has since been for each President and his Cabinet to make a large number of changes in the offices, and when a new party comes into power, to make pretty nearly a clean sweep. The new appointments are made as rewards of political services to the party in power. The case has never occurred that all the officers were removed who could be. In the various bureaus, some clerks have such knowledge of the methods of business that their services could not be spared. But the general fact is that a new President makes many changes, and a change of the party in power makes nearly a complete change of the civil service.

The effect of these changes has not been so disastrous upon public business as it would seem to be. The new officers are usually selected not merely with reference to political services, but with reference to special abilities for their work. And such is the general business adaptability of Americans that a politician appointed to a post office, or a revenue office, or an office in one of the departments, learns its duties in a month or two, and performs them as well as if he had been doing them for years. Nor is there very much corruption in office, and probably no more than there would be under any system of appointing or electing government officers.

The chief evil of our civil service is that it is a huge machine to control the politics of the country. While politics have not very largely corrupted the civil service, the civil service has greatly corrupted our politics. In order to purify our politics, it is necessary to take the civil service out of politics, just as the military and naval service is now out of politics.

SECTION 3.

OTHER SOLE POWERS OF THE PRESIDENT.

He shall from time to time give to the Congress information of the state of the Union, and recommend to their consideration such measures as he shall judge necessary and expedient; he may on extraordinary occasions, convene both Houses or either of them, and in case of disagreement between them, with respect to the time of adjournment, he may adjourn them to such time as he shall think proper; he shall receive ambassadors and other public ministers; he shall take care that the laws be faithfully executed, and shall commission all of the officers of the United States.

I. THE PRESIDENT'S MESSAGE.— The President sends to Congress at the beginning of each regular session a message which contains:

1. A general account of the doings of the executive during the year.

2. A summary of the reports of departments, which reports are published separately.

3. Suggestions and recommendations as to legislation needed.

The President also sends special messages whenever there is occasion for them, to give information or to make recommendations.

Washington and Adams followed the custom of the sovereigns of England, by going in person to deliver their messages, and by receiving a reply from each House. But Jefferson sent a written message, and did not expect a reply. This usage has been followed since.

Congress does not always follow the recommendations of the President.

II. THE POWER TO CONVENE CONGRESS.— Congress meets regularly on the first Monday in December, and remains in session in the odd years until the fourth of March, and generally much longer in the even years.

This is enough for all ordinary legislation. But occasionally there will come an extraordinary occasion when legislation is needed on some subject which cannot be put off till the regular session. Presidents have used their power to convene Congress in special session only ten times in all.[1] These occasions were all extraordinary.

The President has frequently convened the Senate at the close of a regular session of Congress to consider appointments.

The President can only convene Congress at the capitol, if the capitol can be used. If the capitol should be captured by foreign enemies, or by rebels, or a great pestilence or fire should make it uninhabitable, it would probably be in the power of the President to convene Congress at some other place, either at a regular or special session. But the case has never arisen since the Constitution was adopted.

When Congress is convened in special session, it is

---

[1] The following table will show the special sessions of Congress, and the reasons for them:

WHEN.	BY WHOM.	WHY.
May 15, 1797.	Adams	Difficulties with France.
Oct. 17, 1803.	Jefferson	Purchase of Louisiana.
May 22, 1809.	Madison	Difficulties with England.
May 24, 1813.	Madison	Difficulties with England.
Sept. 4, 1837.	Van Buren	Financial distress of the country.
May 31, 1841.	Harrison	Financial distress of the country.
Aug. 21, 1856.	Pierce	Kansas troubles.
July 4, 1861.	Lincoln	Civil war.
Oct. 15, 1877.	Hayes	No appropriations for the army.
Mar. 15, 1879.	Hayes	No appropriation bills passed.

not confined to any special time. It can sit as long or as short a time as it pleases. Nor is it confined to any class of subjects. The President calls it together for special reasons, which he names in his proclamation or in his special message; but Congress is at liberty to consider any other subject, and generally takes that liberty. A special session only differs from a regular session in beginning at a different time.

After a Congress has once met and organized, it can adjourn to any future time, and thus make special sessions, without any call of the President. But before a Congress has met, or if it has adjourned without determining on a special session, it can only meet before the time of the next regular session by a call of the President.

III. THE POWER TO ADJOURN CONGRESS. — When the Senate and House of Representatives cannot agree as to the time of adjournment, the President may adjourn them to such time as he thinks proper. This cannot be construed to mean that he can adjourn them any longer than till the time for the next regular session, as that is fixed by law.

The case has never arisen in which both Houses have disagreed as to the time of adjournment, and the President has never been called on to exercise this power. But the case might well arise when the value of this provision would be seen.

In England the sovereign can prorogue, that is adjourn, Parliament at any time, and can even dissolve Parliament and order a new election. A Parliament in England never adjourns itself, but is always prorogued by the sovereign when it has finished its work. And a Parliament rarely sits the full seven years for which it is elected without a dissolution.

IV. RECEPTION OF AMBASSADORS. — To receive an ambassador or other public minister is to formally recognize him as an ambassador. A foreign minister must present his credentials to the President at a formal audience, and be received, before he can perform any public act. The same thing is done by our ambassadors abroad.

The power to receive implies the power to refuse to receive, and the power to dismiss. The executive of any country may refuse to receive or may dismiss the ambassador of another country on one of the following grounds:

1. If the nation he represents has not yet been recognized as a nation by the government to which he is accredited.

2. Often when the country he represents and the country to which he is accredited have a very serious quarrel, and always when they are at war.

3. When the ambassador is personally objectionable to the government to which he is accredited. In that case some other person will be sent in his place.

The act of receiving ambassadors is to nations what it is to individuals to be on calling terms, or on speaking terms, except that it is done by agents instead of in person.

This power of the President is one of great responsibility at times. When in consequence of civil war there are two rival governments in a foreign nation, the question which government we shall recognize is decided by the President, and this recognition might even sometimes involve us in war with the side which we did not recognize. Or if the President should dismiss the ambassador of some other country on account of a difference with that government, it might easily lead us into a war. We are favored by Providence by having the Atlantic between us and any formidable foe, so that the mistakes of our President are not so dangerous to us as they would be in another situation. We have also been fortunate in having Presidents who, with the advice of their Cabinets, have managed our foreign relations discreetly, whatever may be said of their home policy.

V. EXECUTION OF THE LAWS. — This is the most important duty of the President, and of the executive officers under his direction. The President does not make or repeal the laws (except so far as his veto power extends). If he thinks a law a bad one, it is nevertheless his duty to enforce it until it is repealed. He can recommend its repeal by Congress, but he must enforce it until it is repealed.

If the President or any officer should enforce that as law which is not law, or should go beyond his powers or duties as given in the Constitution and Statutes, any one aggrieved by such action has a remedy in the courts, by some of the various writs used by the courts, and by a suit for damages, if any damages have been sustained. The President and all his subordinate officers are thus subject to the laws. They do not make the laws; Congress does that. They do not interpret the laws; the courts do that. But it is their duty to enforce the laws, and to enforce them in lawful ways.

If any one violates the law, he can be arrested and tried, and punished. If any one refuse to obey the law, the executive officers can compel him to obey it, either by citing him before the courts for trial and punishment, or, if necessary, by armed force.

The President cannot himself do all the work of enforcing the laws, but he can take care that the laws are faithfully executed. He frequently instructs the District Attorneys and Marshals as to suits or criminal cases in the courts, by which violations of law are punished. All executive officers of the United States act under his direction, and must obey his orders, or risk being removed from office. Thus he has ample power to see th..t the laws are enforced.

VI. COMMISSIONING OFFICERS. — When an officer is appointed, he receives a commission, signed by the President and certified by the great seal, which is affixed by the Secretary of State. An officer's term of office begins when the President signs his commission, whether the officer receives it or not. The following things are necessary to holding any office to which the President can appoint with the advice and consent of the Senate:

1. The President must nominate.

2. The Senate must confirm (except during their recess).

3. The President must commission.

4. The person appointed must accept.

Other officers only require to be appointed by the proper authority and to accept the appointment.

Under this clause the President might be required by law to commission officers, appointed by the courts or by heads of departments, but this has not been required as yet by law.

SECTION 4.

IMPEACHMENTS.

ANALYSIS OF THE SUBJECT OF IMPEACHMENT.

The President, Vice President, and all civil officers of the United States, shall be removed from office on impeachment for, and conviction of treason, bribery, or other high crimes and misdemeanors.

I. WHO CAN BE IMPEACHED. — Only civil officers of the United States can be impeached. Military and naval officers are not civil officers, and cannot be impeached; but they can be tried by court martial.

Senators and Representatives are not officers, but representatives of the States or the people; they can be expelled by the House to which they belong; but they cannot be removed by impeachment.

Judicial and executive officers (except military or naval) are civil officers within the meaning of this sec-

tion, and can be removed from office by impeachment
and conviction. Any officer who can be removed by
the President or by other authority would usually be
removed in this way, if he deserved it, rather than to
wait for the slow process of an impeachment trial.

II. FOR WHAT CAN OFFICERS BE IMPEACHED? — Not
for their private conduct, but only for their official acts.
For instance, an officer could not be impeached for
drunkenness, unless it rendered him unfit to perform
the duties of his office. The Constitution specifies
three causes for impeachment:

1. Treason. As this is defined elsewhere in the Constitution, it consists in "levying war against the United
States, or in adhering to their enemies, giving them aid
and comfort."

2. Bribery, that is, receiving money or its equivalent for using their office to the advantage of some one.
For instance, if a judge should take a present for deciding for one party to a suit rather than the other, that
would be bribery. Or if a revenue officer should take
money from an importer to let his goods pass the custom house with less than the legal duty, that would be
bribery.

3. Other high crimes and misdemeanors. What these
are is not defined, nor was it meant to be. Cases will
sometimes arise which cannot be included under any
law previously enacted, and the Senate must exercise its
own discretion as to what constitutes these high crimes
and misdemeanors. It will be guided, however, largely
by the precedents already made in impeachment trials
in this country and England.

III. DISPUTED QUESTIONS — 1. *Can an officer avoid
impeachment by resignation?*

No. In 1876, the House of Representatives impeached W. W.

Belknap, Secretary of War, for corruption, and he was tried by the Senate and acquitted. The proof of his crime seemed to be plain. But he had offered his resignation, and it had been accepted by the President before the House of Representatives had voted to impeach him. In his case the resignation was expressly for the purpose of avoiding impeachment. The Senate by a majority, but not a two-thirds vote, decided that it had jurisdiction of his case, notwithstanding his resignation. But upon the final vote, more than one-third of the Senators present voted "not guilty" upon each charge, and he was acquitted. A part of the Senators voting "not guilty," did so expressly upon the ground of want of jurisdiction, because he was no longer an officer of the United States. This decision of the Senate established the precedent that a civil officer of the United States cannot escape impeachment by resignation.

2. *Can an officer be impeached when he is no longer in office?*

Probably he can. The case of Belknap would not positively decide this question, but would lead to a presumption that an officer can, at any time in the future, be impeached for acts done while in office. The case of an officer whose term of office had expired, perhaps many years before the impeachment, would be a different one from that of an officer who had resigned in order to escape impeachment. As such a case has never been decided by the Senate, this question cannot be answered positively.

IV. A TABLE OF IMPEACHMENT TRIALS.

The following is a table of impeachment trials before the United States Senate:

WHEN.	WHOM.	WHY.	RESULT.
1798....	Senator Blount...	Intrigues with Indian tribes	Case dismissed for want of jurisdiction.
1803....	Judge Pickering..	Intemperance and Insanity	Removed.
1804....	Judge Chase	Partiality and Injustice	Acquitted.
1830....	Judge Peck	Abuse of Judicial Power.............	Acquitted.
1862 ...	Judge Humphries	Treason	Removed and disqualified.
1868 ..	Pres't Johnson...	Violation of Tenure of Office Act	Acquitted by one vote.
1876....	Secretary Belknap	Accepting Bribes	Acquitted.

This table of course does not include impeachment trials in the several States, of which there have been several.

ARTICLE III.

THE JUDICIARY DEPARTMENT.

" Law is the deep, august foundation, whereon peace and justice rest.
On the rock primeval, hidden in the past its bases be,
Block by block the endeavoring ages built it up to what we see."
—JAMES RUSSELL LOWELL.

I. THE JUDICIAL DEPARTMENT DEFINES AND APPLIES THE LAW. — The third department of the government is the judicial department. As the legislative department *makes* the laws, and the executive department *enforces* them, so the judicial department *applies* and *interprets* the laws. It is the business of the judicial department, in any cases brought before it, to decide whether the law applies to those cases, and how far it applies to them.

Thus if a crime is committed, the criminal ought to be punished. But in doing this, each department of the government has its share. The legislative department has already made a law forbidding that crime, and affixing certain penalties for committing it; an executive officer arrests the criminal on a warrant issued by a judicial officer; after certain preliminaries, the accused is tried before a judge and jury, who are judicial officers. The question is, whether the accused is guilty of the crime charged, and whether that is a violation of law; that is, whether the law with its penalties applies to this particular case. If it is proved that it does, then the criminal is handed over to some executive officer to be punished. Now although it is the business of the executive department of the government to enforce the law, no executive officer has a right to punish a criminal until he has been found guilty of some violation of law; that is, until the judiciary department has decided that the law applies to this particular case.

So with civil suits. It is the business of the judicial department to decide upon the proof shown in any case, how far the laws apply to the dispute between the parties to the suit. When that is decided, it is the duty of some executive officer to carry out the law, as it has been applied to this case by the courts.

Now in thus applying the law to particular cases, it often becomes necessary to know just what the law is. Either the law is not worded clearly or two laws conflict. It then becomes the duty of the courts to decide what the law really means, or which of the two laws is really law and which is not. In such cases the judicial department *defines* and *interprets* the law.

II. THE CONSTITUTIONALITY OF LAWS. — Here comes in the power of the courts to decide the constitutionality of laws. The highest law is the United States Constitution, and all United States and State laws must conform to it. If they conflict with it, they are null and void, and are no laws. If in any case which comes before the courts, a law or a part of a law is found to be in conflict with this Constitution, the courts decide that the law is unconstitutional, and therefore void. Such a decision by any court is entitled to respect unless the decision is reversed by a higher court. But when such a decision is made by the Supreme Court of the United States, the highest court of the land, it is regarded as settling the question that the law is unconstitutional.

It is a mistake to suppose that the Supreme Court is constantly deciding constitutional questions, and that all constitutional questions come at once before that court. Nothing comes before any court except in connection with an actual suit or trial. An unconstitutional law may stand for years before a case under it is carried up to the Supreme Court. Some things from their nature cannot be taken into court. And the courts always hesitate to decide a law to be unconstitutional, and only do so when the case is plain.

SECTION 1.

ORGANIZATION.

THE JUDICIARY.	I. ORGANIZATION OF JUDICIARY.	1. Courts.........	(a.) Supreme court		III, 1
			(b.) Inferior courts	Circuit court.. / District court. / Court of claims / Supreme court of the District of Columbia..	III, 1
		2. Judges	(a.) Term of office— for life or during good behavior....		III, 1
			(b.) Salary not to be diminished		III, 1

The judicial power of the United States shall be vested in one Supreme Court, and in such inferior courts as the Congress may from time to time ordain and establish. The judges both of the Supreme and inferior courts, shall hold their offices during good behavior, and shall at stated times receive for their services a compensation which shall not be diminished during their continuance in office.

I. IN WHAT COURTS THE JUDICIAL POWER IS VESTED. The judicial power of the United States is vested in one Supreme Court, and in such other courts as Congress may establish.

The number and manner of organization of the courts have been changed from time to time. There are now three classes of United States courts, with two special courts.[1]

---

[1] The Territorial courts are not, properly speaking, United States courts. A Territory is a State under guardianship, not yet come of age. The Su-

1. The Supreme Court of the United States, composed of one Chief Justice and eight Associate Justices.

2. United States Circuit Courts,[1] each composed of one Supreme Judge, one Circuit Judge, and one District Judge, or by any one of them sitting alone, or by any two of them sitting together.

3. United States District Courts,[2] each composed of one District Judge. At least one of these District Courts is located in each State, and in several States more than one.

Special Courts — 1. The Supreme Court of the District of Columbia, composed of a Chief Justice and four Associate Justices. Any one of these may hold a District Court for the District of Columbia with the same jurisdiction as other District Courts of the United States.

2. The Court of Claims, composed of a Chief Justice and four Associate Justices.

II. OFFICERS OF THE COURTS. — These courts, besides the judges, have the following officers:

1. Each court has a clerk, appointed by the court and removable by it, who keeps all the records of the court, and prepares all documents issued by the court.

2. Each District Court has a marshal, who is the executive officer of the court, with the same powers as those exercised by sheriffs. He is appointed by the President, with the consent of the Senate, and is also

preme Court of the United States has decided that Territorial courts are not United States courts, in any such sense as to give Territorial judges a life tenure of their offices. These judges are appointed for four years unless sooner removed.

[1] There are now nine circuits, corresponding to the number of justices of the Supreme Court. One of these is assigned to each circuit, and a circuit judge is also appointed for each circuit.

[2] There are now fifty-nine districts. Of these, Alabama, New York, Tennessee and Texas have three each. Arkansas, Florida, Georgia, Illinois, Michigan, Mississippi. Missouri, North Carolina, Ohio, Pennsylvania, South Carolina, Virginia and Wisconsin have two each, and the other States one each. But as the States of Alabama, Georgia, Mississippi, North Carolina and South Carolina have but one district judge for each State, and Tennessee but two, the whole number of district judges is fifty-two. The Indian Territory is attached to the western district of Arkansas.

marshal for the Circuit Court whenever it sits in his district.

3. The Supreme Court has a marshal, appointed by the court, and the Court of Claims has a bailiff.

4. Each District Court has a district attorney, who represents the United States in the prosecution of all criminal cases, and is the lawyer for the United States in all civil suits to which the United States is a party. The district attorney is appointed by the President, with the consent of the Senate, and acts as United States attorney also in the Circuit Court, when held in his district. In the Supreme Court, the Attorney General of the United States, or one of his assistants, acts as United States attorney.

5. The Supreme Court has also a reporter, appointed by the Supreme Court, who prepares and publishes the official reports of all cases brought before it. The reports now fill many volumes.

III. TERM OF OFFICE OF JUDGES.— The term of office of all United States judges is for life, or during good behavior. As the only legal way of determining that a judge has not behaved well is by impeachment, this practically means that United States judges hold office for life, unless removed upon impeachment. Only two judges have thus been removed. A judge may, however, resign; and if he has served ten years, and is seventy years old, he will be paid his full salary for the remainder of his life.

The object of making judges hold office for life, is to make them independent in their decisions. A judge ought not to be influenced in his decisions by the fear of removal from office, or by the hope of reappointment or re-election.

IV. SALARY OF JUDGES.— The amount of the salaries of judges is left to Congress. But the Constitution provides that their salaries shall not be diminished. They may, however, be increased. The object of this is to make the judges independent of Congress.

If it ever should be thought best to decrease the salaries of the judges, or of any class of them, it could be done in regard to all judges thereafter to be appointed, but the salaries of those then in office would not be changed. But Congress can raise the salary of all judges at any time, and has done so several times.

SECTION 2.

JURISDICTION OF THE COURTS.

THE JUDICIARY.

II. JURISDICTION.

1. EXTENT.

Cases........
- (a.) Arising under this Constitution, the laws of the U. S. or treaties.. III, 2, 1
- (b.) Affecting ambassadors or consuls............. III, 2, 1
- (c.) Of admiralty or maritime jurisdiction...... III, 2, 1

Controversies
- (a.) To which the U. S. is a party .... III, 2, 1
- (b.) Between two or more States .... III, 2, 1
- (c.) Of a State against citizens of another State .... III, 2, 1, and Am. XI
- (d) Between citizens of different States.. .... III, 2, 1
- (e.) Concerning land grants of different States..... III, 2, 1
- (f.) Of a State against foreigners ... III, 2, 1, and Am. XI
- (g.) Between foreigners and citizens . ... III, 2, 1

2. ORIGINAL JURISDICTION OF SUPREME COURT..
- (a.) In cases affecting ambassadors and consuls.... III, 2, 2
- (b.) When a State is a party. III, 2, 2

3. APPELLATE JURISDICTION......
- (a.) In all other cases........ III, 2, 2
- (b.) Except as modified by Congress .... III, 2, 2

CLAUSE 1.

EXTENT OF JURISDICTION.

The judicial power shall extend to all cases, in law and equity, arising under this Constitution, the laws of the United States, and treaties made or which shall be made, under their authority; to all cases affecting ambassadors, other public ministers, and consuls; to all cases of admiralty and maritime jurisdiction; to controversies to which the United States shall be a party; to controversies between two or more States; between a State and citizens of another State; between citizens of different States; between citizens of the same State claiming lands under grants of different States, and between a State or the citizens thereof, and foreign States, citizens or subjects.

I. MODIFIED BY THE ELEVENTH AMENDMENT. — This clause has been modified by the eleventh amendment, which reads as follows:

"The judicial power of the United States shall not be construed to extend to any suit in law or equity, commenced or prosecuted against one of the United States by citizens of another State, or by citizens or subjects of any foreign State."

This amendment abolishes the power of individuals to sue a State in the United States courts. It leaves everybody the power of suing a State in its own courts, if the States allow it.

II. CASES IN LAW AND EQUITY. — A *case* is an alleged state of facts, brought before a court in a legal way by some one who is aggrieved thereby. The courts can only act on cases. They cannot decide on legal questions, except as they are brought before them in actual cases, either as criminal trials or civil suits. Thus a legal question may be disputed a long time before it is settled by a judicial decision, because no case has been brought before the courts which involves that question.

There are questions in regard to the meaning of some clauses of the Constitution which have never been decided, because no case has arisen which brought them before the courts.

These words "cases in law and equity," refer to distinctions made by English law, from which our law is derived. When the Constitution was adopted, there were four classes of courts in England, each having its own officers, its own methods of procedure, and its own system of law. These courts were called law courts, equity courts, admiralty courts and ecclesiastical courts; and the law administered by each was called common law, equity, admiralty and maritime law and canon law. As there was to be no State church in this country, canon law and ecclesiastical courts were needless, and are therefore not mentioned in this Constitution. The other three divisions of English law are named in this paragraph. This clause of the Constitution gives the United States courts all cases in admiralty or maritime law, and takes them away from the State courts. It also gives the United States courts a part of the cases which may arise in law or equity, and leaves the rest of the cases in law and equity to the State courts.

Under the power given Congress to organize inferior courts, three sets of courts, for law, equity and admiralty, might have been organized in imitation of the English courts. Congress did not do so. Only one set of courts was organized, and they were made courts of law, equity and admiralty alike. But the forms of procedure and the body of law remains different for each class of cases.

No brief definition can be given of the difference between law and equity. Two distinctions in the methods of procedure, however, can be easily remembered. There are no juries in equity cases, and there are no criminal trials.

III. THE COMMON LAW. — The common law of England, in its widest sense, is that body of customs, precedents and forms which had gradually grown up in the course of English history. These were law in the colonies as well as in the mother country. The colonists, in rebelling against the rule of England, did not wish to lose all that was valuable in the institutions of England. Just as their State and National governments were formed largely on the model of the English government, so the practice of their courts has been largely the same as the practice of the English courts. In the United States courts, and in most of the State courts, the English common law as it stood at the time of the Revolutionary War, and so far as it has not been repealed by our Constitution and statute laws, is held as good law to-day. A notable exception is the case of Louisiana, which we acquired from France, where the courts follow the forms and customs of French law.

IV. CASES UNDER THE CONSTITUTION, LAWS AND TREATIES. — It is plain that the United States courts should have jurisdiction of all cases arising under the laws of the United States. By Article VI, Clause 2, these are made the supreme law of the land, and overrule all State laws or constitutions, when there is any conflict between them.

The United States courts are bound to maintain this supreme law of the land in any case brought before them.

It should be remembered that the subjects upon which the United States can make laws are limited by this Constitution. The United States has full jurisdiction only in the District of Columbia, in the territories, on the high seas, in the United States forts, arsenals and dockyards, and on United States ships. Everywhere else its jurisdiction is limited. Thus if a robbery is committed in any of the places named above, the person accused of it will be tried in the

N

United States courts and by United States law;[1] but if it is committed in the jurisdiction of a State, it will be tried before the courts and by the laws of that State. But robbery of the mail, although committed within a State, would be tried before a United States court and by United States laws, because the United States has jurisdiction over post offices and post roads.

Cases may arise under the Constitution, directly, where there is no United States statute law involved. Thus the State of New Hampshire passed a law changing the charter of Dartmouth College. As the State courts refused to declare the law unconstitutional, the case was carried into the United States Supreme Court. The Supreme Court decided that the charter of a corporation is a contract between the State and the corporation, which cannot be changed without the consent of both parties. As the State law impaired the obligation of a contract (I, 10, 1), the Supreme Court decided it to be unconstitutional, and therefore null and void. This was a case under the United States Constitution.

Cases may also arise under treaties made with foreign powers. These treaties, while they last, are laws of the United States, and binding on every citizen. The punishment for violation of treaties necessarily belongs to the United States courts. Under the Confederation, when we had no United States court, these cases came before State courts, which generally failed to punish their violation. The consequence was, our reputation as a nation suffered, and we might easily have been involved in a war, because of neglect to compel our citizens to obey our own treaties.

V. Cases affecting ambassadors, etc.— All cases affecting ambassadors, other public ministers, or consuls, are tried in the United States courts. These are officers of foreign nations, and the United States are bound to protect them, and treat them according to the rules of international law. It is therefore necessary that all cases affecting them should be tried in the United States courts, not in State courts, as the United States is responsible for their treatment.

---

[1] If in an organized territory, the trial would be under the laws of that territory. But these territorial laws are only made laws because an act of Congress has allowed the territory to make its own laws within certain limits. Territorial laws are thus virtually United States laws.

But not all cases affecting ambassadors can be tried by our courts, for by the law of nations, ambassadors and other public ministers are not subject to the criminal or civil law of the country to which they are ambassadors, but are subject to the laws of their own country. Thus, if the English ambassador to this country should commit a crime, he could not be tried here, but our government would have to write a statement of the case to the English government, whereupon he would be recalled and tried in England under English laws. The same is true of civil suits. The ambassador of a foreign power cannot be sued in this country, but if he run in debt and refuse to pay, he must be sued in the country to which he belongs. The family and officers and servants of an ambassador share in these privileges in a less degree. But consuls have no such privileges under the law of nations, except in heathen or Mohammedan countries.

VI. CASES OF ADMIRALTY AND MARITIME JURISDICTION.— These are cases arising on the high seas and navigable waters. It is a very difficult question to exactly define the limits of this kind of jurisdiction. The courts have not been able to do it; but have made many conflicting decisions in regard to the extent of maritime jurisdiction.

In general terms, we may say admiralty and maritime jurisdiction include:

1. All questions of prizes and captures at sea.

2. The trial of all crimes committed on the high seas or waters of the sea outside of any country, and of all offenses against the law of nations.

3. *All cases* involving damages done on the high seas, and *some cases* on waters of the sea where the tide ebbs and flows.

4. *Many cases* concerning contracts or claims for services or sales at sea or in foreign ports.

Most of the above classes of cases evidently belong to the United States courts, because States have no jurisdiction over them. (Sec. I, 8, 10 and 11.)

VII. CONTROVERSIES TO WHICH THE UNITED STATES IS A PARTY. — The United States may be a party to a controversy either,

1. *As prosecutor in a criminal case* arising under United States law. All such cases are prosecuted in the name and by the authority of the United States. The actual work of the prosecution is done by the Attorney General, or by the District Attorney of the district in which the case belongs. He may be assisted by other lawyers, if necessary.

2. *As plaintiff in a civil suit.* These are prosecuted when the United States has a legal claim against any one.

In violations of the revenue, there may be both a criminal prosecution and a civil suit.

3. *As defendant in a civil suit.* If any one has a claim against the United States, which the proper officer refuses to pay, he may begin a suit in the Court of Claims and in no other court. But if the case is decided against the United States, the claim cannot be paid until Congress makes an appropriation for it (I, 9, 6).

VIII. CONTROVERSIES BETWEEN TWO OR MORE STATES. — It is evident that these controversies must be tried in the United States courts, unless they can be settled by arbitration. These suits must be begun in the Supreme Court.

No District or Circuit Court has jurisdiction in any case in which a State is a party (see Clause 2). When the Constitution was adopted, there were many unsettled controversies between States, especially in regard to territory. Before the Revolution, controversies between the colonies were heard before the King in council. During the Revolution, there was no tribunal to decide controversies between the States. The disputes between them in regard to land grants led to much trouble and violence, and might easily have led to war between the States.

The Articles of Confederation provided for the trial of such controversies by commissioners. These commissioners acted really as arbitrators, but had no authority to enforce their decisions. The Supreme Court can now decide cases between States, with authority, and its decision is final, and must be obeyed.

IX. CONTROVERSIES BETWEEN A STATE AND CITIZENS OF ANOTHER STATE. — Suits brought by a State against citizens of another State must be tried in the Supreme Court. Other United States courts have no jurisdiction (Clause 2). Citizens of one State cannot sue another State, except in the courts of that State (Amendment IX).

X. CONTROVERSIES BETWEEN CITIZENS OF DIFFERENT STATES. — A United States court will be likely to be more impartial than a State court, in a suit between its own citizens and the citizens of another State. Controversies between citizens of different States are therefore tried in the United States courts.

But the law which regulates such cases is the law of the State in which the case occurs. Thus if a citizen of Wisconsin owes a citizen of New York, the citizen of New York may sue in one of the United States district courts in Wisconsin. But that court will try the suit according to the laws of Wisconsin; and in levying an execution, the Wisconsin debtor would be entitled to the exemption provided by Wisconsin law. Congress cannot legislate, except for certain things, within the limits of a State (I, 8). But the United States courts do not always follow the decisions of the State courts upon the law of each State.

Therefore, when the United States courts take jurisdiction of controversies between citizens of different

States, they do not take United States law, but State
law, when the subject in dispute is not one of those covered by the powers of Congress.

A citizen of the United States is a citizen of the State
in which he resides (Amendment XIV). But a citizen
of a territory or of the District of Columbia is not a citizen of any State, and is not included in this provision.

XI. CONTROVERSIES ABOUT LAND GRANTS OF DIF-
FERENT STATES. — Even in cases between citizens of the
same State, when the controversy is respecting land
claimed under grants from different States, the United
States courts have jurisdiction. Thus all controversies
respecting conflicting land grants go into the United
States courts. In these cases, although the States are
not, in form, parties to the suit, they are involved in it.
When a State grants land to individuals, it guarantees
the title to the land. If the title is not good, the State
is bound in good faith to make the title good or pay
damages. Every State is therefore interested in the
titles to land it has granted, and all the more so because
a single case will usually involve the questions of law
and fact on which the titles to many tracts of land
depend.

XII. CONFLICTING CLAIMS OF STATES TO LAND.
The charters of several of the colonies and the grants to proprietors, given by different sovereigns of England, were generally
drawn very loosely, and often overlapped one another. As the
country settled, this led to controversies between the colonies, some
of which had been settled by the King in council, and some of
which were left undecided at the time of the Revolutionary War.
The States had granted land under these conflicting claims to two
or more sets of settlers, who fought it out in legal and illegal ways,
as men will fight when the title to their homes is in question. The
chief disputes in regard to territory and land grants made by States
were:

1. The whole State of Vermont, which was claimed both by New Hampshire and New York.

2. A large part of western New York was claimed by Massachusetts, as well as by New York.

3. Northern Pennsylvania was claimed by Connecticut, as well as by Pennsylvania.

4. The Northwest Territory (Ohio, Indiana, Illinois, Michigan and Wisconsin) was claimed by Virginia by right of conquest, and parts of it by other States under their charters.

Besides these, there were questions of the exact boundary line between almost all neighboring States. These questions were some of them settled just before the Constitution was adopted, and others afterwards. In general we may say, that men who had bought land and settled on it were secured in their titles to it, but only after a great deal of trouble; and that the State boundaries were settled as they now stand.

XIII. CONTROVERSIES BETWEEN A STATE, OR THE CITIZENS THEREOF, AND FOREIGN STATES, CITIZENS OR SUBJECTS. — All cases to which foreign states or their citizens or subjects are parties, come before the United States courts. It is the United States government which is held responsible for our treatment of foreigners. The United States ought therefore to have jurisdiction over cases in which foreigners are parties. But foreigners cannot sue a State in the United States courts. (Amendment XI.)

XIV. JUDICIAL POWERS EXERCISED BY OTHER DEPARTMENTS OF THE GOVERNMENT.

A. *Judicial powers of the legislative department:*

1. Power of punishing members for misconduct. (I, 5, 2.)
2. Power of punishing other persons for contempt.
3. Power of impeachment and removal from office. (I, 2, 5, and I, 3, 6 and 7, and II, 4.)
4. But no bill of attainder or ex post facto law. (I, 9, 3.)

B. *Judicial powers of the executive department:*

1. The President's power to pardon. (II, 2, 1.)
2. Powers of courts martial. (I, 8, 14, and Am. V.)
3. Power under military law. (I, 9, 2.)
4. But cannot make unwarrantable searches and seizures. (Am. IV.)
5. And cannot hold persons for trial without a presentment or indictment of a grand jury. (Am. V.)
6. Nor hold a person for trial twice for the same offense. (Am. V.)
7. Nor deprive any person of life, liberty or property without due process of law. (Am. V.)

CLAUSE 2.

ORIGINAL AND APPELLATE JURISDICTION.

In all cases affecting ambassadors, other public ministers and consuls, and those in which the State shall be a party, the Supreme Court shall have original jurisdiction. In all the other cases before mentioned, the Supreme Court shall have appellate jurisdiction, both as to law and fact; with such exceptions, and under such regulations as the Congress shall make.

I. ORIGINAL JURISDICTION OF THE SUPREME COURT. — When it is said that the Supreme Court has *original jurisdiction* in certain cases, it is meant that these cases must be begun in the Supreme Court.   Other cases may reach the Supreme Court, but only when they have been tried in lower courts, and an appeal has been taken from their decisions to the Supreme Court.

The Supreme Court has original jurisdiction in two classes of cases only:

1. In all cases affecting ambassadors, other public ministers and consuls.

2. In all cases where a State is a party.

In these cases original jurisdiction is given to the Supreme Court, not because the cases are always important, but because there are important parties to the suit.

II. Appellate Jurisdiction of the Supreme Court. When it is said that the Supreme Court has *appellate jurisdiction* in other cases, it is meant that other cases must be begun in some lower court, but may be taken to the Supreme Court on an appeal from the decisions of the lower courts. This appellate jurisdiction is to have such exceptions and be under such regulations as Congress shall make by law.

CLAUSE 3.

TRIAL OF CRIMES.

The Judiciary. — III. TRIAL OF CRIMES.

1. By jury, except in impeachment .... III, 2, 3
2. Held in State and district where the crime is committed .... III, 2, 3, and Am. VI
3. If not committed in any State, where directed by law .... III, 3, 3
4. Forms of trial. (See Bill of Rights.)

The trial of all crimes, except in cases of impeachment, shall be by jury; and such trial shall be held in the State where the said crimes shall have been committed; but when not committed within any State, the trial shall be at such place or places as the Congress may by law have directed.

[See also Amendments V, VI, VII.]

I. Trial by Jury. — A jury consists of twelve men impartially chosen. All questions of fact in criminal trials are decided by the jury; and questions of law are decided by the judge, with some exceptions. No person can be convicted of any crime in a United States court unless a jury unanimously find him guilty. If the jury unanimously find him not guilty, he is released, and can never be tried again on that charge. If the jury disagree, a new trial must be had with a new jury.

It is required by amendment VII, that in all suits at common law, where the amount is more than twenty dollars, the right of trial by jury shall be preserved. This does not include equity cases, or admiralty or mar-

itime cases, which are not governed by the common law.
These cases are often so complicated that it requires
skilled judges to decide them, and a jury might do great
injustice through ignorance of the law which governs
these cases.

Cases of impeachment have already been provided
for. An impeachment trial is not a criminal trial, but
a political proceeding to remove from office an unworthy officer. This does not prevent such an officer
from being also tried in the courts for a crime, if he has
committed one. Cases of impeachment are therefore
not tried before a jury, but before the Senate sitting as
a high court of impeachment.

A large part of all the cases which come before the
district and circuit courts require the aid of a jury. A
jury is thus a part of the judicial department, for the
time being. This is one of the checks and balances of
our Constitution, that judges shall not decide the
plainer questions of fact; but that these are left to the
judgment of twelve citizens, who are not lawyers.

II. WHERE TRIALS ARE HELD.— Criminal trials must
be held in the State where the crime was committed.
Each State has at least one district court, so that there
is no difficulty to the United States. This provision is
intended as a benefit to the accused. It leaves him
nearer to his friends, makes it easier to procure his witnesses, lessens his expenses, and gives him the benefit
of the natural prejudices of the jury for a citizen of
their own State.

Where crimes are not committed in any State, they
are tried in some specified court. When committed
on the high seas, they are tried in the State where the
vessel first arrives.

III. Privileges of accused persons.

For these, see Amendments IV, V, VI and VIII. These privileges regulate the methods of procedure in courts, and therefore might be treated here. But they belong properly under the Bill of Rights, where trial by jury really also belongs.

SECTION 3.

TREASON.

1. Definition	(a.) Leving war against the U. S.	III, 3, 1
	(b.) Or adhering to their enemies, giving them aid and comfort	III, 3, 1
2. Mode of Conviction	(a.) Testimony of two witnesses to the same act	III, 3, 1
	(b.) Confession in open court	III, 3, 1
3. Punishment	(a.) Declared by Congress...	III, 3, 2
	(b.) But no corruption of blood or forfeiture, except during the life of the traitor	III, 3, 2

THE JUDICIARY. — IV. TREASON.

CLAUSE 1.

THE TRIAL OF TREASON.

Treason against the United States shall consist only in levying war against them, or in adhering to their enemies, giving them aid and comfort. No person shall be convicted of treason unless on the testimony of two witnesses to the same overt act, or on confession in open court.

I. The reasons for this section.— Treason is the highest crime against society. It is an attempt to subvert the government, and it deserves severe punishment. But the history of England is full of instances of that being called treason which was not really treason; of innocent persons being convicted of treason, and of extreme and oppressive punishments for treason. To prevent such things in this country, this section was put into the Constitution.

II. THE DEFINITION OF TREASON.—Treason against the United States is defined to consist only in levying war against them, or in adhering to their enemies, giving them aid and comfort.   These words are taken from an old English statute, passed five hundred years ago,[1] which defines treason against the King of England, and which was in force at the time of the Revolution. Other things were made treason by this statute, but these two things were the only ones which the framers of the Constitution thought should be made treason against the United States.

It is not treason to conspire against the United States, or to agree to levy war, any more than it is murder to conspire to commit murder.   But it is a less crime.   It is not until the war is actually levied that there can be treason.   But as soon as a rebellion against the government or a war by a foreign power is actually begun, then any assistance given the enemy is treason.   In time of war or rebellion we ought to be careful of our acts, that we do not aid the enemy indirectly.   When the country is at war, she calls for the help of all her citizens, and at least demands that they shall not help her enemies.

III. THE PROOF OF TREASON.— No person ought to be convicted of so odious a crime as treason except on

---

[1] This is the famous statute of 25 Edward III., which defines treason to be:

1. To compass or imagine the death of the King, Queen, or their eldest son and heir.

2. To violate the King's wife, or his eldest daughter unmarried, or the wife of his eldest son and heir.

3. To levy war against the King in his realm.

4 To adhere to the King's enemies in the realm, by giving them aid and comfort, or by sending them intelligence or provisions, or selling them arms.

5. To slay the chancellor, treasurer, or the King's justice, while in their place administering justice.

Many other things were at one time or another made treason in England. Our Constitution adopts the third and fourth of the above only.

the clearest evidence. The Constitution, therefore, requires that the charge should be proved, either —

1. By the testimony of two witnesses to the same act. This act must be an overt act, that is, an open act. These witnesses must testify to the same act; any number of witnesses each to a separate act are not allowed. This is to give an opportunity to compare the testimony together and to detect false swearing.

2. Or by a confession in open court. A confession in private may easily be misunderstood or misstated by the person to whom the confession was made. The confession, therefore, must be made in open court. It would be sufficient for the accused to simply plead guilty at the trial to make it a confession in open court.

<h2 style="text-align:center">CLAUSE 2.</h2>

<h3 style="text-align:center">THE PUNISHMENT OF TREASON.</h3>

The Congress shall have power to declare the punishment of treason, but no attainder of treason shall work corruption of blood or forfeiture except during the life of the person attainted.

I. THE REASON FOR THIS CLAUSE. — The punishment of treason under English law was very severe. The traitor was put to death in a barbarous manner;[1] his whole property was confiscated, he was attainted, and this corruption of blood descended to his posterity so that no one could inherit from him or through him.

---

[1] The details of the death of a convicted traitor in England were:

1. He was drawn to the place of execution on a hurdle or sledge. In ancient times he was dragged on the ground.
2. He was hanged by the neck, but cut down before he was dead.
3. His heart and entrails were drawn out of his body while he was still alive, and burnt in his presence.
4. His head was cut off, and his body divided into four quarters, which were in ancient times stuck over the gateways of London or other cities.

The above named punishments are commonly referred to as hanging, drawing and quartering. The King could commute this punishment to beheading. Women were only hanged.

Such extreme and barbarous punishments are forever forbidden in the United States by the Constitution. Congress has declared the punishment of treason to be death by hanging. A less punishment may be inflicted, but not less than imprisonment for five years and a fine of ten thousand dollars.

II. ATTAINDER OF TREASON. — The conviction of treason under the common law of England involved *attainder*, that is, it tainted the person so convicted. Persons could also be attainted by a *bill of attainder* without a trial, which has the same effect. A conviction of treason of itself brought an attainder of treason on the person convicted. No bill of attainder was needed in such a case.

This attainder in either case worked corruption of blood and forfeiture. Any person attainted, by that fact became corrupt in blood, and forfeited all his property, titles and honors.

The Constitution forbids bills of attainder (I, 9, 3, and I, 10, 1), so that no person can be attainted except by a regular trial, and then only for treason as defined in this section. But it does not abolish attainder of treason. It only limits its effects to the person thus attainted.

III. CORRUPTION OF BLOOD. — Under the common law, corruption of blood follows from any attainder. "By corruption of blood all inheritable qualities are destroyed, so that an attainted person can neither inherit lands nor other hereditaments from his ancestors, nor retain those he is already in possession of, nor transmit them to any heir. And this destruction of all inheritable qualities is so complete that it obstructs all descents to his posterity, whenever they are obliged to derive a title through him to any estate of a remote ancestor. So that if a father commits treason, and is attainted and suffers death, and then the grandfather dies, his grandson cannot inherit any estate from his grandfather, for he must claim through his father, who could convey to him no inheritable blood. Thus the innocent are made the victims of a guilt in which they did not, and perhaps could not, participate, and the sin is visited upon remote generations."[1] This injustice of the English common law is forbidden by this clause.

IV. FORFEITURE. — By the English common law, an attainder of treason worked not only corruption of blood but also forfeiture; that is, a person convicted of treason forfeited all his property of every description, and all his titles and honors. Persons were often convicted of treason purposely to confiscate their property. "Rapacity has been thus stimulated to exert itself in the service of the most corrupt tyranny; and tyranny has been thus furnished with new opportunities of indulging its malignity and revenge, of gratifying its envy of the rich and good, and of increasing its means to reward favorites and secure retainers for the worst deeds."[2]

The Constitution limits this by providing that no attainder of treason shall work corruption of blood or forfeiture, except during the life of the person attainted. A conviction of treason in the United States does not of itself carry any corruption of blood or forfeiture. Treason can be punished in such way as is prescribed by law, like any other offense; but the common law punishments of treason are abolished by the Constitution. If the Constitution had not abolished them, it might have been claimed that as the common law is in force in this country so far as it is not expressly repealed,

---

[1] Story on the Constitution, section 1299.
[2] Story on the Constitution, section 1300.

that these common law punishments for treason were in force in the United States.

V.   DISPUTED QUESTIONS.

1. *Can Congress prescribe, as the punishment of treason, the confiscation of all the traitor's property ?*   It is agreed that a fine can be imposed, which might be in some cases the same thing as a confiscation of all the traitor's property.   It is also agreed that Congress can by law confiscate all the property of persons duly convicted of treason, if the confiscation lasts only during their lives, and if at their deaths the property confiscated is allowed to revert to their heirs.   But if Congress should provide by law that the property of persons convicted of treason should be confiscated forever, would that be constitutional?   The case has never been decided by the courts.   Most writers on the Constitution seem to think that such a law would be constitutional.   But because of the doubt, such a law has never been passed.

2. *Can States punish treason ?*   As a fact, the Constitutions and statutes of all or nearly all the States provide for the punishment of treason against themselves.   Persons have been convicted and hung for treason against a State.   The case of John Brown, who was hung for treason against Virginia, is the most noteworthy one. But some writers on the Constitution hold, that as a State has no complete sovereignty, there can be no treason against it.   No case has ever been decided in the Supreme Court.

A State cannot punish treason against the United States.   But if, under this Constitution, there can be such a thing as treason against a State, then the State can define and punish it.

VI.   TREASON TRIALS.

During and after the Revolutionary war many persons were attainted of treason against their States for acting with the royal troops.   A large amount of property was confiscated, much of which was afterwards restored.   This was before the adoption of this Constitution.   Under the United States laws, no person has ever been convicted of treason.   The two most famous cases, were the trial of Aaron Burr and the case of Jefferson Davis.

Aaron Burr had been Vice President of the United States, and had lacked only one vote in the House of Representatives of an election as President.   Disappointed of his ambition to be President, he engaged in a scheme, the object of which was supposed to be to set up an independent nation west of the Alleghany Mountains. But his scheme, whatever it was, was frustrated, and he was arrested and tried for treason in 1807. He was acquitted for lack of legal proof; but was universally despised.

Jefferson Davis was one of the conspirators in the plot of the Southern leaders to force the Southern States into secession, and organize a separate nation in the South. When the scheme was accomplished, he was elected President of the Southern Confederacy. When the civil war was closed by the victory of the Union arms, he was captured and held for trial. But his case was never brought to trial, and he still lives. No other nation ever went through a civil war without trials for and punishments of treason.

O

ARTICLE IV.

RELATIONS OF THE STATES.

A slow-developed strength awaits
Completion in a painful school;
Phantoms of other forms of rule
New Majesties of mighty States."
— TENNYSON.

ANALYSIS OF THIS ARTICLE.

RELATIONS OF THE STATES.

I. STATE RECORDS ....
1. Each State shall give full faith to the records of every other State.   IV, 1
2. Congress shall prescribe the manner of proof ....   IV, 1

II. INHABITANTS OF OTHER STATES......
1. Privileges of citizens shall be equal.............. ....   IV, 2, 1
2. Fugitive criminals shall be given up..... ....   IV, 2, 2
3. Fugitive slaves shall be given up.   IV, 2, 3

III. NEW STATES AND TERRITORIES ......
1. *Admission of new States.*
   (a.) Admitted by Congress ..   IV, 3, 1
   (b.) States not changed without their own consent ...   IV, 3, 1
2. *Territory of the United States.... .*
   (a.) Congress may dispose of it..   IV, 3, 2
   (b.) Congress may legislate for it..   IV, 3, 2
   (c.) State claims not affected   IV, 3, 2
   (d.) U. S. claims not affected   IV, 3, 2

IV. PROTECTION OF STATES ..
1. Guarantee of republican government........................ ...   IV, 4
2. Protection against invasion ......   IV, 4
3. Protection against domestic violence ....   IV, 4

RELATIONS OF THE STATES.

V. POWERS OF STATE GOVERNMENT OVER U. S. GOVERNMENT.......
1. To e'ect U. S. Senators............ I, 3, 1
2. To prescribe details of elections to Congress (subject to the action of Congress) .... I, 4, 1
3. To prescribe the manner of appointing presidential electors.. II, 2, 1
4. To vote on proposed amendments, V.

VI. Other powers of State governments (see 000).

VII. STATES SUBORDINATE TO U. S.........
1. State judges bound by U. S. Constitution, in spite of State laws, VI, 2
2. State officers and legislators to swear to support U. S. Constitution............................ VI, 3

SECTION 1.

STATE RECORDS.

Full faith and credit shall be given in each State to the public acts, records and judicial proceedings of every other State. And the Congress may by general laws prescribe the manner in which such acts, records and proceedings shall be proved, and the effect thereof.

I. THE REASON FOR THIS SECTION.—The laws and records of one nation are not accepted in the courts of another nation with full faith and credit, but only under certain limitations and conditions. But as we are one nation, and not a collection of nations, it is provided that the official records of one State shall have full faith and credit given them in every other State. These records are not to be treated as the records of a foreign State, but as the records of another part of the same nation.

II. WHAT DOCUMENTS ARE EMBRACED IN THIS SECTION.—The following documents are embraced in this clause:

1. *Public acts;* that is, the Constitutions and statute laws of the States.

2. *Public records;* such as registration of deeds and

wills, records of marriages, and journals of the legislature.

3. *Judicial proceedings;* that is, judgments, writs and processes of courts, and published reports of decisions.

III. MANNER OF PROOF. — Congress may by law prescribe the manner of proving these documents, and the effect thereof. Congress has done this, and there is now one uniform manner of proving public documents. And such documents have the same effect in any State as they have by law or usage in their own State.

IV. THE VALUE OF THIS SECTION.— The principal value of this clause is to prevent endless controversies over the titles to property. Where these have been settled in one State, they are held good in every other State. A man cannot begin over again a law suit which has once been settled, by simply moving from one State into another.

SECTION 2.

RELATIONS OF STATES TO THE INHABITANTS OF OTHER STATES.

CLAUSE 1.

PRIVILEGES OF CITIZENS.

The citizens of each State shall be entitled to all privileges and immunities of citizens in the several States.

I. PRIVILEGES OF CITIZENS OF ONE STATE IN ANY OTHER STATE. — As this is one nation, not a collection of nations, it is plain that intercourse between the States should be as free as possible. This clause provides that no State shall give its own citizens any special privileges over the citizens of sister States. If any one is a citizen in Illinois, for instance, and goes into Wisconsin, he is entitled to all the privileges of a citizen of Wisconsin, and under the same limitations. He can engage in any business, hold any property, be married or divorced, and be protected by the laws, under the same conditions as a citizen of Wisconsin. But if the State of Illinois gives its citizens some special privilege which the State of Wisconsin does not give, he does not carry that privilege with him in going to Wisconsin. When there he has all the privileges of citizens of Wisconsin, but no more.[1]

This clause should now be studied in connection with the first clause of the fourteenth amendment. Two questions are reserved for that place: 1. Who are citizens of the United States? 2. What are the privileges and immunities of citizens?

CLAUSE 2.

FUGITIVE CRIMINALS.

A person charged in any State with treason, felony, or other crime, who shall flee from justice, and be found in another State, shall, on demand of the executive authority of the State from which he fled, be delivered up, to be removed to the State having jurisdiction of the crime.

I. EXTRADITION LAWS. — In ancient times, criminals who escaped into another country, generally escaped punishment thereby. Civilized nations now generally give up escaped criminals to one another. This is done by virtue of special treaties, called *extradition treaties.* Criminals are usually given up by one nation to another only for such crimes as are named in the treaties and

---

[1] Thus the Supreme Court decided that a law of Maryland was unconstitutional, which imposed a license on all traveling salesmen who were not citizens of Maryland. If the law had imposed the license on all traveling salesmen, it would have been constitutional. But as it discriminated against citizens of other States, it violated this clause of the United States Constitution.

under the forms prescribed by them. But as a matter
of courtesy, nations which have no extradition treaties
with one another, often give up each other's criminals.

II. STATE EXTRADITION OF CRIMINALS. — As we are
one nation, this extradition of criminals between the
States is made to depend not upon treaties, but upon the
Constitution. This provision has been made by act of
Congress to apply to the Territories and the District of
Columbia as well as to the States.

In the case of a person accused of any crime against a State law,
the usual rule in all the States is, that a warrant must first be made
out for his arrest by some proper officer, based on probable evidence.
These warrants are good only within the jurisdiction of the State.
But the person to be arrested on the warrant may escape from the
State, or he may escape from the officer after his arrest and get out
of the State. In either case there is just one course to pursue under this Constitution. The officer who has the warrant applies to
the Governor of his own State, who then issues a requisition upon the
Governor of the State to which the accused person has fled. Upon
this requisition, the Governor who receives it authorizes some officer of his own State to arrest the person called for in the requisition, and hand him over to an officer from the State which demands
him. In the case of a person convicted of a crime who escapes from
prison, the course is the same.

To illustrate, let us suppose that a murder is committed in Illinois,
and that a person who is supposed to have committed it has gone
across the line into Wisconsin. A warrant is made out in Illinois
by some judicial officer, and given to a sheriff or deputy sheriff.
Application is made to the Governor of Illinois in person, or by mail.
He issues a requisition on the Governor of Wisconsin which the
Illinois officer presents to the Governor of Wisconsin. He authorizes some Wisconsin officer to make the arrest and deliver over
the person named in the requisition to the Illinois officer, by whom
he is taken to the county where the crime was committed, and put
on his trial.

III. CONCURRENT JURISDICTION OF STATES.— The
jurisdiction of a State extends to the boundaries of the

State, except where a lake or river lies in several States. In that case they all have concurrent jurisdiction upon the lakes or river. That is, a crime committed on the lake or river may be tried in the courts of any of the States in which it partly lies. Thus, Lake Michigan lies partly in Michigan, partly in Wisconsin, partly in Illinois and partly in Indiana. A crime committed on the waters of Lake Michigan may be tried in the courts of Michigan, Wisconsin, Illinois or Indiana, whichever is most convenient. All questions are thus avoided about the exact boundary line, which would be difficult to determine exactly on the water.

IV. A DISPUTED QUESTION.

Is a Governor obliged to surrender any person called for by the Governor of another State? There is no law to compel a Governor to do so. And Governors do not always give up persons upon the requisition of the Governors of other States. They look into each case for themselves, and decide it upon its merits. Perhaps the most remarkable case occurred in 1878. Many years before, a murder had been committed in Pennsylvania. The supposed murderers, two in number, moved to Illinois, and remained there as good citizens till the year 1878, when an attempt was made by the authorities of Pennsylvania to arrest and try them, by means of a requisition upon the Governor of Illinois. But the Governor of Illinois refused to deliver them up.

As the law now stands, a Governor is not compelled to obey the requisition of the Governor of another State. Whether it would be constitutional for Congress to pass a law to that effect, is an undecided question.

CLAUSE 3.

FUGITIVE SLAVES.

No person held to service or labor in one State, under the laws thereof, escaping into another, shall, in consequence of any law or regulation therein, be discharged from such service or labor, but shall be delivered up on claim of the party to whom such service or labor may be due.

I. THIS CLAUSE OBSOLETE.—The same principle applies to fugitive slaves as to fugitive criminals. As we are one nation, runaway slaves were not to gain their freedom by crossing the boundary line of any State. The free States were to respect the institution of slavery in the slave States. If a master carried his slaves to a free State, they became free; but if a slave ran away to a free State, he still remained a slave, and should be given up on demand.

All this is changed by the Civil War, and the abolition of slavery which it brought about. Under the thirteenth amendment, there can be now no slavery in any State, and consequently no fugitive slaves.

II. PERSONS TO WHOM IT APPLIED.—The persons included in the phrase, "persons held to service or labor," were:

1. Slaves, who were owned like cattle, and who were held to service for life, and their children after them.[1]

2. Apprentices, who are boys bound out for a term of years to learn a trade. They are not slaves, but their masters have a right to their services during the time for which they are bound out. The old system of apprenticeship, however, has almost gone out of use.

3. Other persons bound out to service for a term of years. It was once common for persons to bind themselves out for a term of years, to secure a passage to this country. When they arrived, their services for that time were sold to any one who would buy them. This practice has also passed away. In some States, pauper children are still bound out till they come of age.

[1] The student should notice here, as elsewhere in the original Constitution, the words *slave* and *slavery* are carefully avoided. The framers of the Constitution, when drawing up a form of government for a free nation, were ashamed to confess in the same document the existence of slavery in the nation. They hoped it would soon be peacefully abolished. But Providence ordered otherwise.

This clause would still apply to any persons of the second or third classes who ran away from one State to another. But as their numbers are very few, and as slavery has been abolished, this clause has lost its importance.

SECTION 3.

NEW STATES AND TERRITORIES.

CLAUSE 1.

ADMISSION OF NEW STATES.

New States may be admitted by the Congress into this Union; but no new State shall be formed or erected within the jurisdiction of any other State; nor any State be formed by the junction of two or more States or parts of States, without the consent of the legislatures of the States concerned as well as of the Congress.

I. NEW STATES MAY BE ADMITTED.— The United States of America here announces a new principle of national life. Nations before this had not been in the habit of admitting their dependencies, whether conquered provinces or colonies, to equal political privileges. It was because Great Britain refused the colonies a representation in Parliament, and attempted to govern them without their consent, that they rebelled, and made themselves into the United States. They now provided against repeating the mistake. New States may be admitted into the Union. When they shall be admitted, or under what conditions, is a matter left to the discretion of Congress. But when a State is admitted, it is entitled to all the privileges of any other State, as guaranteed by this Constitution.

II. THE CONSENT OF STATES IS REQUIRED TO CHANGE THEIR BOUNDARIES.— Congress may carve out

States as it pleases from the territory outside of any State. But it cannot change the boundaries of a State without its consent.

1. No new State can be formed within the limits of another State without its consent. Maine and West Virginia were thus formed.

2. No new State can be formed by joining two or more States, without the consent of all the States affected. No such case has occurred.

3. No new State can be formed from parts of other States, without the consent of the States affected. Vermont was formed by land claimed by both New Hampshire and New York.

4. It is plainly implied, though not stated directly, that a part of one State cannot be taken from it and added to another State, without the consent of both the States. But disputes in relation to the boundary are settled by the Supreme Court (III, 2, 1–2). The consent of States is to be given by their legislatures, which represent the sovereign people of the States.

III. How STATES ARE ADMITTED. — The method of admitting States is not always the same; but the usual method is this: The legislature of a Territory sends a memorial to Congress asking to be admitted as a State. Congress passes an "enabling act" giving authority to call a convention. This convention frames a constitution which may or may not be voted by the people. Congress then passes an act admitting the new State to the Union.

But Congress has several times refused to pass either the enabling act or the act admitting the State, and the people have several times voted down a constitution proposed by a convention. In either case the Territory fails at that time to become a State.

Congress has generally required a Territory to have population enough to be fairly entitled to one representative in Congress, before admitting it as a State. No Territory which had so much population ever was long kept out of the Union. In some cases, States have been admitted directly without passing through the condition of Territories.

IV. DISPUTED QUESTIONS.

1. *Can Congress create a State against the wish of its inhabitants?* Probably not. As a fact, Congress has never admitted a State, except upon the request of its inhabitants.

Nor is it likely that Congress will ever offer the privilege to people who do not wish it enough to ask for it; and it seems to be the spirit of the Constitution that States shall not be admitted without their own consent, although the letter of the Constitution does not demand it.

2. *Can a State be admitted with less population than the ratio of representation?* Yes. Congress has lately admitted several States which had less population than would regularly be entitled to one Representative. In the case of Nevada there was only one-third enough population, but there were so few women and children, it was claimed it had its fair proportion of voters. The unwritten constitution — the fixed political habits of the people — are, however, opposed to such hasty admission of States. But there is nothing in the Constitution to prevent it. And no law of Congress, such as has recently been passed on this subject, can bind even the same Congress, much less succeeding Congresses. The whole subject is in the discretion of Congress.

3. *Can a State leave the Union?* In one sense, yes; in another sense, no. A State can secede so far as to renounce its privileges as a State, but not so far as to rid itself of the rights of the United States toward its territory and its inhabitants. When a State secedes, it loses its privileges as a State, and stands in the relation of a Territory, and can only become a State again in the same way in which any other Territory can become a State.

If it succeeds in its rebellion by force of arms, of course it becomes independent, not by any law or clause in the Constitution, but by the right of revolution, the right of successful force. But if it is defeated in its rebellion, it becomes conquered territory, which is at the disposal of the United States, and which can only be re-admitted to the Union by Congress on such conditions as Congress may impose.

This was what was done in the case of the seceded States. (See Am. XIV.) The only power which could decide this question was Congress (subject to the President's veto). This is a political question, not a judicial one, and the Supreme Court will not undertake to decide political questions. We need not, therefore, go to the Supreme Court for an answer to this question, but to the acts of Congress. Congress, over the President's veto, acted on these principles in reconstructing the seceded Southern States, and thus established this principle.

It is true that there was much opposition to this view. It was maintained by many that a State could not secede. If this meant that a State could not constitutionally secede, it is true, for the Constitution has made no proviso for a State's seceding. If it was meant that a State could not successfully rebel, and thus in fact withdraw from the Union, it was not true, for such a thing is very possible. A State can of course rebel, and if it succeeds in its rebellion, it is of course out of the Union, although it was unlawful for it to thus rebel. But, thirdly, if it is meant that a State can rebel (as was meant at that time by those who put in this claim), and if successful, enjoy the fruits of that success, but if unsuccessful, be liable to no punishment, but reassume at once all its privileges as a member of the Union, this is a premium upon rebellion of States, and a political absurdity of the first magnitude.

It is absurd to claim that the United States can conquer territory from Mexico, and govern it as long as it pleases, and only admit States formed from it to the Union at such times and under such conditions as it pleases; and at the same time to claim that the United States can conquer the rebellious State of South Carolina and gain no rights from that conquest. The absurdity is only exceeded by the preposterous claim made at the beginning of the Civil War, that we could not constitutionally coerce a sovereign State, as if the rights of self-defense and of conquest were not rights inherent in all nations and superior to all Constitutions.

V. TABLE OF THE ADMISSION OF STATES.

The following table gives the original States, and the States since admitted to the Union, with the date of admission:

ORIGINAL STATES.

1 New Hampshire.
2 Massachusetts.
3 Rhode Island.
4 Connecticut.
5 New York.
6 New Jersey.
7 Pennsylvania.
8 Delaware.
9 Maryland.

10	Virginia,	readmitted	Jan. 26, 1870.
11	North Carolina,	readmitted	June 25, 1867.
12	South Carolina,	readmitted	June 25, 1867.
13	Georgia,	readmitted	July 15, 1870.

NEW STATES.

		Admitted.	*Readmitted.*
14	Vermont.	March 4, 1791.	
15	Kentucky.	June 1, 1792.	
16	Tennessee.	June 1, 1796.	July 24, 1866.
17	Ohio.	November 29, 1802.	
18	Louisiana.	April 8, 1812.	June 25, 1867.
19	Indiana.	December 11, 1816.	
20	Mississippi.	December 10, 1817.	Feb. 23, 1870.
21	Illinois.	December 3, 1818.	
22	Alabama.	December 14, 1819.	June 25, 1867.
23	Maine.	March 15, 1820.	
24	Missouri.	August 10, 1821.	
25	Arkansas.	June 15, 1836.	Jan. 22, 1867.
26	Michigan.	January 26, 1837.	
27	Florida.	March 3, 1845.	June 25, 1867.
28	Texas.	December 27, 1845.	March 30, 1870.
29	Iowa.	December 28, 1846.	
30	Wisconsin.	May 29, 1848.	
31	California.	September 9, 1850.	
32	Minnesota.	May 11, 1858.	
33	Oregon.	February 14, 1859.	
34	Kansas.	January 29, 1861.	
35	West Virginia.	June 30, 1863.	
36	Nevada.	October 31, 1864.	
37	Nebraska.	January 15, 1867.	
38	Colorado.	July 4, 1876.	

Vermont was claimed by both New York and New Hampshire. The controversy was settled by both giving their consent to the act of Congress admitting Vermont as a State.

Kentucky was a part of Virginia, and was erected a State with her consent.

Maine had been a part of Massachusetts, and was erected into a State with her consent.

Texas had rebelled against Mexico, and had been nine years an independent nation, and was admitted to the Union on her own request.

West Virginia was formed from a part of Virginia during the Civil War. That part of the population of Virginia which remained loyal reorganized their State government, and then voted to set off West Virginia as a separate State, which was concurred in by Congress.

Kentucky, Tennessee and Missouri, by their legislatures or conventions, voted to secede. In Kentucky the State government finally returned to its allegiance. In Tennessee and Missouri there were two governments during the war. In each State one government was loyal, and was recognized by Congress. Congress was therefore precluded by its own previous action from reconstructing these States, as it did the other seceded States, where the government, as well as the most of the people, had been in rebellion.

CLAUSE 2.

THE TERRITORIES.

The Congress shall have power to dispose of and make all needful rules and regulations respecting the territory or other property belonging to the United States; and nothing in this Constitution shall be so construed as to prejudice any claims of the United States, or of any particular State.

I. THE POWER TO ACQUIRE TERRITORY.— The power to acquire territory or other property is not expressed in this Constitution. It does not need to be so expressed. This power is an attribute of sovereignty. If the United States is a nation, it can, of course, acquire and hold territory or other property.[1]

---

[1] When Jefferson signed the treaty to purchase Louisiana, he said that he "had stretched the Constitution until it cracked." He was an advocate of a strict construction of the Constitution. But the force of circumstances compelled him to purchase Louisiana in spite of his theories, and now no one pretends that it was unconstitutional, although not expressly stated in the Constitution.

Before the Constitution was adopted, the United States acquired territory from several States by the cession of their claims; and since the Constitution was adopted, the United States has trebled its territory by purchase and by conquest, by discovery and annexation.

II. THE POWER TO DISPOSE OF TERRITORY.— The power to dispose of territory or property is also an attribute of sovereignty. It would exist if it was not expressed in this clause. But this clause puts the power in the hands of Congress. Thus, Alaska was bought of Russia, under the general power of any nation to acquire and dispose of territory. It was therefore done by treaty, not by act of Congress. The President with the consent of two-thirds of the Senate bought Alaska. But if we should grow tried of our bargain and wish to sell Alaska again, an act of Congress would be needed to authorize the sale, under this clause. Otherwise it could be sold as it was bought, by the treaty-making power. So also ships of war, arms, clothing, etc., of which we had more than was needed at the close of the Civil War, were sold under authority of an act of Congress. No territory of the United States has ever been sold to another nation. But Congress ceded that part of the District of Columbia south of the Potomac river, back to Virginia, under this clause.

III. THE POWER TO GOVERN TERRITORY.— The power to govern the territory it holds, is also an attribute of a nation's sovereignty. Every nation has this right, subject to the limitation of treaties and constitutions. But this clause gives the power to govern the territory of the United States to Congress rather than to any other branch of the government.

Congress has generally acted in the relation of a State legislature as well as of the National legislature to the District of Columbia, and to the unorganized territory of the United States, and has made all their laws. But in all the organized territories Congress has authorized the people to govern themselves, subject to the government of the United States.

Territorial legislatures are elected by the people; but the governor and judges are appointed by the President with the consent of the Senate. In such case, Congress really governs indirectly. It delegates the actual work of governing to the territorial government, but it reserves the right to reverse their action, or even abolish their government, at any time. These territorial governments are very much like the colonial governments before the revolution. The territories are really colonies of the United States, and are governed as such.

IV. No prejudice to state or United States claims. — It is provided that nothing in this Constitution shall be so construed as to prejudice any claims of the United States or of any particular State. This was inserted to satisfy some States whose claims to territory had not yet been settled. The conflicting claims of the States to territory west of the Alleghanies had nearly all been settled just before the Constitution was framed. But some of these claims still remained at that time unsettled. All these claims were finally settled peaceably.

V. Claims and cessions of territory by the States.

The original settlements of the English colonies were made along the Atlantic coast. The English crown claimed this territory by virtue of the discoveries of the Cabots, and other later explorers. The crown granted these lands to the companies and proprietors that settled them, with very little regard for geographical accuracy. Massachusetts, Connecticut, New York, Virginia, the two Carolinas, and Georgia, all had grants of the land within their present boundaries, but stretching westward to the "South Sea," that is the Pacific Ocean. The other six colonies had grants not quite so vague and extensive, but indefinite enough to give rise to many disputes about boundaries. If the student will refer to a map, he will see that the claims of Massachusetts overlapped the claims of New York; that the claims of Connecticut overlapped those of New York and Pennsylvania, and that the claims of the Carolinas and of Georgia were likely to conflict. Besides these, New York and New Hampshire each had a claim on what is now Vermont, by virtue of English charters, and almost every colony had an unsettled question of boundary with its neighbor.

When the Revolution made the colonies independent States, no power was left to settle these conflicting claims. To add to the confusion, Virginia, in 1777, sent an expedition under John Rogers Clarke, which captured the country between the Ohio, the Lakes, and the Mississippi, from the English, and Virginia claimed this territory by right of conquest. It was certain that we should not have got this territory at the close of the Revolution, if Virginia had not conquered it, so that the claim of Virginia had a show of reason.

These claims were to two things — to jurisdiction and to the right of eminent domain over the soil; that is, each State claimed certain territory to govern, and also claimed all the land in it not held by private persons, with power to extinguish the Indian titles, and to give away or sell the land. On the strength of these claims, the States had sold land or given it away to revolutionary soldiers. But the conflict of State claims produced a conflict of titles to land. Thus, Connecticut had sold lands in the Wyoming Valley, in northeastern Pennsylvania, to settlers. But Pennsylvania claimed that territory, and also sold the same land. Thus there were two sets of proprietors of the land, the actual settlers from Connecticut, and the speculators who had bought of Pennsylvania. The result was that the two States almost went to war. Again, New Hampshire sold lands in Vermont to her own citizens, who settled what was called "the New Hampshire Grants." New York claimed the territory and tried to enforce the claim. The "Green Mountain Boys" organized and armed to resist the claim, and if the Revolution had not broken out, there would have been a little war between the colony of New York and the settlers of Vermont. It is not to be wondered at that each State claimed all it could. But it was necessary to the peace and safety of the Union that these conflicting claims should be settled as soon as possible.

P

During the war, the State legislatures and Congress passed various resolutions. At last New York led the way in giving up her claims to the west for the general good in 1780, Virginia followed in 1784, Massachusetts in 1785, and Connecticut in 1786. All this was done before the Constitution was adopted. As soon as all the conflicting claims to the territory between the Ohio, the lakes and the Mississippi had been ceded to the United States, Congress passed the celebrated ordinance of 1787, for the government of that territory, which has been the model for all territorial governments since. The conflicting claims of Massachusetts and Connecticut with New York and Pennsylvania, were adjusted by arbitration.

New Hampshire and New York both gave up their claim to Vermont, and it was admitted to the Union in 1791. Virginia gave its consent to Kentucky being set off from her territory into a separate State in 1792. Other cessions of western territory were made by South Carolina in 1790. and by Georgia in 1802. Thus all these conflicting claims were settled by peaceable means.

The United States in all these cases gained the entire jurisdiction of the territories ceded, but the title to the land was not all given to the United States. Most of the States kept a part of the land and granted it to their Revolutionary soldiers. So now when the United States erects a State out of its territory, it gives up such part of its jurisdiction, as a State is entitled to under this Constitution, but it keeps its lands, unless it specially gives a part of them to the State.

VI. TERRITORY SINCE ACQUIRED.

The original limits of the United States were between the Atlantic, the Mississippi, and the boundary of Canada. But on the south, the United States did not touch the Gulf of Mexico. Spain held what is now Florida and a strip extending west to the Mississippi, and all west of that river.

In 1803, we purchased of France all of what was then called Louisiana. France had just acquired it from Spain by a secret treaty. Louisiana then included "the island and city of New Orleans," and all the Valley of the Mississippi which lies west of that river, with some vague claim to the country west of the Rocky Mountains.

The coast of Oregon had been discovered by two trading ships from Boston in 1788, and the Columbia (or Oregon) river, in 1792, by one of the same ships. In 1804, an exploring expedition under

Lewis and Clark was sent across the country, which explored the valleys of the Missouri and of the Columbia. This was followed by settlement in 1811. We thus acquired Oregon by discovery, if we did not already have a title to it by the purchase of Louisiana. We claimed as far north as the latitude of 42° 40', and the English claimed all down to California. We finally compromised on the present boundary.

In 1819 we purchased Florida of Spain. Texas revolted from Mexico in 1835, and declared its independence in 1836. It was independent for nine years, and in 1845 was annexed to the United States, at its own request. In this case, Texas retained the title to her soil, and was admitted at once as a State on the same footing as the other States.

At the close of the war with Mexico, we gained by a mixture of conquest and purchase what was then called New Mexico and California, including all the territory westward to the Pacific and south of Oregon. The southern part of Arizona was added to this by purchase from Mexico in 1853, and lastly, in 1867, we purchased Alaska of Russia.

It should be remembered that in acquiring all this territory we acquired rights of sovereignty only. The title to the land has been purchased of the various Indian tribes, and a large part of the land thus acquired has been sold or given away to encourage settlement. And as fast as the territory has been settled sufficiently, it has been made first into organized Territories and then into States. It is not the policy of the United States to govern the territory it acquires, as dependent provinces; but to erect it into free States, as fast as it can wisely be done. It is the glory of the States of the Union that they are not jealous of admitting other States to their sisterhood. Already the center of population and of power has passed to the westward of the Atlantic States. The new States which have been erected out of the territory of the United States already surpass the original thirteen States in number, in size, in population and in wealth.

SECTION 4.

FEDERAL PROTECTION OF STATES.

The United States shall guaranty to every State in this Union a republican, form of government, and shall protect each of them against invasion, and on application of the legislature, or of the executive (when the legislature cannot be convened), against domestic violence.

I. GUARANTY OF A REPUBLICAN FORM OF GOVERN- MENT.— This section provides that the United States shall guaranty to every State in this Union a republican form of government. This means that no State government shall be a monarchy or an aristocracy. States have had very various details of government in their Constitution, and no attempt has ever been made to interfere with those, on the ground that they are not republican. But should a tyrant ever usurp power in a State, or a few men, not the lawful choice of the people, ever seize on the government of a State, then it would be the duty of the United States to step in and overthrow the unrepublican government and call on the people to organize a more suitable one. Congress alone could do this, and the President could only act as authorized and directed by Congress in such a case. Nor could the Supreme Court have any jurisdiction in such a case. The question would be purely a political one, and therefore wholly beyond their jurisdiction. Congress alone can decide when a State no longer has a republican form of government, and how such a government shall be guaranteed to it.

Fortunately no such case has ever arisen. But the whole history of our States shows a constant tendency toward a more republican rather than a less republican form of government.

II. PROTECTION AGAINST INVASION. — The United States is required to protect every State in the Union against invasion. Even if this clause did not expressly state this, it would be the duty of the government to protect the States against invasion. It is one of the greatest things for which governments are organized, to protect against foreign invasion; and if nothing were said about it in the Constitution, it would still be the duty of government.

Besides, the preamble of the Constitution gives, among the objects of this Constitution, "to provide for the common defense," and this would include defense against invasion.

What department of the government is entrusted with this power? The executive. The President generally, by his orders to the army and navy, defends the whole United States against invasion. But in sudden danger, the officer of the army or navy who is in command at the point of danger, does all he can, until he hears from the President.

III. PROTECTION AGAINST DOMESTIC VIOLENCE. — The Constitution also guarantees every State in the Union protection against domestic violence. But for fear that the Federal government might make riots or local insurrections a pretext to meddle too much with State affairs, it is provided that this protection shall only be given on the application of the proper State authority. This is the State legislature, or the governor, if the legislature is not in session or cannot be convened.

The President can only interfere to put down an insurrection in a State when he is properly summoned, and it is fair to infer that his interference can only last until the domestic violence is suppressed, and that he must then cease his protection.

Several cases have arisen, of domestic violence in a State, and the federal power has been found most use- . ful to protect against riot and insurrection.

IV. RIVAL STATE GOVERNMENTS.— But the most delicate case is that which has several times occurred, when there are two rival governments, each claiming to be the lawful one, and one or both appealing to the President for help against the other. In such cases, who shall decide which is the lawful government? This case differs decidedly from the case of a riot or insurrection, where there is no pretense of legality. When two rival governments exist in a State, and one calls for aid against the other, the President must know which is the lawful government before he can help either. His help will be the practical decision as to which shall be the government of the State, and will decide the question of fact, if not of law.

The answer is that in such a case, if Congress has recognized either government, the President is bound to follow that decision. But if not, then the President must decide to the best of his ability. But Congress may at any time reverse that decision and direct a change of policy.

ARTICLE V.

AMENDMENTS.

" The world advances, and in time outgrows
The laws that in our father's day were best."
                                    — LOWELL.

ANALYSIS OF THIS ARTICLE.

AMENDMENTS

I. PROPOSED ....
  1. By two-thirds of each House of Congress.
    Or
  2. By a Convention.
    (a.) Applied for by legislatures of two-thirds of the States.
    (b.) Called by Congress.

II. RATIFIED.....
  1. By legislatures of three-fourths of the States.
    Or
  2. By Conventions in three-fourths of the States.

III. LIMITATIONS..
  1. No amendment before 1808 to abolish the slave trade.
  2. No amendment before 1808 to change the direct taxes.
  3. No amendment to change equality of States in Senate.

The Congress, whenever two-thirds of both Houses shall deem it necessary, shall propose amendments to this Constitution, or, on the application of the legislatures of two-thirds of the several States, shall call a convention for proposing amendments, which, in either case, shall be valid to all intents and purposes, as part of this Constitution, when ratified by the legislatures of three-fourths of the several States, or by conventions in three-fourths thereof, as the one or the other mode of ratification may be proposed by the Congress; provided that no amendment which may be made prior to the year one thousand eight hundred and eight, shall in any manner affect the first and fourth clauses in the ninth section of the first article; and that no State, without its consent, shall be deprived of its equal suffrage in the Senate.

I. THE METHOD OF MAKING AMENDMENTS.— Amendments to the Constitution may be made in two ways:

1. Congress may by a two-thirds vote of each House propose amendments. If these amendments are ratified by the legislatures (or by conventions) of three-fourths of the States, they shall be valid; otherwise not.

2. The legislatures of two-thirds of the States may ask for a constitutional convention.

In that case Congress *must* call such a convention.

This convention *may* propose amendments to the Constitution.

If these amendments are ratified by the legislatures (or by conventions) of three-fourths of the States, they shall be valid; otherwise not.

This method of proposing amendments is somewhat tedious and complicated. But it is nearly the same process by which this Constitution was adopted in the first place. The reason which makes it difficult to amend the Constitution is well stated in the Declaration of Independence: "Prudence, indeed, will dictate that governments long established should not be changed for light and transient causes; and accordingly all experience hath shown that mankind are more disposed to suffer, while evils are sufferable, than to right themselves by abolishing the forms to which they are accustomed."

II. RESTRICTIONS ON THE POWER OF AMENDMENTS.— These are three:

1. In the interest of the slave-holding States, it was provided that Article I, section 9, clause 1, should not

be amended before 1808. This clause allows the importation of slaves until that time.

2. It was also provided that Article I, section 9, clause 4, should not be amended before 1808. This clause provides that direct taxes shall be assessed on the States in proportion to the representative population, thus favoring the slave-holding States again.

3. In the interest of the smaller States, it was provided that the equal representation of States in the Senate should never be changed. Under this restriction, the number of Senators from each State may be changed to one, or three, or any other number. But the number of Senators must be the same from each State. This is now the only provision of the Constitution which cannot be amended or repealed.

III. DISPUTED QUESTIONS.

1. *Is the approval of the President necessary to a proposed amendment?* Both the Supreme Court and Congress have decided that it is not necessary.

2. *Can a State withdraw its ratification of an amendment?* Congress has decided that it cannot, and that if a State has once ratified an amendment, it cannot reverse that action. But if a State has rejected an amendment, it may afterwards adopt it, and have its vote counted.

3. *When is an amendment, once proposed, dead?* This question has never been decided by authority; but probably a proposed amendment never dies. We may suppose that at any time in the future, new States, or those which have rejected it, may ratify it, and whenever three-fourths of all the States have ratified it, it becomes a part of the Constitution.

4. *When States are in rebellion, must a proposed amendment be ratified by three-fourths of all the States, or by three-fourths of the loyal States?* By three-fourths of the loyal States. It has been decided by Congress that rebel States lose their rights as States, until restored to the Union by act of Congress. As rebel States have lost their rights as States, they need not be counted in making up the number of States, three-fourths of which must ratify a proposed

amendment before it becomes a part of the Constitution. It is true that Congress, while reconstructing the seceded States, required them to ratify the recent amendments. But this was not done for the sake of securing their votes to make the amendment valid, but as a guarantee that the seceded States had accepted the results of the war in good faith.

5. *When does an amendment become valid?* When it is ratified by the requisite number of States. But it is the duty of the Secretary of State, as soon as he receives official notice from the requisite number of States, to publish the amendment, with his certificate that it is ratified.

IV. LIST OF AMENDMENTS PROPOSED.

The following amendments have been proposed, the most of which have been adopted:

1. The first ten amendments were proposed in 1789, and ratified in 1791. These were designed as a Bill of Rights.

2. Two other amendments were proposed in 1789, but were not adopted. One of these was to regulate the number of Representatives. The other was to prevent members of Congress voting an increase of salary to themselves.

3. The Eleventh Amendment was proposed in 1796, and ratified in 1798.

4. The Twelfth Amendment was proposed in 1803, and ratified in 1804. This was proposed in consequence of the contested election in 1801.

5. An amendment to prohibit citizens of the United States receiving titles of nobility, presents or offices from foreign powers, was proposed in 1811, but not ratified.

6. An amendment to make slavery perpetual, in hopes of averting the Civil War, was proposed in 1861, but was not ratified.

7. The Thirteenth Amendment was proposed in 1865, and ratified before the close of the same year.

8. The Fourteenth Amendment was proposed in 1868, and ratified in 1868.

9. The Fifteenth Amendment was proposed in 1869, and ratified in 1870.

NOTE.— Those amendments which were ratified will be found in full in their proper place. Those which were not ratified read as follows:

1. After the first enumeration required by the first article of the Constitution, there shall be one Representative for every thirty thousand, until the

number shall amount to one hundred, after which the proportion shall be so regulated by Congress that there shall be not less than one hundred Representatives, nor less than one Representative for every forty thousand persons, until the number of Representatives shall amount to two hundred; after which the proportion shall be so regulated by Congress that there shall not be less than two hundred Representatives, nor more than one Representative for every fifty thousand persons. (Proposed in 1789.)

2. No law varying the compensation for the services of the Senators and Representatives shall take effect until an election of Representatives shall have intervened. (Proposed in 1789.)

3. If any citizen of the United States shall accept, claim, receive or retain any title of nobility or honor, or shall, without the consent of Congress, accept and retain any present, pension, office, or emolument of any kind whatever, from any emperor, king, prince, or foreign power, such person shall cease to be a citizen of the United States, and shall be incapable of holding any office of trust or profit under them or either of them. (Proposed in 1811.)

4 No amendment shall be made to the Constitution which will authorize or give to Congress the power to abolish or interfere, within any State, with the domestic institutions thereof, including that of persons held to labor or service by the laws of said State. (Proposed in 1861.)

ARTICLE VI.

SUPREMACY OF THIS CONSTITUTION.

ANALYSIS OF THIS ARTICLE.

SUPREMACY OF THIS CONSTITUTION.

I. All debts and engagements still as valid as under the confederation .... VI, 1

II. THE SUPREME LAW OF THE LAND ....

  1. *Consists of .....*
  - (a.) This Constitution.   VI, 2
  - (b.) Laws of U. S. made in pursuance thereof .... VI, 2
  - (c.) Treaties made under the authority of the U. S ... VI, 2

  2. *Is binding on.*
  - (a.) The judges in every State, in spite of State Constitutions or laws .... VI, 2
  - (b.) All executive officers of the State, VI, 3
  - (c.) Members of the State Legislatures .... VI, 3
  - (d.) The President of the U. S......... VI, 1, 8
  - (e.) Senators and Representatives ..... VI, 3
  - (f.) All U. S. executive officers .... VI, 3, 2
  - (g.) All U. S. judges .. VI, 3, 2

  3. *Is expressed by .....*
  - (a.) An oath of office, II, 1, 8 and VI, 3
  - (b.) Liability to impeachment ...... II, 4

III. No religious test for office shall be required .... VI, 3

CLAUSE 1.

DEBTS AND ENGAGEMENTS.

All debts contracted and engagements entered into before the adoption of this Constitution, shall be as valid against the United States under this Constitution as under the confederation.

ALL DEBTS AND ENGAGEMENTS STILL VALID.—When a nation changes its form of government, it does not lose its identity and become another nation. It remains the same nation, with a different government. A change of government does not release a nation from the debts and engagements it has entered into. In such a case, the law of nations requires the new government to assume the debts and fulfill the engagements of the old.

This would therefore have been the duty of the United States whether this clause had been inserted or not.

But it was inserted to show the world that we intended to pay our debts and to live up to our treaties. Of course all debts and engagements due *to* the United States are also equally binding.

CLAUSE 2.

THE SUPREME LAW OF THE LAND.

This Constitution, and the laws of the United States which shall be made in pursuance thereof, and all treaties made, or which shall be made, under the authority of the United States, shall be the supreme law of the land; and the judges in every State shall be bound thereby, anything in the Constitution or laws of any State to the contrary notwithstanding.

I. UNITED STATES LAW THE SUPREME LAW.— As we are one nation, and not a confederacy of nations, it is necessary that the national laws should be supreme over State laws. If not, we should have thirty-eight supreme laws instead of one, and the laws of the United States would be obeyed only as far as it suited each State to obey them.

South Carolina, in 1832, refused to obey certain laws of the United States. This was called nullification, because South Carolina wished to nullify those laws, that is, to treat them as null and void. This attempt was speedily put down by President Jackson.

II. WHAT IS UNITED STATES LAW? — United States law consists of three things:

1. The Constitution of the United States. This may be amended, but while in force is always the highest law for the United States and every State.

2. All laws of the United States made in pursuance of the Constitution. This includes all laws of the United States which are not unconstitutional. Only the courts can decide whether a law is constitutional or not, and until so decided as unconstitutional, it must be obeyed as law.

3. All treaties made under the authority of the United States, that is, by the President, with the consent of two-thirds of the Senate. When a treaty is made, it repeals all laws that are in conflict with it, as long as the treaty lasts. When the treaty expires, these laws come into force again.

These taken together constitute the supreme law of the land. They cease to be the supreme law in these cases:

1. When the Constitution is amended, the part abolished by the amendment ceases to be law.

2. If a revolution should occur, which should destroy our government, the Constitution and law would practically cease to be law.

3. When a statute is repealed by Congress it ceases to be law.

4. When a statute is decided by the courts to be unconstitutional, it ceases to be law. If the decision of a lower court is thought to be wrong, the case may be carried up to the Supreme Court, whose decision is final.

5. When a law conflicts with a treaty made after the law was was made, the law ceases to be law.

6. When a treaty is broken by mutual consent, is repudiated successfully by either party, or expires by its own limitation, it ceases to be law.

III. STATE LAW AS CONTROLLED BY UNITED STATES LAW. — The law of each State consists of its Constitution, and its laws made in pursuance thereof. If this law is in conflict with United States law, it is null and void. The States cannot nullify United States law, but the United States can nullify State law. But this can only be done within the limits fixed by the Constitution of the United States.

IV. STATE JUDGES MUST DECIDE ACCORDINGLY.— The Constitution makes every judge of a State court bound to follow United States law in preference to State law. When they come in conflict the State law must yield.

CLAUSE 3.

OATH OF OFFICE.

The Senators and Representatives before mentioned, and the members of the several State legislatures, and all executive and judicial officers, both of the United States and of the several States, shall be bound by oath or affirmation to support this Constitution; but no religious test shall ever be required as a qualification to any office or public trust under the United States.

I. OATH TO SUPPORT THE CONSTITUTION.— An oath to support the Constitution of the United States is required of all departments of the State and National governments. The persons required to take this oath are:

1. All Senators and Representatives in Congress.

2. All officers of the United States, executive and judicial. This includes military and naval officers.

3. All members of every State legislature in each branch.

4. All State officers executive and judicial. This includes all county, town, village and city officers.

This oath of office must be taken in every case before entering upon the duties of the office.

The form of the oath in the United States is prescribed by Congress, except that of the President, which is prescribed by the Constitution (II, 2, 7).

The form of the oath in each State is prescribed by the States. All the States require also of their officers and legislators an oath to support the State Constitution.

II. No RELIGIOUS TEST FOR OFFICE.— In England at the time this Constitution was adopted, no one could hold office who could not take a test oath, which excluded all who were not members of the Church of England. A religious test was at that time required in many States of the Union, and still is in some.

This Constitution was in advance of the age in abolishing all religious tests for office. This is now generally acknowledged to be wise. We do not now ask of any person elected or appointed to any position, "What is your belief?" or "To what religious body do you belong?" There is no legal hindrance to a person of any religion, or of no religion, holding office under the United States.

ARTICLE VII.

RATIFICATION OF THE CONSTITUTION.

The ratification of the conventions of nine States shall be sufficient for the establishment of this Constitution between the States so ratifying the same.

I. THE MANNER OF RATIFICATION.— 1. The Constitution was to be submitted, not to the legislatures of the States, but to conventions elected for that purpose by the people of each State. When Congress called this constitutional convention which prepared this Constitution, it expressly provided that the work of the convention should be submitted to Congress and to the State legislatures for approval by them. But the convention disregarded these instructions, and submitted their work to popular conventions in each State. This, however, was done in due form, by submitting the Constitution to Congress with the request that it be submitted to conventions called by the legislatures in each State, but elected by the people; and Congress did so submit it. The legislature of Rhode Island refused to call such a convention for several years, but did so in 1790. Rhode Island had constantly opposed the Constitution from the first, and had refused to send delegates to the convention which framed this Constitution.

2. Nine States were required to ratify the Constitution. This was two-thirds of the thirteen States. The Articles of Confederation required the consent of all the States to make any change valid. But if a unanimous vote had been required to adopt this Constitution

Q

in place of the Articles of Confederation, that vote could never have been secured. Rhode Island and North Carolina would have stood out, and thus defeated the Constitution. The framers of the Constitution knew this well, and therefore made this Constitution go into effect when a two-thirds majority should be secured. But in that case the Constitution was to be established only between the States ratifying it.

II. THE HISTORY OF THE RATIFICATION.— The Constitution was signed and forwarded to Congress September 17, 1787. Congress voted unanimously September 28 to send the Constitution to the several State legislatures, to be by them submitted to " conventions of delegates chosen in each State by the people thereof." It was ratified by nine States in rapid succession, beginning with Delaware on December 7. As soon as the ninth State ratified the Constitution, Congress proceeded to make arrangements for putting the new government into operation. Elections were held for Presidential electors, and for Senators and Representatives, and March 4, 1789, was set as the day on which the new government should be organized and New York as the place. Meanwhile two more States had .ratified the Constitution, so that only North Carolina and Rhode Island still stood out.[1] The government did not actually go into operation on March 4, owing to the difficulties of traveling in those days. But Congress met and waited until April 1 for a quorum. April 6, the electoral votes for President and Vice President were counted by a Presi-

---

[1] The Constitution was ratified by the States as follows:

By Delaware,	Dec. 7, 1787.	By South Carolina,	May 23, 1788.
By Pennsylvania,	Dec. 12, 1787.	By New Hampshire,	June 21, 1788.
By New Jersey,	Dec. 18, 1787.	By Virginia,	June 26, 1788.
By Georgia,	Jan. 2, 1788.	By New York,	July 26, 1788.
By Connecticut,	Jan. 9, 1788.	By North Carolina,	Nov. 21, 1789.
By Massachusetts,	Feb. 6, 1788.	By Rhode Island,	May 29, 1790.
By Maryland,	April 28, 1788.		

dent of the Senate (John Langdon, of New Hampshire), who was elected for that purpose by the Senate·
John Adams entered on his duties as Vice President
April 21, and George Washington as Presid nt April 30.

III. DISPUTED QUESTIONS.

1. *As the Articles of Confederation required the consent of all the States to any amendment to them, by what right was this Constitution adopted and carried into effect against the wish of two of them?* By the right of revolution; a peaceable revolution, it is true, but none the less a revolution. It is to the honor of the American people that they were able to accomplish such a revolution, and establish a new form of government by peaceful discussion, without the use of force. Such a thing has rarely been done in the history of the world.

2. *What would have been done if North Carolina and Rhode Island had stood out, and refused to ratify the Constitution?* They would have been compelled to ratify it. The other States would never have allowed them to exist as independent nations within the limits of the United States. As it was, Congress passed an act laying a heavy tonnage duty on foreign vessels, but suspended it temporarily for Rhode Island and North Carolina vessels. North Carolina yielded and ratified the Constitution. A year later the Senate passed a bill prohibiting all commerce with Rhode Island, and demanding of her a sum of money as her proportion of the expenses of the Revolutionary war. These were steps which could mean nothing but war; and Rhode Island so understood them. Rather than risk a war alone against the other twelve States, Rhode Island hastened to ratify the Constitution before the bill could pass the House of Representatives. Had Rhode Island not yielded in time, there can be no doubt that armed force would have been used to compel her.

3. *By what right could the United States have compelled reluctant States to assent to the Constitution?* By the right of self-preservation; the same right by which, at a later time, the United States coerced rebel States. The United States is a nation, and as a nation it has the inherent right to do whatever is necessary for self-preservation. This right is not given by constitutions, and is superior to all constitutions. It is the inalienable right of a nation; and a nation which cannot or will not hold its several parts together and compel their obedience to the general good of the whole, does not deserve to be called a nation.

AMENDMENTS I-X.

BILL OF RIGHTS.

"We hold these truths to be self evident: that all men are created equal; that they are endowed by their Creator with certain unalienable rights; that among these are life, liberty, and the pursuit of happiness; that to secure these, governments are instituted among men, deriving their just powers from the consent of the governed; that whenever any form of government becomes destructive of these ends, it is the right of the people to alter or to abolish it, and to institute a new government, laying its foundation on such principles, and organizing its powers in such form, as to them shall seem most likely to effect their safety and happiness."— *Declaration of Independence.*

ANALYSIS OF THIS BILL OF RIGHTS.
(And of other personal rights guaranteed in the Constitution.)

BILL OF RIGHTS

I. FREEDOM OF THOUGHT ....

1. *Religious Freedom..*
   - (a.) No establishment of religion...... Am. I
   - (b.) No prohibition of religion...... Am. I
   - (c.) No religious test for office .... VI, 3

2. *Freedom of expression.*
   - (a.) Freedom of speech..... Am. I
   - (b.) Freedom of the press.. Am. I

3. *Freedom of political agitation ..*
   - (a.) Right of assembly..... Am. I
   - (b.) Right of petition...... Am. I

II. FREEDOM FROM MILITARY OPPRESSION,.

1. Freedom to organize militia...... Am. II
2. Freedom from forcible quartering of soldiers.................... Am. III

III. FREEDOM FROM EXECUTIVE OPPRESSION..

1. No unreasonable searches and seizures .... Am. IV
2. No person deprived of life, liberty or property, without due process of law .... Am. V
2. No private property taken for public use without just compensation .. .. Am. V
4. Writ of *habeas corpus* not suspended, except in war......... I, 9, 2

BILL OF RIGHTS.

IV. FREEDOM FROM JUDICIAL OPPRESSION ....

1. *Before trial* ..

- (a.) Indictment of grand jury required, except under military law .... Am. V
- (b.) If acquitted once cannot be tried again .... Am. V
- (c.) Right to a speedy trial .... Am. VI
- (d.) Excessive bail not required...Am. VIII
- (e.) To be informed of the charges against him... Am. VI

2. *On trial*.

- (a.) Trial public..... Am. VI
- (b.) By impartial jury of the district..III, 2, 3, and Am. VI
- (c.) Not to be compelled to be a witness against himself. .... Am. V
- (d.) To be confronted with witnesses against him... Am. VI
- (e.) To subpœna witnesses for him. Am. VI
- (f.) To have counsel Am. II
- (g.) No excessive fines, or cruel or unusual punishments ...... Am. III
- (h.) Definition of treason limited III, 3, 1
- (i.) Stricter evidence required to convict of treason. III, 3, 1
- (j.) Punishment of treason lessened.......... III, 3, 2

3. *In civil suits* ..

- (a.) Trial by jury where twenty dollars is in controversy.... Am. VII
- (b.) Verdict of jury settles the question of fact .... Am. VII

BILL OF RIGHTS.

V. Freedom from Legislative Oppression.

1. Bills of attainder forbidden..... I, 9, 3
2. *Ex post facto* laws forbidden.. I, 9, 3
3. No titled aristocracy created .... I, 9, 7
4. No slavery.................. ....Am. XIII
5. Right to vote not denied on account of color.................. Am. XV

VI. Freedom from Oppression of States.

1. No bill of attainder .. .. I, 10, 1
2. No *ex post facto* law........... I, 10, 1
3. No law impairing the obligation of contracts.................. I, 10, 1
4. No law creating a titled nobility, I, 10, 1
5. Citizens of each State entitled to privileges of citizens in all States . ... IV, 2, 1
6. No slavery......................Am. XIII
7. Citizenship defined.. .... Am. XIV
8. No State shall abridge privileges of citizens..................... Am. XIV
9. Nor deprive any person of life, liberty or property, illegally.. Am. XIV
10. Nor deny any person the equal protection of the laws..... Am. XIV
11. Right to vote not abridged or denied.............. Ams. XIV and XV

VII. Strict construction of personal rights .... Am. IX
VIII. Limited powers of U. S. government................. Am. X

I. THE REASONS FOR THIS BILL OF RIGHTS.—A bill of rights is a statement of those rights of citizens on which the government ought not to encroach. Monarchies are liable to be arbitrary and to have little regard for the rights of their subjects. In England the people secured themselves against the tyranny of the king and his officers by various laws. The first of these was the famous *Magna Charta*, or Great Charter, forced from King John in 1215, and the last was the Bill of Rights, passed by Parliament in 1689, just after the English Revolution. Each of the States had adopted a bill of rights during the Revolutionary war or before.

One of the chief objections to the Constitution was that it did not contain a bill of rights. True, there were several things in the Constitution which properly belonged in a bill of rights (see analysis). But it was claimed that there ought to be a complete bill of rights, covering many points not given in the Constitution.

II. THE ADOPTION OF THESE AMENDMENTS.— As the States ratified the Constitution, several of them recommended that a bill of rights be added. When the First Congress met, it took into consideration these requests, and prepared a list of amendments to form a bill of rights. The House of Representatives proposed seventeen amendments. The Senate only agreed to twelve of these, and the State legislatures only ratified ten. These ten now form the first ten amendments of the Constitution.[1]

These ten amendments were proposed by Congress Sept. 25, 1789, and ratified Dec. 15, 1791.

III. THE NEED OF A BILL OF RIGHTS.— Under a monarchy a bill of rights is needed, but under a republic, there is not so much need of it. Still a bill of rights, even under a republic, can do no harm, and may sometimes do good. Undoubtedly the principles of this bill of rights would have been embodied in our laws, whether they were in our Constitution or not.

Yet the tyranny of a majority over a minority may be as unjust as the tyranny of a despot, although less likely to occur; and this bill of rights is a safeguard against such tyranny.

IV. THE SCOPE OF THIS BILL OF RIGHTS. — These amendments were intended as limitations upon the

---

[1] For the two amendments not ratified, see page 250, note.

government of the United States, but not upon the
State governments. Each of the State Constitutions
had a bill of rights, embracing all and more than all
those named in these amendments, and the State constitutions still contain these bills of rights, designed to
protect individual citizens of those States from oppression by the State governments.

This bill of rights only extends so far as the civil and
criminal jurisdiction of the United States goes. But
that is of no consequence, because the State constitutions also guarantee nearly all these personal rights.

Cases may, however, arise, in which this fact would
be of consequence. Thus, the fifth amendment requires
the indictment of a grand jury to hold a person for
trial, except in cases of court martial. But the State
of Wisconsin has lately returned to the old English
practice of a preliminary examination before a justice
of the peace. In that State, persons are constantly
tried without the indictment of a grand jury; and yet
the United States Constitution is not violated, because
the first eleven amendments were not intended as limitations on the State governments, but on the United
States government. It would be perfectly constitutional, but very unjust, for any State to violate the personal rights named in these amendments, so far as it
affected its own citizens merely. Such a case, however,
would be very unlikely to occur.[1]

---

[1] "These amendments to the Constitution are exclusively restrictions upon
the federal power, to prevent interference with the rights of the States, and
of their citizens." *Fox v. Ohio*, 5 Howard, 434.

ARTICLE I.

FREEDOM OF RELIGION, OF SPEECH, AND OF ASSEMBLY.

Congress shall make no law respecting an establishment of religion, or prohibiting the free exercise thereof; or abridging the freedom of speech, or of the press; or the right of the people peaceably to assemble, and to petition the government for a redress of grievances.

I. FREEDOM OF RELIGION. — One of the worst oppressions of European governments has been their attempt to make the people all adopt the religion of the government. A large part of the early settlers of this country fled from Europe expressly to secure religious freedom.

And now in organizing the government of a new nation, their descendants demanded that the Constitution should guarantee religious freedom.

The freedom guaranteed is not freedom *from* religion, but freedom *of* religion. This country is a Christian country, in the sense that nearly all its inhabitants are Christians, but not in the sense that any one is compelled to accept the Christian religion, or any particular form of it. Any one can believe any religion, or no religion at all, and the law will not interfere with his faith or practice so long as he does not interfere with any one's legal rights.

This religious freedom, however, does not mean that the government of the United States is irreligious. It only means that it forces no religion upon the people. Prayer is offered at the inauguration of a President; each House of Congress has its chaplains and the daily sessions are opened with prayer. The army and navy have chaplains. The President recommends Thanksgiving. day to be observed.

II. FREEDOM OF SPEECH AND OF THE PRESS. — In most countries, to speak or write against the government is a great crime, and every one has to be careful of what he says on political subjects. In this country there is a complete freedom of speech, and of writing on political subjects, and on all other subjects so far as the rights of others are not interfered with.

The freedom of speech and of the press is limited by the rights of other people. We have no right, under the laws of the United States, to slander or libel, or to publish obscene books. But so far as our freedom does not injure others, we have a right to speak or write upon any subject.

III. FREEDOM OF ASSEMBLY AND PETITION. — The right of holding political meetings, and of sending petitions to Congress or to any officer of the government, is frequently exercised. Together with the freedom of speech and of the press, it enables the people to influence the government constantly, as well as by means of the elections. Despotic governments always forbid or discountenance efforts to express public opinion by petition or public meetings. This article guarantees us the right to assemble for any political purpose, but it must be in a peaceable manner.

ARTICLE II.

THE RIGHT TO BEAR ARMS.

A well regulated militia being necessary to the security of a free State, the right of the people to keep and bear arms shall not be infringed.

I. THE MEANING OF THIS RIGHT.—This provision is to secure the rights of citizens to bear arms, and to be trained in military exercises. Under it, Congress has power to make rules for the militia, but not to forbid the organization of the militia. Congress can only prescribe the methods under which they can organize (I, 8, 16).

Should the time ever come when a usurper tries to gain power against the will of the people, this provision may be found of value. In that case, the people could organize and defend their liberties.

This provision was abused in the south just before the. civil war, by the organization and arming of military companies to resist the authority of the United States. And it may be abused in like manner again in times when sectional strife or party feeling runs high. But that is better than to take away from the people the means of defending their liberties.

II. OUR NEGLECT TO EXERCISE THIS RIGHT.— It is remarkable that while the founders of our government were so tenacious of a militia system, their descendants should have neglected it so entirely. No people can long maintain their freedom who depend upon a standing army for their defense against foreign and domestic foes. A good militia system is the only safe defense for a free country. We are fortunate in being protected by the ocean from any foreign foe, but there is danger of civil wars, and of mob violence from the dangerous classes of our population, and for these contingencies we need an efficient militia system, such as we do not have now.

ARTICLE III.

QUARTERING SOLDIERS.

No soldier shall, in time of peace, be quartered in any house, without the consent of the owner; nor in time of war, but in a manner to be prescribed by law.

I. QUARTERING SOLDIERS IN PEACE.— To quarter soldiers, means to give them board and lodging. Strictly with soldiers, board is called *rations*, and lodging *quarters*. But actually, when soldiers are quartered in a house, they have to be fed as well as lodged. No one needs to be told how annoying this may be to families to have rude soldiers quartered upon them, nor how expensive it may become if long continued. In peace, under this article, soldiers cannot be quartered on the citizens without their consent, which is not generally given. The result is that soldiers in peace generally lodge in barracks built for them by the government, and are fed by government rations.

II. QUARTERING SOLDIERS IN WAR. — But in time of war, soldiers must be moved about from place to place so rapidly sometimes that this cannot be thus provided for. In summer, they can carry tents with them; but in winter, it may be necessary for them to be quartered upon the inhabitants. But this must be done, not arbitrarily, but according to law.

The "owner," whose consent must be obtained, is the person who lives there, whether he owns the house or not.

ARTICLE IV.

UNREASONABLE SEARCHES AND SEIZURES.

The right of the people to be secure in their persons, houses, papers and effects against unreasonable searches and seizures shall not be violated, and no warrants shall issue, but upon probable cause, supported by oath or affirmation, and particularly describing the place to be searched, and the persons or things to be seized.

UNREASONABLE SEARCHES AND SEIZURES. — This article forbids arrests of persons, seizure of property or search of buildings without a legal warrant. And this warrant must name the particular place to be searched or the particular persons to be seized. Thus, if property be stolen, neither the loser nor the officers can search a single house without a search warrant; nor can they have a general warrant to search any house they please. The loser must make oath that he believes the goods are in such a place, and on that oath the search warrant will be issued to search that place.

ARTICLE V.

RIGHTS OF ACCUSED PERSONS BEFORE TRIAL.

No person shall be held to answer for a capital or otherwise infamous crime, unless on a presentment or indictment of a grand jury, except in cases arising in the land or naval forces, or in the militia, when in actual service in time of war or public danger; nor shall any person be subject for the same offense to be twice put in jeopardy of life or limb; nor shall be compelled in any criminal case to be a witness against himself, nor be deprived of life, liberty or property without due process of law; nor shall private property be taken for public use without just compensation.

I. THE OBJECT OF THESE TWO ARTICLES. — The object of this and the next amendment is to secure accused persons every chance to prove their innocence. It is thought better that ten guilty persons should escape punishment than that one innocent person should be punished. Therefore every possible chance is given to an accused person in the ways provided in this article, and in other ways.

II. PERSONS CANNOT BE TRIED UNTIL INDICTED BY A GRAND JURY. — A *capital* crime is one that may be punished with death. An *infamous* crime is one that may be punished by death or imprisonment. A grand jury makes a *presentment* against a person on their own motion, but they make an *indictment* upon the complaint of some one else. In either case they must have evidence enough to make it probable that the person

presented or indicted is guilty of the crime with which
he is charged. There must be some probable evidence
against a person before he can be presented or indicted
by a grand jury. The grand jury therefore prevents
accusations being made that have nothing in them.
It is an annoyance and disgrace and expense to be tried
for crime, even if not found guilty. The grand jury
therefore prevents persons being held for trial merely
to persecute them.

III. EXCEPT UNDER MILITARY LAW.— Armies cannot be governed by the slow processes of the courts.
The army and navy regulations (I, 8, 14) require certain duties of soldiers and sailors, and prescribe certain
punishments for the violations of these regulations.
These punishments are administered by the officers, at
once, or by courts martial. All soldiers and sailors in
actual service are liable to be tried by this military law,
and when the militia is called out in actual service they
also are subject to this military law. Soldiers are also
responsible to the ordinary courts for any crime committed by them.

In case of actual war or insurrection, martial law
may be proclaimed in the country actually the theater
of war. In that case the writ of *habeas corpus* is suspended (I, 9, 2), and citizens as well as soldiers may be
tried and punished by court martial.

IV. CANNOT BE PUT IN JEOPARDY TWICE FOR THE
SAME OFFENSE.— No person can be tried twice for the
same offense. But if the jury disagree, he can be tried
before a new jury. That is not another trial, but the
same one continued. If a verdict of "not guilty" is
given by a jury, the case can never be tried again. But
if a person is found "guilty" by a jury, he has the right
to appeal the case to a higher court. In that case, if a

new trial is granted, he is not put in jeopardy; for if the new trial were not granted he would be punished, but in the new trial he has a chance of being acquitted.

V. CANNOT BE COMPELLED TO BE A WITNESS AGAINST HIMSELF.— No accused person can be compelled to be a witness *against* himself. And, as there is no object in making him testify *for* himself, if he does not wish to, an accused person is not *obliged* to testify upon his trial at all. But if an accused person wishes to make any statements, or to testify on his trial, he has the right to do so.

VI. CANNOT BE DEPRIVED OF LIFE, LIBERTY OR PROPERTY WITHOUT DUE PROCESS OF LAW. — This means that the government of the United States cannot lawfully deprive any person of life, liberty or property without some lawful process. By the fourteenth amendment, the same thing is forbidden to the States. "Due process of law" means a trial before some regular court, or before a court martial, in cases where a court martial has legal power. As this is only for soldiers and sailors while in service, or for persons near armies that are at war, "due process of law" means for almost all cases, a regular trial before a court of law. No person can be arbitrarily put to death or imprisoned or fined. It must be for some violation of law of which he has been duly convicted.

VII. PRIVATE PROPERTY CANNOT BE TAKEN FOR PUBLIC USE WITHOUT COMPENSATION. — Cases often happen where private property is taken for public use. Thus, if the United States needs a certain piece of land for a fort or arsenal, the land will be taken whether the owner wishes to sell it or not. In such a case, if the price can be agreed upon between the owner and the government, it is paid; but if the owner asks more than the government is willing to pay, the case is referred to a jury, who assess the value of the property, which is then paid.

In case of war, the army frequently seizes provisions or horses, or other property, to be used at once. The value of this is paid by the government, if it is taken from loyal citizens of the United States, but if taken from rebels or foreign enemies, the property seized is not paid for.

ARTICLE VI.

RIGHTS OF ACCUSED PERSONS ON TRIAL.

'In all criminal prosecutions, the accused shall enjoy the right to a speedy and public trial, by an impartial jury of the State and district wherein the crime shall have been committed, which district shall have been previously ascertained by law, and to be informed of the nature and cause of the accusation; to be confronted with the witnesses against him; to have compulsory process for obtaining witnesses in his favor, and to have the assistance of counsel for his defense.

I.   A SPEEDY AND PUBLIC TRIAL. — When any one is arrested on a criminal charge, he is held for trial, either in jail or on bail (see page 276). It would be unjust to hold an accused person in jail for a long time. An accused person is therefore guaranteed a *speedy* trial. That will usually be at the next term of court. But an accused person often asks to have his trial put off for some reason. This request is generally granted. But if an accused person wishes a speedy trial, he can have it, under this article.

All criminal trials are *public*, to secure fairness in the trial. Records are kept by the clerk of the court; spectators are admitted, and newspapers often publish an account of the proceedings.

II. TRIAL BY A JURY OF THE STATE AND DISTRICT.—
It has already been provided (III, 2, 3) that all crimes
shall be tried by jury, and in the State in which the
crimes were committed. This amendment provides further, that the trial shall be in the district in which the
crime was committed. As all the larger States are divided
into two or more judicial districts, this restricts the court
before which a crime can be tried to the district court
for the particular district in which the crime was committed. This district cannot be created for the purpose
of trying some one. It must have been previously ascertained by law.

The impartiality of the jury is secured (1) by care in
selecting jurors, who, in the United States courts, are
always men of character and position; (2) by giving both
sides the privilege of challenging jurors, either for cause
or peremptorily. If any cause is shown why a certain
person would be prejudiced as a juror, he is challenged
for cause, and his name withdrawn from the list. Each
side can also challenge a certain number peremptorily,
that is, without giving any reason.

A jury always consists of twelve persons, and their
verdict must be unanimous. A grand jury (see page
269) consists of from thirteen to twenty-four persons,
and a majority can indict.

III. THE RIGHT TO KNOW OF WHAT HE IS ACCUSED.—
The *warrant* on which a person is arrested, and the
indictment on which he is held for trial, both state the
offense with which he is charged and the time and place
of the offense. An accused person has the right to see
both these writs, or certified copies of them. Knowing
exactly of what he is accused, he has an opportunity to
prepare his defense.

IV. THE RIGHT TO CROSS-EXAMINE THE WITNESSES.—

R

This article gives an accused person the right to be confronted with the witnesses against him. The object of this is to give him the right to cross-examine the witnesses. After they have told their story, he, or his lawyer for him, questions them closely, to make them contradict themselves or to bring out something in favor of the accused. By such an examination by both sides, the whole truth is much more likely to be brought out.

V. THE RIGHT TO SUBPŒNA WITNESSES.—The "compulsory process for obtaining witnesses" is called a *subpœna*. Any person who knows anything of his own knowledge about the case may be subpœnaed as a witness on one side or the other, and is thus obliged to appear and testify at the trial. The government already has the right to subpœna witnesses against an accused person. By this article, the accused also has the right to subpœna witnesses in his favor.

VI. THE RIGHT TO HAVE COUNSEL.—Any accused person may, if he choose, act as his own lawyer. But the technicalities of the law are so many that even an intelligent and careful person would better entrust his defense to a good lawyer, much more an ignorant or a timid person. If an accused person is not able to employ a lawyer, the judge will appoint a lawyer to defend the prisoner, and the government will pay him.

ARTICLE VII.

TRIAL BY JURY IN COMMON LAW CASES.

In suits at common law, where the value in controversy shall exceed twenty dollars, the right of trial by jury shall be preserved, and no fact tried by a jury shall be otherwise re-examined in any court of the United States, than according to the rules of the common law.

I. THE RIGHT OF TRIAL BY JURY IN COMMON LAW CASES.— The right of trial by jury in criminal cases has already been guaranteed (III, 2, 3, and Am. VI). The same right is now guaranteed in common law cases, where the value in controversy exceeds twenty dollars. Where the amount in controversy is smaller, it is not worth while to empanel a jury. The time and expense of a jury trial is considerable, and it is not fair to cause that expense to the government, and that delay to more important cases, for the sake of a trifling suit.

II. FACTS FINALLY DETERMINED BY A JURY TRIAL.— In the Constitution (III, 2, 3), the Supreme Court is given appellate jurisdiction both as to law and fact. This was meant to cover cases in equity, cases in admiralty, and maritime cases, all of which are tried by the court alone without a jury. But for fear it should be held to give the Supreme Court appellate jurisdiction in suits at law, both as to law and fact, this clause was added to the bill of rights.

The common law of England is that whole body of customs, precedents and forms which grew up in England in the course of English history. (See page —.) The American courts recognize this common law, so far as it is not abrogated by any express provision of this Constitution or of a statute. Under the common law all suits are tried before a judge and jury. The judge determines the law and the jury the facts of the case.

The rules of common law allow only one way of re-examining facts once tried by a jury, and that is by a new trial before the same court for good reasons. The law as applied to any case may be re-examined by a writ of error or an appeal to a higher court; but in such cases the verdict of the jury is held conclusive as to the facts.

The effect of this provision is —

1. To allow equity, admiralty and maritime cases to be carried up to an appellate court and re-examined both as to the law and the facts.

2. But to prevent common law cases, which include most ordinary law suits, from being re-examined as to the facts, unless a new trial is granted before the same court.

ARTICLE VIII.

EXCESSIVE BAIL, FINES AND PUNISHMENTS.

Excessive bail shall not be required, nor excessive fines imposed, nor cruel and unusual punishments inflicted.

I. EXCESSIVE BAIL FORBIDDEN. — *Bail* is the security given, that a person arrested for any offense will appear in court and stand his trial, when the time comes. When no bail is given, the accused person will be kept in jail till his trial; not to punish him, for he has not yet been convicted of any crime; but to make sure that he will be on hand to be tried. Bail is not allowed in capital cases, because a man who expects to be hung will be likely to forfeit any security in order to escape.

If excessive bail is required, the accused will not be able to furnish it, and it amounts to the same thing as to refuse to admit the prisoner to bail. What is excessive bail in any case, must be determined by the seriousness of the offense charged, and the wealth of the prisoner or his friends.

II. EXCESSIVE FINES FORIDDEN. — Many offenses are punished by fine alone, or by fine and imprisonment. If excessive fines are imposed, they may easily amount to confiscation of the prisoner's property. The punish-

ment by fine is intended to be a light punishment for a
light offense. But an excessive fine may be made a very
heavy punishment. The laws regulate the amount of
fines for those offenses which are finable.

III. CRUEL AND UNUSUAL PUNISHMENTS FORBID-
DEN. — Cruel and unusual punishments are understood
to mean such punishments as whipping, branding with
a hot iron, maiming, torturing on the rack, burning at
the stake, breaking on the wheel, drawing and quartering. These were, until a century or two ago, inflicted
everywhere; but have now been abolished in all civilized countries. These are forbidden by this article.

ARTICLE IX.

STRICT CONSTRUCTION OF PERSONAL RIGHTS.

The enumeration in the Constitution of certain rights shall not be construed to deny or disparage others retained by the people.

It is impossible to enumerate fully all the personal
rights which the tyranny of government might possibly
violate, and certainly they are not all enumerated in the
Constitution. For fear that it might be inferred that
the government could infringe on any personal rights
not expressly guarded by the Constitution, this article
was inserted.

ARTICLE X.

LIMITED POWERS OF THE U. S. GOVERNMENT.

The powers not delegated to the United States by the Constitution, nor
prohibited by it to the States, are reserved to the States respectively, or
to the people.

I. THE POWER GIVEN TO THE GENERAL GOVERN-
MENT.— In the first Congress the motion was twice
made to amend this article so that it should read, "The

powers not *expressly* delegated to the United States by
the Constitution," and was twice lost.   It was pointed
out by Madison then, that a government, to be a government, must have *implied* as well as *express* powers;
that it is impossible to foresee and name in a Constitution all the cases which will arise; and this argument
prevented this word being inserted.   Notwithstanding
this fact, it has been the habit of lawyers and statesmen
to quote this article with the word "expressly" inserted,
the very thing which its authors purposely refused to
do.   Had this been made the reading of the Constitution,
we could never have bought Louisiana or Florida or
Alaska constitutionally; nor could we constitutionally
have built a light house or established the signal service.
As it is, the United States has all the powers granted
to it by this Constitution, and all other powers that are
fairly implied in these.   All other powers are prohibited to the United States government.

II.   THE RESERVED POWERS BELONG TO THE PEOPLE,
NOT TO THE STATES. — Who has these reserved powers
then?   The advocates of State rights say that all rights
not expressly given to the United States are reserved
for the States.   We have already seen the falseness of
that word "expressly."   But are all the reserved powers
given to the States?   No,   For in the first place we
have certain powers expressly forbidden to the States
(I. 10), some of which are also prohibited to the United
States.   And this article says that certain powers are
reserved to the people.

The truth is that in this country the people are the
source of all power.   They have delegated certain
powers expressed or implied to the United States government by this Constitution, certain others to the
State governments, and have reserved the rest, not to

be exercised by either till called for by the people. And, moreover, lest certain powers extremely liable to abuse should be exercised, they have expressly prohibited one or both governments from exercising them.

But it does not follow that the States, any more than the United States, can exercise any powers not expressly prohibited to them. All powers not given expressly or by fair implication to the United States government or to the several State governments, are held in reserve by the people.

The people of the United States may grant additional powers to the general government, or take away some already granted, by an amendment to this Constitution. The people of any State may do the same with their State government, subject to the limitations of this Constitution.

MISCELLANEOUS AMENDMENTS.

.

ARTICLE XI.[1]

STATE REPUDIATION.

"Let us speak plain; there is more force in names
Than most men dream of; and a lie may keep
Its throne a whole age longer, if it skulk
Behind the shield of some fair-seeming name."
— LOWELL.

The judicial power of the United States shall not be construed to extend to any suit in law or equity, commenced or prosecuted against one of the United States by citizens of another State, or by citizens or subjects of any foreign State.

I.   CAUSE OF THIS AMENDMENT. — At the close of the Revolutionary War, the States, as well as the United States, were burdened with the debts incurred in that struggle, and scarcely able to pay them. Article III, Section 2, of the Constitution, gave the United States courts jurisdiction over controversies "between a State and citizens of another State." After a time suits were begun in the Supreme Court (III, 2, 2) by their creditors. The Supreme Court decided that,[2] under the Constitution, a State could be sued for a debt the same as a private person.

This decision led at once to this amendment, which cuts off all suits against a State by private individuals, those already begun as well as future suits. Most of the States were not in a situation to pay their debts on demand, and this amendment operated as a stay-law, to give them time in which to pay their debts, as well as a bankrupt law for those which could never pay them.

---

[1] This amendment was proposed by Congress, March 5, 1794, and ratified January 8, 1798.

[2] Chisholm vs. Georgia.

II.   RESULTS OF THIS AMENDMENT.— The States were
at once freed from the fear of any power which would
compel them to pay their debts.   A creditor of a State,
like a creditor of the United States, must now depend
upon the good faith of his debtor.

Most of the States eventually paid their Revolutionary War debts.   But other debts, since contracted, have
been repudiated by many States, especially the newer
States.   These States have not often repudiated their
whole debt, but some part of it, where there was some
special provocation, as where the debt had been incurred
by corrupt officials, or where the proceeds had been mis-
applied in the construction of railroads.

But these provocations are not sufficient excuse, and
it remains the disgrace of the United States, that while
it own obligations have been paid with scrupulous good
faith, so many State debts have been repudiated in
whole or in part.

III.   THIS AMENDMENT DOES NOT COVER MUNICIPALI-
TIES WITHIN A STATE.—Although a State cannot be sued
in the United States courts by a private person, the parts
of the State, such as counties, towns, villages or cities,
can be sued, and are frequently sued, by private persons.
If the creditor lives in the same State, he of course sues
in the State courts.   But if he does not live in the same
State, he can sue in the United States courts.

AMENDMENT XII.[1]

THE ELECTION OF PRESIDENT.

"Th' older a guv'ment is, the better 't suits;
New ones hunt folks's corns out like new boots;
Change jes' for change is like them big hotels,
Where they shift plates, an' let ye live on smells."
— BIGELOW PAPERS.

THE REASON FOR THIS AMENDMENT.— The disputed election of 1801 showed the dangers of the method of electing President and Vice President under the Constitution as it then stood. This amendment was passed, making such changes as the experience of that election had shown to be necessary. Another experience of a disputed election in 1877, will probably call for another amendment embodying another method of electing President.

This amendment has already been treated of in another place as a substitute for Article II, Section 1, Clause 3.

---

[1] This amendment was proposed by Congress December 12, 1803, and was ratified September 25, 1804. For the text of this amendment, see p 155.

AMENDMENTS XIII–XV.

RESULTS OF THE CIVIL WAR.

> " If New and Old, disastrous feud,
>   Must ever shock, like armed foes;
> And this be true, till Time shall close,
> That principles are rained in blood."
> —TENNYSON.

I. ANALYSIS OF THESE AMENDMENTS.

1. *Slavery abolished* (Am. XIII).
2. *Citizenship and its privileges defined* (Am. XIV, 1).
    (a.) Citizenship defined.
    (b.) States cannot abridge the privileges of citizens.
    (c.) States must do equal justice to all persons.
3. *Representation in Congress* (Am. XIV, 2).
    (a.) Representatives apportioned according to population.
    (b.) Representation abridged as the right to vote is abridged.
4. *Disability of rebels to hold office* (Am. XIV, 3).
    (a.) Rebels who have broken their oaths excluded from office.
    (b.) But their disabilities may be removed by Congress.
5. *The public debt versus the rebel debt* (Am. XIV, 4).
    (a.) Public debt declared valid.
    (b.) Rebel debts declared illegal and void.
    (c.) Claims for the loss of slaves declared illegal and void.
6. *Negro suffrage established* (Am. XV).

II. THE ADOPTION OF THESE AMENDMENTS.—The great Civil War, from 1861 to 1865, drew with it many important consequences.   Chief among these is the entire reorganization of society in the slave-holding States. These amendments mark a great social and political revolution; and they were meant to secure the results of the Civil War in the surest manner possible under our government.

The reconstruction measures, which went along with these amendments, took the political power from the former ruling class of the south, the white aristocracy, and put it in the hands of the former slaves and their white friends. It is not wonderful that counter revolutions should have since taken place in all those States, which have put their governments back into the hands of the former ruling class, the white aristocracy.

But these counter revolutions have not restored the state of society as it was before the war. These three amendments have made the negro *free*, a *citizen* and a *voter*. These three great facts will remain as legal facts, although the negro in some parts of the south may be defrauded of some of the privileges of a citizen by unlawful violence or fraud.

III. A DISPUTED QUESTION.

Were these amendments constitutionally adopted? Yes, on either theory of the relations of the rebel States. Congress held that rebel States have lost their rights as States, and therefore that only three-fourths of the loyal States are needed to ratify the amendments. This decision by the only lawful authority (for the Supreme Court cannot decide political questions) binds us legally, whether it was a right or a wrong decision. Three-fourths of the States then recognized as in the Union ratified each of these amendments, and they are therefore legally a part of the Constitution.

But even if we accept the State rights theory, these amendments were legally ratified, for three-fourths of all the States ratified each of them. It is true the rebel States adopted them under a sort of compulsion, for Congress required them to ratify these amendments as one of the conditions of receiving them into full membership in the Union. But that did not make their ratification of these amendments invalid. It was the legal act of each State.

For a time there was a disposition on the part of some to repudiate these amendments as soon as possible. But all political parties have repeatedly declared that these amendments are valid. And it is not likely that any political party will ever seriously raise any doubts as to the validity of these amendments. They have been recognized by Congress, by the President and by the Supreme Court.

ARTICLE XIII.

SLAVERY ABOLISHED.

Neither slavery nor involuntary servitude, except as a punishment for crime, whereof the party shall have been duly convicted, shall exist within the United States, or any place subject to their jurisdiction.

Congress shall have power to enforce this article by appropriate legislation.

I. SLAVERY THE CAUSE OF THE CIVIL WAR. — One of the chief causes of the Civil War was the "irrepressible conflict" between two social organizations so diverse as those of the free and of the slave States, bound together in one nation. Other causes may be found; such as the difference in climate, and therefore in the character of the inhabitants and in the nature of their industries; the difference of character and ideas between the first settlers of north and south; or the fatal poison of the "State rights" doctrine. But whatever effects these had, all clustered around the institution of slavery, to attack or to defend it. Slavery perhaps was not the chief *cause* of the difficulties between north and south, but it was certainly the chief *expression* of those difficulties. Without it, the war perhaps would never have come, and certainly not at the time and in the way it did. And thus slavery came to be popularly called the *cause* of the war. It was natural that when the war closed with the victory of the north that slavery should be abolished.

II. THE ORIGIN AND SCOPE OF THIS ARTICLE.— The form of this article is taken from article VI of the ordinance of 1787, for the Government of the Northwest Territory (now the States of Ohio, Indiana, Illinois, Michigan and Wisconsin). "Any place subject to their jurisdiction," includes not only the States, but also the Territories, the District of Columbia, forts, arsenals and dockyards, United States vessels or naval stations owned by us in other parts of the world.

Congress would have power to enforce this article by appropriate legislation (I, 8, 18) without the power being expressly granted here, and this section is therefore superfluous. The same thing can be said of the similar sections at the close of articles XIV and XV.

ARTICLE XIV.

MISCELLANEOUS PROVISIONS RELATING TO THE CIVIL WAR.

SECTION 1.

CITIZENSHIP AND ITS PRIVILEGES.

All persons born or naturalized in the United States, and subject to the jurisdiction thereof, are citizens of the United States and of the State wherein they reside. No State shall make or enforce any law which shall abridge the privileges or immunities of citizens of the United States, nor shall any State deprive any person of life, liberty or property without due process of law, nor deny to any person within its jurisdiction the equal protection of the laws.

I. CITIZENSHIP DEFINED.— The question of who are and who are not citizens had been left somewhat vague till this amendment was adopted. And the exact position of free negroes was in doubt. The thirteenth amendment had made all negroes *free persons.* This amendment now made them *citizens.* Hereafter there can be no question as to who are citizens of the United States.

All persons born in the United States, except wild Indians, are natural-born citizens, and any foreigner may become an adopted citizen by being naturalized. (See page 88.)

II. STATE CITIZENSHIP.— Any person who answers
to the above definition of a citizen of the United States
may become a citizen of any State by taking up his
residence in it. But he cannot be a citizen of two
States at the same time. Nor can he become a citizen
of any State in any other way than by gaining a residence within its jurisdiction. Whether a person has
his legal residence in one State or in another, is a question which is sometimes hard to decide. But once
establish the residence in a particular State, and the
citizenship in that State follows.

Not all citizens of the United States are citizens of
any particular State. They may be residents of the
District of Columbia or of a Territory. Nor is it necessary that all citizens of a State should be citizens of
the United States. Several States give the privilege of
voting and holding office to persons who have merely
declared their intention of becoming citizens. This
certainly makes them citizens of the State, but not of
the United States. Thus we see that citizens of the
United States and citizens of the several States are not
necessarily the same. A person may be one of them
without being both.

III. PRIVILEGES AND IMMUNITIES OF CITIZENS.—
As the Supreme Court of the United States has refused
to enumerate these privileges, we need not expect to be
able to give these completely. But in general terms we
may say that citizens of the United States, as such, are
entitled to the protection of the government in foreign
lands, and to the equal benefits of the laws of the United
States at home. Thus:

(a.) A citizen of the United States is entitled to the protection of
the United States against any unjust treatment by foreign governments.

(b.) If he is of age, he may take up government land under the homestead act, on certain easy conditions, the chief of which is that he shall live on it five years, and thus have a farm given to him free. But a married woman cannot take up a homestead, because that would give two homesteads to the same family. An unmarried woman, who is of age, may take up a homestead on the same conditions as a man.

(c.) He is entitled to the use of the post office, the navigable rivers and lakes, and the mining lands, on the same terms as other citizens.

(d.) He is entitled to the equal protection of the laws of the United States, and also to equal punishment for violating those laws. It should be remembered that within the States, United States law has a limited scope only.

(e.) He is entitled to hold any United States office for which he is legally qualified, and to which he has been regularly elected or appointed.

Now the privileges and immunities of citizens of the United States belong to all citizens of the United States, without regard to color, birthplace, religious opinions, party, sex or age; and no State can infringe them lawfully.

IV. PROTECTION TO LIFE, LIBERTY AND PROPERTY. — Our two-fold system of government, United States and State governments, limits the privileges of citizens of the United States as such, and leaves a wide margin for oppression by the States within their own jurisdiction. This amendment, therefore, goes on to guarantee not only to the citizens of the United States, but to all persons, equal justice by the State governments. By this clause the United States guarantees to all persons within its borders, whether citizens or aliens, the inalienable rights named in the Declaration of Independence. "We hold these truths to be self-evident, that all men are created equal; that they are endowed by their Creator with certain inalienable rights; that among these are life, liberty, and the pursuit of happiness; that to secure these rights, governments are instituted among men, deriving their just powers from the consent of the governed." [1]

Except in the case of the slaves, the practice of our government has been in accordance with these principles. The great argument against the Constitution, as it was prepared by the convention, was that it did not sufficiently secure these personal rights to life, liberty, and the pursuit of happiness. These rights were made perfectly secure by the first ten amendments, as against any oppressions of the United States government. And at last, after slavery was abolished, these rights are by this amendment secured as against the oppressions of the State governments, and thus the Constitution guarantees to every person within the reach of its authority the inalienable rights to life, liberty and property, and to the equal protection of the laws. To the citizens of the United States, it guarantees this not only in this country, but in foreign lands, so far as the government has power to protect them; to foreigners, it guarantees them so long as they remain within the United States.

V. DISPUTED QUESTIONS.

1. *Can a State have citizens who are not citizens of the United States ?* This is left an open question by this section. It is probable, however, that a State has this power. Several States have made voters of a large number of foreigners who have only declared their intention to become citizens, and, if they are voters, they must of course be citizens of the States; and no act of any branch of the United States government has ever questioned this right of the States.

2. *What is the status of aliens who have declared their intention to become citizens ?* They are not citizens, but they have taken the first step toward becoming citizens, and are therefore entitled to the

---

[1] The student should memorize this extract from the Declaration of Independence.

protection of the government, but not to any of the special privileges of citizens.   The government has several times protected
them against injustice in foreign lands.

3. *Can a Chinaman be naturalized?*   No, he cannot be naturalized as the law now stands.   White men and negroes may be, but
not Chinamen.   The law is plain, notwithstanding a difference on
this point in the practice of the United States courts.   But Chinamen can become citizens of some of our States under the State laws.

4. *How can an Indian become a citizen?*   An Indian cannot be
naturalized in the manner prescribed for foreigners.   The practice
has been to declare a tribe or a part of a tribe citizens by a special
act of Congress on their renouncing their tribal government.   In
some cases, tribes or parts of tribes have been again allowed, by
act of Congress, to give up their citizenship, and reassume their
tribal government.   Under this section, it would seem that any
individual Indian ought to be allowed to renounce his tribe and
become a citizen; but Congress has passed no law to that effect.

5. *Does this section give women the right to vote?*   No, it does
declare them citizens, which they were before, but it does not make
them voters.   Citizenship and suffrage are not equivalent terms.
But in any State women may be made voters, if the State chooses,
without any violation of the United States Constitution.   The Constitution does not make women voters, but it does not forbid the
States making them voters.

SECTION 2.

SUFFRAGE.

Representatives shall be apportioned among the several States according to
their respective numbers, counting the whole number of persons in each
State, excluding Indians not taxed. But when the right to vote at any
election for the choice of electors for President and Vice President of the
United States, Representatives in Congress, the executive and judicial
officers of a State, or the members of the Legislature thereof, is denied to
any of the male inhabitants of such State, being twenty-one years of age,
and citizens of the United States, or in any way abridged, except for participation in rebellion or other crime, the basis of representation therein
shall be reduced in the proportion which the number of male citizens
shall bear to the whole number of male citizens twenty-one years of age
in such State.

I.   THE OBJECT OF THIS SECTION.—This is an attempt to secure indirectly that which was secured

directly by the fifteenth amendment — negro suffrage. The effect of this section would have been to put a powerful inducement before the Southern States to give negroes the right to vote; and the result would undoubtedly have been that they would have gradually conceded that right to them. But as this is secured directly by the fifteenth amendment, we need only consider what effect this section may have in the future.

II. THE EFFECT OF THIS SECTION.— The effect of this section, as things now are, is as follows:

1. It changes the basis of representation from that given in Article I, section 2, and makes it the whole population except uncivilized Indians. This had already been practically done by abolishing slavery.

2. It is assumed that manhood suffrage shall be the rule — that all citizens of the United States who are of the male sex and twenty-one years old are voters, unless specially disqualified.

3. It is established, that no State ought to abridge the right to vote for any cause except for participation in rebellion or other crime. And this extends to State elections as well as to United States elections.

4. The penalty for a State thus abridging the right to vote is, that it shall have its representation in Congress proportionately reduced. If a State chooses to take this penalty, it may abridge the right to vote in certain ways. No State has yet been deprived of a part of its representation under this section.

III. WHAT POWERS OVER THE SUFFRAGE ARE LEFT TO THE SEVERAL STATES. — Assuming that manhood suffrage of citizens of the United States is the standard qualification for voting, the States may constitutionally increase the number of voters as much as they please; and they may reduce that number in the following ways:

1. They may shut out traitors from the right to vote.
The justice of this is evident. After the Civil War, for
some time in many of the Southern States those who
had aided in the rebellion were shut out from voting.
But it was found impossible to disfranchise permanently
the most intelligent and wealthy people of the south.
These restrictions have now all been removed and the
former rebels now control the Southern States.

2. They may disfranchise criminals. In every State
persons convicted of crimes are disfranchised; but they
are frequently restored to their civil rights by a pardon.

3. They may require an educational qualification subject to the penalty of having their representation reduced. In a few of the Northern States, it is required
of every voter that he be able to read and write: but
in those States the number of illiterate persons is very
small. If such a qualification should be required in the
Southern States, it would shut out such a large fraction
of their natural voters, that their representation in Congress would be greatly reduced. In Georgia and Alabama, according to the census of 1870, more than one-
half of the voters are unable to read and write. In these
States, such a qualification for the suffrage would reduce
their Representatives in Congress to less than half the
number they now have.

4. They may require a property qualification, subject
to the penalty of losing a part of their representation
in Congress. If a considerable amount of property were
required for a voter, it would reduce the number of
voters very much, because the mass of the voters are
men who live by their labor, and have no great amount
of property. The total value of property in the United
States, by the census of 1870, is over $300 for each man,
woman and child in the United States, or $1,500 for each

family. A property qualification of $100 would only shut out the paupers, the tramps, and a few young men just beginning in life, and would not greatly reduce the number of voters. But a property qualification of $1,000 would shut out more than one-half of the voters of every State. It is safe to say that any considerable property qualification will never be required of voters while our present form of government lasts.

But many States require a poll tax of $1.00 to $1.50 of each voter before he is allowed to vote. This is not a violation of this section, because no one is really prohibited from voting as long as the amount of tax is so small.

SECTION 3.

REBEL DISABILITIES.

No person shall be a Senator or Representative in Congress, or elector of President or Vice President, or hold any office, civil or military, under the United States, or under any State, who, having previously taken an oath as a member of Congress, or as an officer of the United States, or as a member of any State Legislature. or as an executive or judicial officer of any State, to support the Constitution of the United States, shall have engaged in insurrection or rebellion against the same, or given aid or comfort to the enemies thereof; but Congress may, by a vote of two-thirds of each House, remove such disability.

I. POLITICAL DISABILITIES THE ONLY PUNISHMENT OF REBELS IN THE CIVIL WAR. — The disability to hold office provided for in this section is the only punishment inflicted by the United States upon the rebels in the Southern States. Every person who had borne arms against the government, or who had given aid and comfort to the rebel army or government, was guilty of treason. (III, 3.) This made nearly every white man in the seceded States a traitor, and liable to punishment for his treason. But not a single person was ever brought to trial on that charge, not even Jefferson

Davis, the President of the Southern Confederacy. The only punishment inflicted was that prescribed in this section.

II. THE EXTENT OF THESE DISABILITIES. — The extent of these disabilities is limited:

1. Not all rebels are punished, but only those who had previously held a position under the United States or any State, in which they had sworn to support the Constitution of the United States. Rebellion alone was not punished, but only rebellion joined with violation of an official oath.

2. The punishment is only a disability to hold office. It is not death, or imprisonment, or fine, or even disfranchisement; but only that the guilty person shall not hold office.

3. These disabilities were only to last until Congress by a two-thirds vote of each House removed them. Within a very few years these disabilities were removed from nearly all; and now the persons from whom these disabilities have been removed fill most of the positions to which the votes of the Southern States can elect them in the State governments and in Congress.

No government in the world was ever so lenient toward conquered rebels. It should be noted that this section applies to future rebellions as well as to one that is past; and that Congress may not always be so lenient if a new rebellion should arise in any part of our land.

SECTION 4.

THE PUBLIC DEBT VERSUS THE REBEL DEBT.

The validity of the public debt of the United States, authorized by law, including debts incurred for payment of pensions and bounties for services in suppressing insurrection or rebellion, shall not be questioned. But neither the United States nor any State shall assume or pay any debt or obligation incurred in aid of insurrection or rebellion against the United States, or any claim for the loss or emancipation of any slave; but all such debts, obligations and claims shall be held illegal and void.

I. THE REASON OF THIS SECTION. — War is an expensive luxury, and cannot be wholly paid for in cash. As carried on in modern times, a great war always causes a great public debt on both sides. Our Civil War was carried on so long, and on such a scale, that great public debts were contracted by both sides.

No conquering power ever pays the debts of the beaten side, and certainly no government in the world ever paid the expenses incurred by rebels who were defeated. On the other hand, good faith to our creditors, and the desire to keep our credit good, would doubtless make us pay our national debt without any constitutional guarantee. But to make assurance doubly sure, this section was added.

II. THE PROVISIONS OF THIS SECTION.— 1. It promises that the public debt of the United States shall never be legally questioned. In fact, we have been paying off our debts quite rapidly, and our credit is now equal to that of any nation in the world.

2. It prohibits the payment by the United States, or by any State, of any debt incurred in support of the rebellion. This lifts a load from the Southern States.

3. It prohibits the payment by either the United States, or by any State, of any claim for the loss of slaves by the war, or by their being set free. The freedom of the slaves was a consequence of the Civil War. Had they been freed by peaceful legislation, they would doubtless have been paid for. But they were freed in consequence of the war undertaken by their masters, and the government therefore rightly refused to pay for them.

SECTION 5.

APPROPRIATE LEGISLATION.

The Congress shall have power to enforce, by appropriate legislation, the provisions of this article.

THE POWER TO ENFORCE THIS ARTICLE. — Congress has undertaken to enforce the provisions of this article by appropriate legislation.

This section is unnecessary, as Congress would have power to pass all needful and appropriate laws to enforce this article under the general power given in Article I, Section 8, Clause 18. Even without that, common sense would teach that where certain things are ordered to be done, the government must be understood to have the power to see that they are done. Else the government would stand in the position of that politician who was in "favor of the Maine law, but opposed to enforcing it." Common sense would teach us that the government must be considered to have all powers necessary to enforce the Constitution.

ARTICLE XV.

NEGRO SUFFRAGE.

The right of the citizens of the United States to vote shall not be denied or abridged by the United States or by any State on account of race, color or previous condition of servitude.

The Congress shall have power to enforce this article by appropriate legislation.

THE NEGRO GUARANTEED THE RIGHT OF SUFFRAGE. — For fear that section 2 of the last article would not be enough to secure the negroes the right to vote, this amendment also was passed. Thus these three amendments each secure an essential right to the negro — the thirteenth, the right to *freedom;* the fourteenth, the right to *citizenship;* the fifteenth, the right to *vote.* Thus at last the principles of our government are carried out consistently, so far as the negroes are concerned. Whether they are carried out in our treatment of the Chinese and the Indians, is a question. But the great blot on our character as a nation which loves *liberty,* has been washed out — washed out in blood. And our nation now carries out the grand words of Daniel Webster:

"LIBERTY AND UNION, NOW AND FOREVER, ONE AND INSEPARABLE."

THE AMERICAN UNION.

I profess, sir, in my career hitherto, to have kept steadily in view the prosperity and honor of the whole country, and the preservation of our Federal Union. It is to that union we owe our safety at home, and our consideration and dignity abroad. It is to that union that we are chiefly indebted for whatever makes us most proud of our country. That union we reached only by the discipline of our virtues in the severe school of adversity. It had its origin in the necessities of disordered finances, prostrate commerce, and ruined credit.

Under its benign influences, these great interests immediately awoke, as from the dead, and sprang forth with newness of life. Every year of its duration has teemed with fresh proofs of its utility and its blessings; and although our territory has stretched out wider and wider, and our population spread farther and farther, they have not outrun its protection or its benefits. It has been to us all a copious fountain of national, social, personal happiness.

I have not allowed myself, sir, to look beyond the Union, to see what might lie hidden in the dark recesses behind. I have not coolly weighed the chances of preserving liberty, when the bonds that unite us together shall be broken asunder. I have not accustomed myself to hang over the precivice of disunion, to see whether, with my short sight, I can fathom the depth of the abyss below; nor could I regard him as a safe counselor in the affairs of this government, whose thoughts should be mainly bent on considering, not how the Union should be best preserved, but how tolerable might be the condition of the people when it shall be broken up and destroyed. While the Union lasts, we have high, exciting, gratifying prospects spread out before us, for us and our children. Beyond that I seek not to penetrate the veil. God grant that, in my day at least, that curtain may not rise. God grant that on my vision never may be opened what lies behind.

When my eyes shall be turned to behold, for the last time, the sun in heaven, may I not see him shining on the broken and dishonored fragments of a once glorious Union; on States dissevered, discordant, belligerent; on a land rent with civil feuds, or drenched, it may be, in fraternal blood! Let their last feeble and lingering glance, rather, behold the gorgeous ensign of the republic, now known and honored throughout the earth, still full high advanced, its arms and trophies streaming in their original luster, not a stripe erased or polluted, not a single star obscured— bearing for its motto no such miserable interrogatory as, What is all this worth? nor those other words of delusion and folly, Liberty first, and Union afterward; but everywhere, spread all over in characters of living light, blazing on all its ample folds, as they float over the sea and land, and in every wind under the whole heavens, that other sentiment, dear to every true American heart—Liberty and Union, now and forever, one and inseparable!

DANIEL WEBSTER, in 1830

INDEX.